My Secret Profession

The Memoirs of Marie Duval

A Novel By Paul Sterling

JoJo

PUBLISHING

First published in Australia in 2005 by
Jo-Jo Publishing
61/189 Beaconsfield Parade
Middle Park, 3206

10 9 8 7 6 5 4 3 2 1
© Paul Sterling
The moral right of the author has been asserted.

National Library of Australia
Cataloguing-In-Publication date:
Sterling, Paul.

My secret profession: the memoirs of Marie Duval : a novel.
ISBN 0 9757471 1 8.
I. Title.
A823.4

ISBN 0 9757471 1 8
Cover image © Corbis
Cover design by Michael Hanrahan (www.mhps.com.au)
Edited and typeset by Damian Alway (www.PublishingServices.com.au)
Printed in China by Everbest Printing Company, Ltd

All rights reserved. Without limiting the rights under copyright reserved
above, no part of this publication may be reproduced, stored in or
introduced into a retrieval system, or transmitted, in any form or by any
means (electronic, mechanical, photocopying, recording or otherwise),
without the prior written permission of both the copyright owner and
the above publisher of this book.

This is a work of fiction and should any characters bare any resemblance
whatsoever to actual persons it is unintentional and purely co-incidental.

Contents

To Cleo, who had faith.

*"We are all in the gutter, but some
of us are looking at the stars."*

– Oscar Wilde

Marie Duval Explains

This is the story of the 13 years I spent in Australia. Once I returned to France, I decided to send my diaries and notes to Paul Sterling, a good friend and a colleague of my husband.

Since I am French and I learned to speak the Australian language mostly in places where there was not a lot of good grammar, my words may be simple, or sometimes crude. If I use coarse or obscene words from time to time, it's because they were used by those around me. I hope that Paul and his wife, Suzanne, will improve on my grammar, but will not remove my real message.

I could not keep these memoirs; I did not want my family and those around me to find them. People here ask me so many questions about Australia, but I can't tell them much and they finally give up, finding me a little boring. There are so many landmarks that I never saw to tell them, and so many other things that I did see but cannot discuss. There are already probably many overseas visitors who have written about their lives, their work or their travels in Australia. My story will be very different. I will tell you about places in Australia which many, many Australians have never visited.

I am sure that Paul will be most surprised when he reads my diaries because he would never have guessed about the work I did when I was in his country. He saw me as the elegant, indolent wife of a successful businessman. Nevertheless, I hope that he will do what I have asked him; adapt my notes into a book and persuade a brave publisher to offer them to the Australian reader.

To those who ignored my real job, and who are shocked, I apologise. To those who knew me under my assumed name, I send my warm greetings. I am sure that many will laugh and cry with me.

I hope that you, my readers, will read, understand and forgive. For what you gave and for what you took, Australia, I love you.

Marie

My name is Paul Sterling, and I am happily married to the delicious Suzanne. Not long ago, on a typical Melbourne winter evening, with the gas fire (imitation Scandinavian logs made in Japan) roaring, I was battling with the August 2001 Census. I was feeling silly, and asked Suzanne, my wife, if she could imagine who would be prepared to write, in capital black letters, 'SEX WORKER' as a response to question 34 (profession).

She agreed that not many would admit to the career. I opened a bottle of Tullamore Dew Whiskey Liqueur, which had been hiding shyly in the cupboard for a few months, and pushed the debate a little further. Providing the person offering professional sexual services was totally honest and declared up-front what he or she did for a living, question 35 would provide an interesting challenge: 'What are the main tasks usually performed in that occupation?'

Have you noticed how a small glass of liqueur can encourage facetious suggestions? We finally agreed that the most popular replies would probably be:

a)   listening to crass compliments

b)   listening to complaints about the legal spouse or customary partner

c)   refusing to have sex without a condom

d)   faking orgasm; and

e)   proposing masturbation as a last resort.

Suzanne even suggested, halfway through the second glass, that we should try to write a book around the idea. We would call it: *Fore Play, For Sex or For Money*. We laughed so hard we needed a third glass to recover.

We then withdrew to the bed chamber for a little inebriated hanky-panky. It was not a success, but Suzanne suggested it was probably worth 100 bucks, nevertheless. We giggled ourselves to sleep.

ℤ   ℥

Two days later a large parcel arrived. It contained Marie's diaries and notebooks with a covering letter, explaining that we would now know about her secret life in Australia.

We were surprised, and wondered what dreadful secrets our good friend was going to unveil. Our immediate thought was that she had been an agent for the French secret service, because she could well have played the role of the beautiful, enigmatic spy. Did she sabotage a Greenpeace vessel? Did she steal some uranium? Worse still, perhaps she had taken secret photographs of Federation Square?

It took the two of us more than three weeks to work our way through the 16 exercise books of fine handwriting which constituted the story of her life in Australia. We read, we paused, and we talked, then we starting reading again. At first we were shocked, and then we discovered the sadness, the joy, the fun and the pleasure she had witnessed, dispensed and even shared. The memoirs also answered the unanswered question concerning the whereabouts of Marie on that dreadful day we all needed to find her so urgently.

We reached three conclusions.

Firstly, we were terribly ashamed of our tasteless jokes about the 2001 Census.

Secondly, with Suzanne's help, I would rewrite Marie's notes, hoping to produce a pleasurable book.

Lastly, we were proud to be the friend of Marie Duval, migrant prostitute, and honoured by the confidence she had graciously bestowed upon us.

I would use my limited literary experience to put Marie's memoirs into form, telling her story and showing the research she had also undertaken. We decided that we would also include the stories from her Parisian episode, because they showed another form of prostitution; the use of sex to promote career ambitions.

Suzanne would help by reading the proofs and providing constructive comments to overcome my total lack of understanding regarding the female of the species. It was decided that she would also write some sections covering aspects of Marie's life that an ordinary Australian male would be unable to comprehend, such as passion, love or orgasm.

It was also obvious that simply by reading Marie's diaries, by writing about her adventures and by listening to Suzanne's enlightened advice, I was going to make a major contribution to my own understanding of Woman.

ജ   ങ

I have one important task, and this is something a primitive male can do best: I must describe Marie Duval. I will do this very carefully, as Suzanne, my beloved wife, is reading over my shoulder. As an author, I must be scrupulously honest. As a husband, with ambitions for everlasting comfort and peace, I must be cautious.

When Marie first came to Melbourne, she was 38 years old, and, dare I say, Suzanne, stunning? Yes, my wife nods, I can. She was small, with dark auburn hair cut in a lovely soft fringe in front, while the rest fell to her shoulders in soft, undulating waves. She had big brown eyes, a small nose and a mouth and lips which looked as if they were made for pleasure. Ouch! Sorry, Suzanne.

She had the most beautiful pair of (whoops... okay Suzanne) breasts I have ever seen, curvaceous hips, beautifully round thighs and a bottom which her husband, Pierre, once described as the world's most beautiful vertical smile. And with all these attributes, she was never arrogant.

Having described the actor, and survived almost unscathed, let me now set the stage.

Marie Duval spent most of her life in Australia as a sex worker. This will be the story of the adventures of a wonderful young lady who secretly dispensed sexual pleasures within a legal environment. It will be occasionally crude, and this is where you decide whether you throw the book away or go on reading, even if it is under the quilt.

I have nothing more to add. The stage is set. Marie will tell you the story of her life, and I hope you will laugh and cry with her. We did.

I was a simple country girl when I met Pierre. It was the summer of 1974; the Beaujolais grapes were ripening on the vines, and, from what I was told by all the young teenage Frenchmen seeking access to my virginal underwear, I was a sunbaked beauty. They believed that my eyes were open invitations to sex, that my mouth was specially designed to provide infinite pleasures and that my breasts were the most beautiful of all.

It was all rather embarrassing. I was terribly shy, not adventurous at all, and dreadfully afraid that if kissed by a handsome boy I might end up with a baby in my tummy. I was not arrogant but I enjoyed the compliments. I did check myself now and again in the mirror and I compared what I saw with the nude tarts in the magazines my father hid above the toilet cistern. I made myself blush by concluding that I was, in fact, and *en toute modestie,* rather pretty.

But despite all, and thanks to, my own timidity and my father's firm supervision, the day I met Pierre I was still a virgin. At 19, this was most unusual for a French country girl. My nation has its origins firmly embedded in agriculture, and many children spent their younger years watching horses, pigs, ducks, cattle, goats and dogs copulate.

Because of these animals' otherwise boring lives, it became quite obvious that this must be a very special form of entertainment. Some of my girlfriends tried the experiment and told me that it was at first painful, but later quite enjoyable. I was determined not to be tempted, and resolute in my intention to offer myself, pure and intact, to the man of my dreams.

Claire, my best friend at the School of Saint Mary of the Marshes, told me that the best bit was getting the boys excited. She finally persuaded me to meet Jerome, the Mayor's son, one evening behind the co-operative wine shop, in her company. She opened my blouse and began to stroke my breasts. In just a few seconds, poor Jerome had his shorts around his ankles and was pumping away on his swollen willy. He fired a wonderful jet of what looked like full cream milk in my direction, and Claire laughed in delight.

She laughed even louder when I said that it looked like milking a cow, but I made Jerome terribly angry. Later, when I would work in a hospital environment, I saw colleagues who discreetly helped some convalescing patients overcome their frustrated ambitions, although I never dispensed such services myself.

Claire was proud to have organised my first encounter with a penis, but admitted that it had proved that I was not only the most tempting, but, above all, the most innocent virgin in the village.

Holding out became quite a challenge when my young sister, Brigitte, reached the age of 15 and showed a strong determination to share physical pleasures with any available and willing male as quickly as possible. People are inclined to say that two peas from the same pod have similar characteristics, above all if the pod, in this instance my mother, was remembered for certain wild escapades of her teenage years.

Luckily, before my sister could entice me to follow her down the outrageous path of temptation, Pierre appeared. He was from Lyon, a young man at the beginning of an exciting career with a large French company, one which was known almost the world over. His cousins were wine growers in our region, and he came to visit the family during the summer holidays. He was quite handsome, and very different from the boys of my village: he was tall, he spoke well, he dressed elegantly, and he had a wonderful smile. I met him at the door of our little *Casino* grocery store: he was leaving, I was arriving. He stepped back courteously, smiled, and held the door open. I blushed, stammered my thanks and stood for almost a minute in front of the counter, cheeks purple.

"Come on, girl, it's only a man," Madame Agostineau muttered. "You'll see plenty more where he came from. And they're all the same shape, you know. Ask your sister."

Then, as an afterthought, "Well, what do you want?"

I could not remember. I went home, empty handed, and my mother, exasperated, sent Brigitte back to the shop to buy the packet of *Lentilles du Puy*.

"I think I'm in love," I told my mother. Brigitte came back ten minutes later and confirmed that I had 'gone all strange' after seeing that young bloke from Lyon in the shop.

"I might have a look at him myself," suggested my sister.

"If you as much as look at your sister's young man, I will disinherit you," my mother warned.

I tried to explain that he was not 'my young man'. Well, not yet, anyway. Brigitte paled. She enjoyed sex, but she liked money and status even more. True to family tradition, this important event was discussed over a glass of *Beaujolais Villages*. We went through the usual stuff about the stupidity of love at first sight, and then my mother sighed and took off her apron.

"I'll go and see Madame Garnier," she announced.

Madame Garnier ran the village post office. She also sold post cards, wrapping paper, souvenirs, sugar licences for wine growers and dried flowers, and delivered telegrams (some say, after reading them). No-one ever did anything to anyone or with anyone else in the village without Madame Garnier knowing about it within 24 hours. It was said that when Monique Trousseau fell pregnant, Madame Garnier not only knew before she did herself, but also knew who had sown the seed. Madame Garnier was a historian, a woman of letters (compulsory for a post mistress), and a person who created, invented or destroyed reputations.

My mother took with her something which Madame Garnier cherished. It was a gift, a bottle of *marc*, the local brandy produced covertly and almost always illegally by some of the best vignerons. My uncle Gerard was the best illegal producer of brandy between Lyon and Dijon. It was an expensive investment, but the dividends were immediate and substantial. We knew almost everything about my future fiancé's family within an hour.

Pierre Duval was from Lyon. His father was a reputed paediatrician, his mother a well-known freelance writer. His father was also rumoured to be a free mason, a member of one of the oldest, most respected and most secret lodges of Lyon. Pierre's elder brother lived in Strasbourg, where he was a partner in a successful legal firm, while his young sister had just married the son of a yacht builder in Toulon. The family lived in a large and sumptuous apartment in Lyon, overlooking the Saône River, and owned a *mas* (country home) in Provence, and a yacht berthed in Fréjus. Pierre's Father drove a BMW while his mother zipped around Lyon in a mandarin-coloured Citroen 2CV. Pierre had driven down in his Renault 12 Gordini.

Madame Garnier had even obtained some interesting information about Pierre himself. He had studied political sciences at the *Université Jean Moulin* and after obtaining his *licence* (Bachelor of Arts) had moved almost immediately into a marketing career with one of the largest corporations in France. He spoke good English, collected postage stamps and loved jazz. He had enjoyed a few short-term flirts but had not yet discovered the ideal partner.

According to my mother, he was a beautiful fruit waiting to be plucked from the tree of expectations by the delicate hand of love. After two glasses of wine, my mother becomes both poetical and romantic.

I now had to plan a chance meeting. There were various solutions: dropping a handkerchief after Sunday Mass, if he stayed that long; falling off my bicycle in front of his Aunt Denise Cherrier's house; or watching from the attic window with father's binoculars awaiting the right moment to throw myself into his arms as soon as he went down to Madame Agostineau's store. I discussed my plans with Brigitte, who laughed and offered a very crude solution.

"Just go and knock on the Cherrier's door, wave those lovely tits of yours in front of his eyes and ask him if he wants to take you for a drive."

It was a typical Brigitte strategy. But I was not that kind of woman, and he was not that kind of man. I was still desperately searching for a suitable plan when Denise Cherrier knocked on our front door. Pierre, her nephew, would like to know if he could present himself to my father to ask his permission to take his daughter to the cinema.

"Do you think he means me?" Brigitte hissed at mother, as soon as the door was closed.

My mother laughed.

"No, my darling, it's not for you. If a boy wants to go out with you he doesn't bother to ask your father."

It was magic. This wonderful boy wanted to take ME to the pictures, and was showing that he understood and respected our rural traditions.

"I am frightened," my father confessed to me, eyes twinkling.

"Oh, don't worry, father. I'm sure he's a gentle young man," I assured him.

My father laughed and flexed his biceps.

"I'm not frightened of that young twig. I'm frightened that my daughter might kill me if I refuse permission."

I laughed with him and clapped my hands with joy.

℘   ℘

It was the first of many outings. On the second, we held hands; on the third we kissed. My mother invited him to dinner to meet my family, including our dear grandmother, who insisted on calling him Thierry.

"Is that an old boyfriend?" he whispered.

"No, it's because she's a little deaf," I explained.

Brigitte made some tasteless jokes and tried to attract his attention, and my mother frowned. My father was more forthright and told her to shut up and behave herself. She sulked for the rest of the evening.

The family analysis of the evening was favourable. Grandmother declared that he was a distinguished young man, Uncle Claude and Aunt Berthe were enchanted by his fine manners and easy conversation, and my mother found him to be well-groomed and intelligent. My father thought that he would not make a craftsman; his fingernails were too clean. But the only real negative comment came from Brigitte who thought that he was probably impotent, because he had ignored her all evening. We all laughed, and she stomped out of the drawing room, face flushed with anger.

It was then my turn to be invited to his parent's home for dinner. I was terrified, but my mother told me that there was no reason to be ashamed of my family or our upbringing. She was right. His father was handsome, elegant, and wonderfully kind. He insisted that I taste a cocktail based on his personal recipe, and he laughed when my eyes watered after the first gulp.

"You remind me of my mother," he declared. "She is also a beautiful woman. She married my father, a carpenter, when she was 17, and spent all her life in a little village near Bourg-en-Bresse. She also has great problems with my cocktails."

Pierre's mother was amazing. Terribly elegant and wonderfully eccentric, she wore a large, stained apron over a truly beautiful dress, and proved to be a magician in the kitchen.

"I love cooking," she explained. "The secret is in the wine you use and taste when you prepare the food."

By the time we sat at the table, she had cooked and tasted liberally and was certainly enjoying herself. The beef burgundy was absolutely delicious, and I was delighted to be served such a healthy and invigorating country dish in such a refined environment.

After the meal, Pierre's father insisted that I try a pear brandy made by his brother who lived near Strasburg. It was terribly strong. Luckily, Pierre was to drive me home, as I'm ashamed to admit I was a little tipsy by the time we left. Pierre told me later that I had thanked his father four times, and congratulated his mother on her qualities of *grand chef*. He added that I had insisted on kissing them both, several times on each cheek, before leaving. He assured me that they had been absolutely charmed and delighted.

ಖಿ   ಆ

From that day on, we moved into heavy and official courtship mode. Looking back, I can laugh about the way we both respected the customs and traditions, both pretending that we had not decided, individually and a long time ago, that we would spend the rest of our lives together. When I told my family that Pierre had proposed, the announcement raised hardly an eyebrow. My father simply turned to the sports page of the *Progrès de Lyon* and muttered 'about time'.

Pierre's parents asked my father if the wedding could be held in our village hall, and offered to share the cost of catering. The two fathers appeared to be becoming good friends. While Pierre's parents were rich and lived in a large city, they had rural origins of which they were truly proud. My father said that Pierre's father was, like him, a self-made man, and mother added, with a gentle giggle, that he had simply self-made it a little better. My father pretended to be offended, and then they kissed and made up. I remember hoping at the time that Pierre and I would be just as much in love when we reached their age.

We were married on the 12th of July 1976. The wedding was a dream and even Brigitte behaved herself, although her *décolleté* was outrageous. During the lunch, Pierre whispered in my ear that he had been seeing a lot of Brigitte recently.

"It all stops here," I warned him.

As we drove away to our honeymoon in Nice, the mothers cried, the guests cheered and waved, and the two fathers stood together, arms linked, raising their glasses to the departing lovers. It was just the beginning for Pierre and I.

2. The Early Years

By June of 1977, I was a blissfully happy married woman. It was no secret to me that Pierre was intelligent, hard working and ambitious. I realised that this offered us a certain mobility in our lives but, as a nurse, I already had a very mobile career, so this was of no great concern for me. There were public hospitals all over France and there was a great demand for qualified nurses everywhere. So while we were first settled in Lyon, close to both families, I knew this would not last.

I realised also that Pierre was determined that I would not spend too many years nursing. While he acknowledged that it was an honourable career and provided a wonderful service to society, he was of the opinion that the profession should be exercised by young girls and old spinsters.

"How will I survive if you are not in my bed tonight, but tending to some smelly old man or screaming child in a faraway hospital?" he asked.

I told him that he would have to wait until the following morning. He shrugged his shoulders theatrically.

"Young, healthy Frenchmen do not wait all night hanging on to their envy until the beautiful wife comes home the next morning, pale and exhausted, to refuse his advances. They cannot wait, they look elsewhere."

I pretended anger.

"If you look elsewhere, *mon chéri*, I will undertake a major operation with my own hands."

He laughed with pleasure.

"I love your hands, those sweet, delicate, small fingers which dispense such delights."

I blushed. It was true that marriage to such a gentle and handsome man had done much to dispel my inhibitions. I delighted in his pleasures, and he taught me slowly, with infinite precautions, the little gestures that brought him joy. When his handsome penis began to grow in my attentive hands, my heart would beat as if it was trying to escape my ribs. When he ejaculated, I would rub his warm sperm over my breasts, massaging them softly with the sticky cream, and he would gasp in wonder at such a sight.

Our most beautiful evenings were when we could enjoy these intimate moments together. I would prepare a fine meal, humming in the kitchen as soft music wafted across the apartment. Pierre would serve the drinks, always pretending that my cooking and sexual skills were honed by a fine, well chilled, white wine. Sometimes, he would begin to undress me before the meal was finished, and I remember a marvellous Friday night when he stood behind me, holding my breasts as I beat the salad *vinaigrette*, then penetrating and filling me as the dressing began to thicken.

An hour later, we were on the bed renewing our passions when we were suddenly interrupted by a burning smell coming from the kitchen. My desire was such that I begged him to put out my fire before concerning himself with the imminent household disaster. We ate little that night, and it was after making love to me for the fourth time that he made a solemn declaration. While, to all appearance, I was a sweet, innocent, beautiful young wife, hidden inside me was the spirit of a wanton hussy. Was this a compliment? I begged an explanation and he laughed.

"I think that life will give you many opportunities to please men, and sometimes you will accept the challenge."

I blushed with anger, but he took me forcefully in his arms, his eyes inches from mine.

"You will always be my wife, because nobody can take you away from me. But you may, in years to come, discover that you have extraordinary powers over men. I know already that many of my friends are greatly impressed by your personality and your beauty."

"I will only, ever, belong to you, Pierre, my husband."

He smiled enigmatically.

"That also is true."

₨   ℃

We did not discuss his fantasies about my erotic future again. I was disturbed by his statements, which frightened and excited me at the same time. Secretly, I had looked at other young men on occasions and tried to imagine them naked and offered to my gentle caresses. At other times, I had tried to imagine that they possessed me, quite forcefully, to satisfy their animal needs. I did know that there had been moments when I deliberately tried to draw attention to my physical attributes, and thrilled with the feeling of lustful eyes running over my body. I was a shy, innocent country girl with terrible hidden passions, which I felt I needed to hide and control forever.

It is true that I succumbed to Pierre's love of photography. He is a great artist and does some wonderful pictures of mountains, streams and forests. He also discovered a passion for portraits of his wife. He was a photographer of beautiful objects, but I became his favourite composition. As we progressed, slowly and shyly, he made me realise that I had physical characteristics which could become quite beautiful when the lights and the shadows were mastered.

As weeks went by, I began to offer more and more of myself to the camera. All the photographs were in black and white, but it was the marvellous grey shades that created the real beauty. Each *séance* would begin with Pierre loading his cameras while I watched his preparations, sipping a glass of chilled wine. When the bottle was empty, I would be ready to pose.

After a few months, Pierre claimed that it was as if I was making love to his camera. It was true. Every inch of my body was portrayed, and it was most fortunate that he had his own little development laboratory in the attic. I would have died with shame if some negatives had been left in the hands of a local shopkeeper.

In some of the enlargements he produced, I was shocked by the deliberate, provocative stance I took, as I offered my intimacy to the inquisitive lens. Sometimes the cameraman would be overcome by pent-up passion and throw his model to the ground to enforce her. Totally satisfied, still panting with desire and covered with perspiration, I would close my eyes and feel the camera probing the secrets of my passion.

My husband terrified me by asserting that one day his collection would be displayed in a famous art gallery. He laughed when I told him that I hoped that the exhibition would be in Greenland or New Zealand, somewhere far, far away where I would never be recognised.

૪૦   ૭૪

Two years later, Pierre rushed home one evening to announce an important promotion. He was to become account manager in the international division.

"Does this mean we will be leaving here soon?" I asked fearfully. I was desperately in love with our little home.

"Not at all, I will continue to work from the Lyon office. But I will have to go to Paris quite frequently."

"Leaving your poor wife alone?" I asked, glumly.

"Sometimes, when she is very, very good, she can come with me, but only if that dreadful hospital allows it, of course."

"Otherwise, I will just take an occasional lover," I suggested, coyly.

"Yes, we can organise that too. You know Henri Chaumond who works with me? I'll ask him; I understand that he has an excellent reputation."

I pouted.

"Sometimes, your jokes are not funny," I protested.

Privately, I was flattered. Henri was a handsome and elegant young man.

"You started it," he replied.

We decided to go upstairs for a little cuddle before dinner, just to celebrate his promotion. He made me come twice and then we both fell asleep. There is a French motto, which says that you can live on love and fresh water. We certainly survived well that night.

Pierre undertook his early Paris trips alone, leaving me to mope alone at home. Henri Chaumond did ring once, when he was away, to invite me to dinner, and I laughed before refusing. I explained that while I enjoyed good food and good company, I was concerned about the aftermath of a good dinner in his company. He assured me that I would not be disappointed, and I explained that this was exactly why I was refusing his invitation.

My husband also laughed when he got back and I told him the story.

Pierre's company believed in entertaining visitors well, and this would include good food, beautiful sights and lovely female company. Pierre explained that on these occasions they hired the services of professional escorting ladies, persons of distinction and class, with attractive physical attributes and a reasonable understanding of the English language.

One day, he explained, tongue in cheek, that for the next meeting, he might ask his boss to hire an extra lady, to keep the numbers even. I suggested that a prostitute might be more appropriate considering the task in hand, and he agreed with a roar of laughter. The next day, I went down to *Milady Boutique* and bought an extravagant red cocktail dress with an outrageous *décolleté*. The salesgirl was delighted to see her erotic dress so beautifully filled.

That evening, Pierre came home early and I told him that I had found the perfect companion for his little Parisian adventures. I sat him in his favourite armchair and disappeared to slip into the dress.

His reaction was vigorous. With great difficulty, I avoided damage to the dress, but could not refuse his urgent decision to take me, there on the living room carpet. For a second time that week, we missed dinner, but the dress was a marvellous investment. The next evening, he announced that his boss had accepted that I should accompany him to Paris on all future 'hospitality' functions, and that the company would pay for all costs. He added that this decision was made on the understanding that for all functions in Paris I would wear the red cocktail dress, preferably with nothing underneath.

I offered to try it on immediately, and he begged me to put the parade off until after dinner. He added that he preferred me without the dress. We ate, almost hurriedly; because it was the first time that I dined totally naked. But, when you are lucky enough to marry a gentle and handsome husband, to whom you are sexually a perfect match, and you learn that your husband is always attentive to ensure your greatest pleasure, then you submit yourself to his fantasies.

After dinner that night, he laid me on the table, on the embroidered cloth, among the breadcrumbs, the empty plates and glass ware, and he sat on a chair at my feet. I welcomed his inquisitive tongue, I opened myself to the linguistic research undertaken by the most beautiful man on earth, and I do believe that the neighbours probably drank a glass of champagne to celebrate my final orgasm. It is a wonderful thing to be loved by your husband with such passion.

80   03

My first official and paid trip to Paris was a great success. On our first evening as a team, Pierre and I were to entertain two Malaysian executives, with the assistance of Vanessa, a redhead, and Désirée, a real blonde, provided by the *Vendôme* agency. I must admit that they were both extremely beautiful.

It was a long evening. First, we enjoyed an elegant dinner near *La Madeleine;* then, we were off to *Le Lido*. The Malaysian gentlemen, particularly one young man named Andrew, found those long-legged dancers from Leeds or Liverpool most enticing. While the gentleman devoted all their attention to the show, Vanessa and I were able to talk. She was surprised to learn that I did not work for an agency and that I was with them simply as the wife of the host.

Vanessa giggled. It appeared that Andrew had already warned his elder partner that he hoped to be spending the night with me. Pierre was going to have to explain my status later on.

Désirée told me that if I ever came to live in Paris I might like to join them. I had, she said, all it takes. I told them that I would not like to have sex with different men every evening, and they both laughed. Firstly, I learned, an escort girl, if she was lucky, got two bookings a week, and this alone produced about three times the income of a bank clerk. Secondly, both the agency and the host (Pierre, in this instance) insisted that sex was not part of the agreement. However, they also forgot to tell their foreign guests of this restriction.

It was not a serious matter. Both girls told me that while sex was often on the post-dinner menu, it was rarely totally carried out, due to the generally advanced state of intoxication of the guests. Nevertheless, sex always generated a generous tip, generally proportional to the pleasure provided by the generous hostesses; and both Vanessa and Désirée, I was assured, were highly competent.

We then moved on to a show in *Pigalle* where the spectators sat around an arena to watch the gladiators, in this case two naked young women fighting for the vaginal possession of an extraordinarily long dildo. The Malaysian visitors were obviously greatly impressed by our culture, and I could see that Andrew was going to need quick relief.

I never did get time to explain to Pierre that there was an imminent misunderstanding. As we drove our guests back to their hotel, I found myself on the back seat of a taxi, the eager Andrew lodged between Vanessa and myself. He needed help, desperately, and to the delight of our driver, I dropped my shoulder straps and let his hands wander over my firm breasts. I discovered that the sensation was enjoyable. Vanessa whispered a few words of encouragement and dragged his swollen penis out of its hiding. She began to stroke, vigorously, the beautiful smooth, round cylinder, and I shivered with delight as his lips found one of my nipples. I murmured words of encouragement in his ear, watching Vanessa bring him to the boil. With a loud cry he ejaculated, and I groaned with pleasure to see the streams of hot semen pour from him.

"You're a natural for the job," Vanessa whispered as we climbed out of the car.

A fortnight later, Pierre announced with pleasure that the Malaysian company had been accepted as a partner for a large tourist investment in French Polynesia. His boss was delighted and insisted that I accompany my husband on all future hospitality activities.

"It appears that all Andrew remembers from his trip to Paris was the beautiful woman in the red dress," Pierre told me, proudly.

I was flushed with embarrassment, and he grinned.

"I had to admit to the boss that he was not talking about one of the professional ladies but my own wife, and now he is eager to meet you."

It was difficult for me to explain how I had got caught up in such a situation, but Pierre was not greatly concerned.

A few weeks later, we took the train up to Paris to have lunch with Pierre's boss, Bernard Courtot. He wore expensive perfume, had a head of dyed silvery hair, bore the *légion d'honneur* on the lapel of his suit, and had eyes which explored me: they wandered, penetrated and gleamed with each new discovery, right through the seven course meal.

He explained that he understood the admiration of their visitor, and suggested that I should always accompany my husband for all future events when he would be entertaining potential foreign investors. He added that any ensuing wear and tear to my clothing, hair, skin or jewellery would be covered by the company. Pierre smiled thinly through the speech.

When I got back to the hotel, I was very angry.

"When I told you I would be your slut, I did not expect you to take the offer seriously," I shouted angrily. "Are you expecting me to amuse all your foreign visitors?"

"Of course not. You are there to be the elegant hostess, welcoming the visitors to your country. The other girls do the dirty work."

"That's not fair," I protested, tongue in cheek.

He laughed uproariously. Then we spoke about his personal philosophy and how it concerned our marriage. I was both pleased and surprised.

My husband believed that my body was not his property, but mine to use as I wished. If I discovered a sudden need to enjoy pleasures with a certain man, he would not stand in my way, providing it was private, hygienic, did not affect our marriage and did not create harm for anyone else. He would also require to be warned of any event of that nature.

I realised that ours was to be a modern marriage, a situation which could prove to be highly unsuitable for an extremely jealous woman such as myself. I asked whether he would be offering his beautiful penis to some appealing lady at some time. He smiled.

"Perhaps, but that would be under the same conditions and subject to your prior approval."

I nodded, reluctantly, my acceptance.

That night, after a particularly active session of mutual pleasure, I whispered in his ear.

"No man will ever satisfy me as well as you. And you will never find a woman more attentive and servile to your needs than me."

"We shall see, we shall see," he muttered, teasingly, and I poked him several times in the back with a stiff finger until he begged me to stop.

"If you apologise, right now, I will offer you a special surprise," I told him.

He did, and stretched out on his back, expectantly. I rose above him, placed myself upon his great mace and rode him to a climax. It was wonderful to confirm, every day, that we loved one another as man and wife, but also as lovers.

☙ ❧

I accompanied Pierre on three other trips to Paris. The second time we were with three Canadian businessmen, and accompanied by three magnificent ladies from *Ebony Magic*. My husband told me that while black women were not appropriate company for rampant executives back in North America, in France, our visitors were eager to experience the wonders offered by the ladies of Senegal. In those circumstances there was no confusion about my role for the evening, but I noted that Alice, Denise and Estelle were all hoping to have sex with our transatlantic visitors. Alice told me privately that the extra money would go straight to a good cause – her parents back in Africa.

The third time we were hosts to two executives from South Africa, and I was delighted to find old friends, Vanessa and Désirée. We went to the same spots and discovered the two same young ladies, still struggling with that massive dildo. The two girls whispered that they were expecting imminent sexual overtures and were both looking forward to a little Zulu extravaganza. They must have performed well, because Pierre was delighted to announce that the brewery deal he was working on went through.

Our last guest was a dour German businesswoman accompanied by her husband, also a director of her company. Wilhelm did NOT enjoy the restaurant, he thought that the Lido was BORING, and considered that the two young ladies from Pigalle were particularly UGLY. On the way back to the hotel, his wife, completely drunk, attempted to explore Pierre's crotch.

We managed to carry her to bed, where she began to snore as soon as she hit the mattress. Wilhelm then whipped out his magnificent Nikon and begged permission to take a photo of me. I looked at Pierre, who nodded encouragingly, and I dropped the straps of my sexy red cocktail dress. Wilhelm shot at me from all angles, muttering phrases of admiration in German between clenched teeth. He quickly ran out of film. He wanted to pay me, attempting to thrust a handful of Marks into my hand, but we both refused.

I never knew the result of the German venture. Two weeks later, Pierre had been promoted, again, and my world was about to become a very large place.

3. Heading South

It was in September of 1980, just after harvesting the Brouilly grapes for Uncle Paul, that I learned the extraordinary news. My clever, handsome, intelligent, gentle and wonderful husband had been promoted to manage a new service within his company, that of developing investment activities in Australia. We would be leaving in eight weeks.

Australia!

Firstly, I checked with my gynaecologist. Not only would my birth control coil work perfectly in the Southern Hemisphere (despite the fact that I would be standing all day upside down), but I would find replacement models over there if required. We did not want an unplanned accident to spoil the immediate future.

We drank a bottle of champagne to celebrate our success and the bubbles went to my head. My imagination moved into overdrive. I could see us on an outrigger, moving from island to island on the Great Barrier Reef. A beautiful Polynesian girl would bring us decapitated young coconuts to quench our thirst, and I would smile indulgently as Pierre made love to her on the hot sand. Then it would be my turn.

We would live in a smart house on the waterfront overlooking Sydney and the Opera House, and Pierre would be driven to his skyscraper office by a chauffeur weaving between the ferries in a silver speed boat. All his secretaries would be tall, blonde and talk like Elle MacPherson. I would be dreadfully jealous.

On weekends, we would take our Range Rover out to the desert where we would search for sapphires, opals and emeralds. On Saturday evenings, we would cook kangaroo steaks on the barbecue and drink a heady Australian red wine before making love on a woven reed carpet. Young Aboriginals would be squatting just at the edge of the firelight, watching intensely as my husband made me cry out with pleasure.

❧   ☙

When I woke up the next morning, I was still in France, feverishly searching for hangover remedies. As I swallowed my fizzy cure, Pierre told me that he would be bringing home some 'briefing papers' about Australia. Life over there would be most enjoyable, but not quite as exotic as I had been imagining the previous evening.

I discovered that Australia was an enormous, dry continent, with a few uninspiring hills, called mountains, small rivers, beautiful rain forests and glorious beaches. There were a dozen large cities, some quite beautiful, but it would take at least a day to drive from one to another. Sydney was 6,000 kilometres from Perth, the distance from Paris to Moscow. The railways were appalling and the roads were unexciting, which explained why people seemed to travel everywhere by plane. Most people lived on the coast and ignored what everyone called the 'outback'.

I learned that Pierre would receive a special allowance, which would effectively double his salary. This was to compensate him for being overseas and without a second income, that of his wife. The brief explained that the cost of living in Australia was about half that of France, so we would be more than comfortable. In fact, the company considered me an important asset to Pierre, so expenses such as hairdressers, beauticians and nice clothing for special events would be paid for by Head Office.

Laughingly, Pierre told me that Bernard Courtot had insisted that our Australian contacts saw 'as much of his beautiful wife as possible'.

"And, I don't think he was talking about frequency," he added.

"You think he means that generous cleavage dresses will be standard issue?"

My darling husband nodded.

"You're probably right. Do you mind?"

"Not really. As long as I am with you and it helps you in your job. In fact, I quite enjoy teasing your clients."

He smiled, grabbed me in his arms, and squeezed tightly.

"My goodness, where is that shy little country girl I married four years ago?"

He released me, and then tugged roughly at the buttons on the front of my dress, to gaze at my breasts.

"You must admit they are beautiful."

I shrugged off the compliment.

"And did your boss add that a firm and friendly hand on an investor's penis might help pull off a big job?" I asked, tersely.

"You have become suddenly dreadfully cynical, and you also have an unfortunate choice of words," Pierre laughed.

I decided to change the subject.

"Do you realise that we will be living in the Southern Hemisphere so that I will be on top most of the time when we make love?" I asked.

He gazed at me in surprise.

"Do you know I never thought of that? Do you think we should practise?"

"Straight away," I agreed, pulling his hand as I headed towards the bedroom.

An hour later we concluded that our love life would be greatly improved in the antipodes. It is wonderful for a shy girl like me to overcome all, well, most of, her inhibitions, thanks to an understanding and supportive husband.

                                                    80   03

The date for our departure approached rapidly. Pierre was busy with preparations, coming home late every evening, and looking very tired. He also worked in his study over the weekends, putting together his plans for the first campaign in the Southern Hemisphere.

He was in Paris for several days, including my last day working as a nurse. The team from my ward decided to organise a farewell party for me. We ate and drank, and I was enjoying myself, although a little angry that Pierre was not with me. It was late in the evening, when most of my friends had already left the party, that Georges Bertin, a young house surgeon, admitted that he had been in love with me ever since he had joined the staff. He told me that my departure would break his heart.

There was, he declared, only one cure. I accepted his conclusion, finished my glass of wine and dragged him by the hand to the linen cupboard. There, he made love to me with an extraordinary vigour and dexterity. I was exhausted, and totally satisfied. Why did I give myself to a man, once married, when I repelled all advances before? I concluded that it must have been something in the wine. Or was it a way of saying farewell to France and my dear hospital?

I was not proud the next morning. Georges had not been discreet, but most of my colleagues thought it was a wonderful send-off. I whispered a brief commentary of his talent to my two best friends, and both Alice and Suzie hoped that he would still be on the staff when the time came for their farewell party.

Although I had been delighted by the extramarital experience, I knew that it had in no way affected my passion for my darling husband. I did not tell him of my adventure, even when he came home and confessed to having spent a farewell evening with Bernard Courtot, Vanessa and Désirée. I suspect that one of the ladies might have 'entertained' my husband that night but, in view of my own misdemeanour, I decided not to ask any questions.

            80   CB

It was a painful separation from both families. Both mothers cried while both fathers tried to keep their emotions contained. Ashamedly, we agreed that it would be a great relief to climb on board the aircraft that was to take us away to our new home. We were to take very little with us, just some clothes, toiletries and Pierre's essential papers. Less important things would follow by air freight, while our furniture would be placed in storage. I sat in our apartment, alone, watching the men carry away the things I loved, and cried with despair. Was my husband's new career this important?

It was a long and tiring flight to Singapore, but luckily I slept much of the way. We travelled in the comfort of Business Class, and wine was plentiful. Our steward was determined that this connoisseur of French wines, travelling to Australia for the first time, should familiarise herself with as many Australian varieties as possible during the flight. He was a true patriot and a terribly handsome man. Pierre told me that I snored quite loudly, but none of the other passengers seemed to mind.

Singapore was hot, noisy, exciting and terribly clean. It was in our smart and heavily air-conditioned hotel that I met Henry Coles, our first local business partner. Pierre had already met him in Paris, and they greeted one another like old friends. Over lunch, I discovered that Henry was a real estate promoter in Queensland and that he hoped to attract French investors to a program he was offering in a place called Surfers Paradise. If the town lived up to its name, it must be truly wonderful.

Henry had been meeting some Singapore investors to discuss similar plans. The State of Queensland was seen as an ideal holiday place for wealthy Singaporeans, and Henry was hoping to set up a triangular financial package. I was not quite sure what all this meant, as I was not a financial expert and my English was still limited.

The next evening, we flew from Singapore to Brisbane. Henry was on the same flight; in fact he was just across the aisle from us. We were the only passengers in Business Class. We dined well, drank too much, and started to settle down for a little sleep. Instead of a steward, this time we had a beautiful, blonde hostess. There was some whispering between Pierre and the lady while our seats were being pulled out in a position to allow us to sleep, and she brought a lovely mohair blanket to cover us both. She then dimmed the lights.

"You are now going to be taken at 30,000 feet, for the first time in your life," my husband announced softly.

I knew what was about to happen. I helped him remove all impediments. I wriggled as my skirt, my blouse, my pantyhose and knickers were withdrawn, and I had a sneaking suspicion that Henry was not really asleep, but was watching through half-closed eyes. I whispered my fears to Pierre, and he whispered back that it didn't really matter. I think I understood. I love my husband, and I think he wanted me to fantasise.

While Pierre entered me, from behind, I closed my eyes and sighed, inadvertently, perhaps, letting the blanket slip. A few minutes later, as my darling husband began to take me more vigorously; I gasped with pleasure and opened my eyes, finding Henry's eyes immediately. He watched me, eyes exploring frankly, with a smile of apparent satisfaction on his face.

I fell as soon as Pierre had finished. Later, I felt the hostess put the blanket back in place, and I think I heard Henry's sigh of disappointment. This time, it was Pierre who was snoring loudly.

∞   ∞

At dawn, I was awakened by the pretty stewardess who was offering refreshing face towels. She brushed my hair back from my face and kissed me lightly on the cheeks.

"Welcome to the sky-high club, I hope it was enjoyable?" she whispered.

I blushed, too embarrassed to reply. Had it been obvious that I had also enjoyed the admiring gaze of the other man? Was I becoming a loose woman?

"Come down to the toilets now," she suggested. "You might like to freshen up."

She stayed with me, embarrassingly close, and helped me clean my legs and buttocks with soft towels. Her hands were wonderfully soft, and I could feel her warm breath on my thighs. I almost hoped to feel the brush of her full, warm lips, but she held back.

"It is a pity, you are so beautiful, but you smell of man," she murmured. "If you ever travel without your husband, I hope I'm on your flight."

She escorted me back to my seat, her hand on my arm, her hip brushing against mine. Henry was asleep and Pierre was enjoying his first coffee of the day.

I explained her comments to my husband, who smiled.

"They say that all the cabin staff on this airline are homosexual," he explained. "In her case, it's a great pity."

"Not necessarily."

He raised a questioning eyebrow, and I grinned.

"She said that she hoped that we would catch up, one day. I agreed."

He laughed softly.

"I discover a little more of you every day."

"I think Henry discovered quite a bit last night, too," I replied, petulantly.

He nodded, sadly.

"It was a silly game, but you loved showing him your body and your pleasure, didn't you?"

My face flushed with embarrassment, but I did not reply.

∞   ⌘

We cleared immigration at Brisbane airport quite quickly and Henry led us towards the long-term car park. He helped us pack our luggage in an enormous Ford station wagon, the biggest car I had ever seen. He gave Pierre a bunch of keys, shook his hand, pecked me cautiously on one cheek, and stepped back.

"Off you go. The address and the map are in the glove box. It's about an hour's drive. I'll see you next Wednesday."

The sky was blue, the car whispered its way to the highway, and I raised my skirt to offer my thighs to the great Australian sun. My wonderful husband, Pierre, was comfortably driving a strange car with the steering wheel in front of the passenger's seat. Suddenly, I realised that he was also driving down the exit ramp from the car park, on the wrong side. I was about to shout a warning, then I remembered the brief. In this country, we drive on the left.

We arrived in Surfers Paradise exactly one hour later, as forecast. The beach was long, with enormous surf waves, but the coast was overshadowed by tall apartment buildings. The streets were narrow and full of traffic and the footpaths were crowded. It was obviously a popular holiday resort.

Pierre found the street indicated on the card in the glove box, and used the remote control to access an underground car park. We took the lift to the 16th floor. The apartment that Henry had lent us was magnificent. The kitchen was enormous, and there were four bedrooms and two bathrooms. The upper floor had a large semi-covered living area with a spa and a sunken swimming pool. I had never seen such luxury in my life, although I found the furnishing a little *nouveau-riche*.

The next day, Pierre took me to see the investment project. I have never been terribly interested in business, but I found the real estate proposed really beautiful. The planned property would consist of two towers of 18 stories each, set in a small park. The ground level would include a park, terraces, a small shopping concourse, palm trees and swimming pools. Under the gardens there would be a two-level car park for nearly 200 cars.

The buildings were designed so that all the apartments (there would be two on each floor) had a view over the beach and the ocean. We visited a sample apartment which had been decorated and furnished to attract the Australian investor. There was lots of chrome, gold leaf and mirrors, and the walls were decorated with a tapestry offering gold bamboo trees on a shiny silver background. I could not imagine my parents or any of my friends being enticed by such décor.

I said as much to Pierre who repeated my comment to Henry. He smiled.

"You see, Marie, Queensland is a little special. Everything here is new and exciting, and people go overboard to try to be different."

I nodded, to show that I understood.

"But who are you trying to attract as investors? Will they like this kind of decoration?"

"Probably not. But, do not forget that there is only one apartment decorated like this, it is the only one people visit. Anyone who buys can decorate to their own taste."

"I understand. But perhaps you should have another sample apartment furnished more simply."

My husband laughed, put his arm around my waist and squeezed me.

"My wife is becoming a little business woman. This is interesting."

Henry nodded thoughtfully.

"I should have thought of that myself!" he answered. "If we are trying to attract French and Singaporean investors, perhaps we should furnish two other apartments in a way to suit their tastes."

Pierre agreed enthusiastically.

"Perhaps we could get Marie to choose how to furnish the French model?"

Henry agreed immediately.

"We also have other attractions for would-be investors. Would you like to see them?"

We agreed and followed him to take the lift to the eighth floor. He knocked on the door and a tall girl with blonde hair opened the door. She greeted us with a big smile, and Henry introduced Samantha.

"Hi, Henry, hi everyone," she said, cheerfully.

The apartment was strangely, if sparsely, furnished. There was a curtain rail across the doorway leading to a passageway serving two bedrooms and a bathroom. Each bedroom was furnished with a thick double mattress, laid on the floor, with pillows and a sheet. Samantha explained that the one on the left was her 'workshop', and that the one on the right was used by Barbara. Barbara did not work on Tuesdays.

I think I was beginning to understand.

"Samantha and her friend entertain some of the potential investors, I suppose?"

Samantha replied herself.

"Mainly the guys from Melbourne looking to invest in a place for their future retirement," she explained with a grin. "Climbing on board a young, tanned Queensland chick does much for their motivation."

"Charming," I muttered. "Is this one of your ideas, Henry?"

"Just another local custom," he protested.

"The mirrored cupboard doors must be a great help," I suggested sarcastically.

Samantha nodded in agreement.

"They love it. Can you imagine a 50-year-old public servant from Geelong playing with a suntanned beauty half his age?"

"I can well imagine," I admitted, thoughtfully. "I even know a few Frenchmen who would find it inspiring. What do you think, Pierre?"

"Wonderfully motivating for some, I am sure," he agreed.

"Would you like me to come down once or twice to help Samantha?" I asked, with an evil smile. "Perhaps a little French flavour for the Singaporeans?"

Poor Henry actually nodded once before Pierre interrupted his salacious thoughts with a very loud, "Certainly not!"

"I think you're becoming just a little too cheeky, young lady," he added.

"Yes, father," I replied, lowering my gaze like a bashful, admonished schoolgirl.

Henry laughed, and then added a strange comment.

"If wives use their talents to promote their husband's business interests, I see no problems."

I was to understand his comment later.

ℴ ℴ

Later that evening I was discussing my ideas for French décor with Pierre and explaining why I had not been at all impressed with the furnishings we'd seen. He agreed with most of what I said, except for my dislike of the mirrors. After a second glass of chilled white wine from Western Australia, he begged me to kneel naked in front of the mirrored wardrobe doors in the spare room, while he took possession of his beloved wife, from behind. I must admit that watching myself being laboured, breasts quivering with each thrust of that beautiful man, was most exciting. My climax was fantastic. I loved my husband with passion.

We drank a third glass, to celebrate our achievement and, after a few minutes, he murmured that it might be quite good with Samantha, too.

"What are you saying?" I asked, angrily.

"Well," he said thoughtfully, "look at it this way. She is working for me, indirectly; it would be reasonable for me to check out her qualifications."

"If you do," I warned him, "you might lose your own qualifications. I might take a knife and remove them!"

He laughed, and I threw a cushion.

He laughed again. Then he ran, and I chased him into the kitchen. He begged for forgiveness.

My punishment was terrible. I placed him on his back on the lounge carpet, stroked his beautiful organ until it was ready to burst, and then placed myself upon the pole. As I rose and fell, and he moaned, I warned him not to forget that I wanted every drop. There were to be no leftovers if he was to see Samantha tomorrow.

I do believe that making love madly with the handsome husband you love is the only way for a woman to enjoy real sexual pleasure. Your body, your soul and your spirit all participate.

ᘓ   ᘔ

After a few days, I left Pierre with his business plans, and began to visit what was called the Gold Coast. It was fascinating, and quite strange. For example, I saw a yellow Rolls Royce convertible, covered in advertising for a real estate agent, and which was used to take tourists for a drive around the city. I saw a Japanese wedding and a Queensland funeral where the whole convoy was comprised of white Cadillacs. People clapped as it went past.

I saw many, many surf boys and surf girls, they were tanned and beautifully shaped, and I noticed that many of the young men looked in my direction. I was wearing a flimsy white cotton dress, cut high above the knees and my cleavage was generous. I was a little curvaceous brunette, quite different from the tall, angular blondes of Broadbeach. Pierre told me that I was dressing provocatively because I wanted young men to look at me with interest in their eyes, and while I protested his claims quite angrily, I knew that he was right.

I had discovered that my body loved the sun. I tanned quickly, offering myself for a couple of hours, every afternoon by our rooftop swimming pool. I was alone, so I wore a very small string and let the sun enjoy my body.

"You are tanning beautifully," Henry commented one afternoon. I had not heard him arrive, and panicked. I searched desperately for a towel to cover my nudity, but there was nothing nearby.

"How did you get in?" I asked, peevishly.

"With my key. It is my apartment, you know."

Of course. What an idiot I was. Suddenly, I noticed my t-shirt a few metres away and, with a silent gesture, invited him to pass it to me. He refused.

"I've seen it all before," he protested. "The only difference is that it is a lot browner than the last time. Come on, Marie. Relax."

I relaxed. I began to enjoy watching his eyes move across me, and I could see a fascinating bulge growing below his trouser belt. Ah, men, they are such pigs. To prove my point, I stirred softly, lifting my breasts towards him, quite inadvertently, of course.

He laughed.

"That's better. Don't worry, my little darling, I can see them. But I am worried for them."

I was startled.

"They are not as nice?" I asked quickly, searching already for the reply in his gaze. But, of course, they were still beautiful. I only had to look at that bulge.

"Do you know that the Australian sun is quite dangerous and that this country has a terrible reputation for skin cancer?"

I did not.

"Do you think I am too exposed?" I asked.

He grinned.

"You will never be exposed enough, in my opinion. No, you just need good protection. I'll show you."

He disappeared inside for a moment and came back a few minutes later with a large brown bottle.

"This is from Tahiti," he explained. "It's made from refined coconut oil, exotic tropical perfumes, vanilla, and... who knows what else."

He offered, I protested. He insisted, I surrendered.

He began with my feet and worked his way upwards, very slowly. When he reached my string, he became quite adventurous, and I smacked his hand. He spent the next ten minutes working the oil into my hot breasts, and I closed my eyes. I believe that I may well have moaned with pleasure, now and again.

He murmured that the tender places must be protected too and, with a reluctant sigh, I allowed him to work a little under the string, parting my thighs slightly to help. He reached an area where protection was most needed, when I heard Pierre ask, "Can I take over?"

I do believe that for a little while there were four hands working the soft, warm oil into every pore of my body. Then Pierre was alone. He removed my string, and I lifted my hips to help, despite knowing that Henry was watching. To hide my embarrassment, I kept my eyes tightly closed. My clitoris is small and shy, but Pierre knew how to find it. However, this time his strong but tender fingers did become openly adventurous, and, eyes still closed, I clasped that saucy hand, willing it to finish its work, and I cried out with great pleasure when it accomplished its task. When I finally opened my eyes, it was Henry's hand that I was holding, and Pierre was wearing a wide and cheeky grin.

That evening I was so angry I told Pierre that he would never take me again.

"You treat me like a slut," I complained. "Maybe I should go and work with Samantha."

"What about Barbara?" he asked. "She works too."

"Ah, the other tart. I have not yet met that one."

"She will be dining one evening with us, and Henry."

"Why would I have a woman like that at my table?" I asked angrily.

"Because she's Henry's wife," he replied simply. "She is Chinese and looks after the French investors – with great success I might add."

I was horrified, but my darling husband always knew how to help me through these bad moments. Firstly, he insisted that I drink a large glass of cool, refreshing wine without stopping to take a breath. Then he asked me what I would like to do next.

I told him, and we did it. However, this time, once he had fulfilled my expectations, he talked severely to me. It was most unusual.

He explained that like most healthy people, I had fantasies. He said that they were good for my health. I protested, but accepted. He told me that as the years went by I would reach my sexual peak, and that my fantasies would grow. I asked how long this would last and he replied that he hoped that with me it would last for a long time. I confessed, blushing, that I might agree with him. He said that whatever happened, I must always confide in my husband. He would be there to guide me, encourage me, and to restrain me when necessary.

"What about Henry?" I asked, finally.

"He certainly wants to make love to you, in my opinion."

I admitted that I had the feeling, too.

"Should I allow him to do that? He is married, after all. But, then, his wife entertains other gentlemen. It is my fault, I have tempted him like a cheap vamp."

"Would you like to be taken by Henry?" he asked, bluntly.

I lowered my eyes.

"I think that perhaps I would. I know that he wants me badly. That is flattering for me, and I wonder whether I should not give him satisfaction. Then, he may give me a great orgasm, which I really should only have with my husband."

"Please," Pierre protested, "let's not get sanctimonious about this. Here are two people who want to have sex together. The woman is married and wants her husband to know and to agree. He is married, and I am sure that Barbara would not mind. It will change nothing in either marriage, believe me."

"Of course, of course. I will still love you until I die."

"Then, I agree. Better, I order you to do it, for your own sake, to affirm your personality and your independence. But, please, not until we leave here."

"Why should I wait? If I am decided, maybe we should do it now. Why not tonight?"

He sighed.

"Because he would then probably want to enjoy you regularly, and that I cannot allow at this stage."

I lowered my eyes, to hide my deception, and nodded.

"When we leave Queensland and this project, I will organise a lovely dinner, and then I will offer him my wife."

I stared at him, amazed.

"You would offer your wife to another man? That is crazy. What about the beautiful Barbara."

He laughed.

"I might have to entertain her. It will be great fun. Henry will have the impression of possessing and using you, he will not realise that it is exactly the opposite that is happening."

I clapped my hands with pleasure.

"That is wonderful, and I agree. And I will say, on that last night, 'Dear husband, get me Henry. I want to use him now.'"

I hesitated again.

"I am not too sure about the beautiful Barbara being entertained by my husband, though."

"We will see. Meanwhile, there is another lover who needs you. Would you like him now?"

"Oh, yes please," I murmured. "He is the one I prefer."

We made love passionately. I think I will love my husband even after my death.

I met Barbara two days later. She looked like an Asian princess: small, terribly slim, with beautiful eyes and long silky hair down to her buttocks. I could imagine that many visiting French investors would be overcome by her charm and beauty. She had just finished entertaining a businessman from Marseille who had bought two apartments. Her cheeks were flushed, her eyes were sparkling, and she laughed as she gave her husband the $50 tip the visitor had just given her.

80   03

A few months later, Pierre announced that we would be leaving Queensland in a few days. Nearly three quarters of the project had investors, and Pierre assured me that Bernard Courtot in Paris was delighted. Henry would be left to run the operation alone, assisted by his wife, Barbara. We invited Henry to a farewell dinner, and he came alone as his wife was in Paris being trained in corporate policy. I am sure that Bernard Courtot took a personal interest in her induction program.

As I was preparing the coffee in the kitchen, Pierre asked me if I was going to offer myself to Henry afterwards. Our guest was very eager. I told him that I had decided against it. It was a little early, but I might like to invite Henry to spend a few days with us once we were finally settled in Adelaide. He smiled and agreed.

"He'll be disappointed, but he'll understand," he assured me.

When Henry said goodbye and wished us well with the next venture, his voice was sad. I nearly changed my mind! Instead, I threw my arms around his neck and kissed him passionately on both cheeks.

"You will come to Adelaide soon," I promised. "I will make you very, very welcome."

Then I pulled away, frightened that he would no longer be able to contain himself. When he finally left, Pierre told me that I was a dreadful little teaser. We made love on the carpet, passionately, and I closed my eyes and imagined Henry was inside me. I think that my lovely partner knew that I was fantasising that night, but he made no comment. It is wonderful to have an understanding husband.

4. Churches, Vineyards and Lovers

Pierre had bought a BMW and announced that we would drive all around the coast to Adelaide on a road called the Pacific Highway. I checked on a road atlas, and discovered that Australia was truly enormous. We drove through small towns whose existence seemed to be totally devoted to beer, the beach and the surf. I saw lots of handsome, tanned young men with long blonde hair and surfboards under their arms, without a worry in the world. I could think of a few French girls who would love to be with them. If Brigitte saw this, she would be mad with jealousy.

It is difficult for a person coming from Europe to imagine the length of this almost deserted coastline. There are literally hundreds of kilometres of dunes, beaches and surf. I had reclined the back of my seat and was offering myself to the hot Australian sun. Pierre had opened the sunroof, and I had not realised that as we passed each big truck on the road the drivers, high in their cabins, were enjoying the view. A long blast from the air horn on a Volvo semi-trailer made me jump, and Pierre laughed as he saw, in his rear vision mirror, that the driver was gesticulating happily.

"I think you had better put those lovely breasts back into their nest," he suggested. "You could create an accident."

I sighed and put them away but I left my skirt around my waist. After all, legs were just legs.

We had pulled into a service station to fill up, when the same Volvo truck drew in behind us. The driver sauntered over and leaned in through the window. He grinned.

"Lady, if you go hitch-hiking one day, I want you to stop my truck."

I laughed.

"I promise I will."

His eyes were wandering and he appeared to be an expert in suntanned thighs.

"If you travel with me, I will invite you to visit the nice little sleeper in the back of my cabin," he offered.

I shook my head.

"That would not be a good idea," I decided.

He feigned surprise.

"And why is that?" he asked.

"Because you and I would never reach our destination."

He was still laughing when Pierre came back to the car.

"Congratulations," he said. "She has a lovely body, a lovely accent and a great sense of humour."

Pierre smiled proudly.

"And you don't know the rest," he retorted.

The truck driver shrugged his shoulders and grinned.

"I can guess."

For the rest of the trip to Sydney, I left my breasts inside my sundress and kept the skirt in a more appropriate position.

∞   ∝

We spent two days in Sydney and at first I thought it must be the most beautiful city in the world. However, it is also obvious that the best views, the best access to the harbour and the best sites are the privilege of the rich. I also saw the ordinary suburbs, which are home to the rest of the population. I thought that the city centre was small, crowded and oppressive. I decided that I would only live in Sydney if Pierre became a millionaire.

I was grateful to see that the English settlers had recognised the contribution of the French explorers, and I discovered the suburb of La Perouse with patriotic pride. As we drove South, towards Antarctica as Pierre explained, the sky became paler, and there were little white clouds in the sky, like those of Europe. The towns and the beaches were smaller, but the farmland was hillier and greener. I noted in my diary that since leaving the Gold Coast I had made love with Pierre in Ballina, in Port Macquarie, in Gosford, in Manly, in Kiama and in Eden. We travelled nearly 1,400 kilometres before reaching the State of Victoria. What an enormous country.

At last, more than 2,000 kilometres later, we arrived in Melbourne. It seemed obvious to me that everyone in this city was trying to pretend to be still living in Europe. The trees, the avenues, the tramways, the cafés, everything looked terribly familiar. I would later tell my friends in France that if they visited Australia they might find Melbourne boring, it would not look like the Australia they wanted to find.

Melbourne people were also dreadfully worried about their image. In the shops, people noticed my accent and asked where I was from, and then they wanted to know if I was happy, if I was enjoying Melbourne and if I did not agree that it was the most beautiful city in the world.

We then drove along the Great Ocean Road and kept going all the way to Adelaide, another 1,000 kilometres. I told Pierre that if we kept going for another week we would be back in France. The coast was pretty and quite savage, but I was getting very tired of car travel. I also found that after more than 3,000 kilometres every country town, and its local motel, looked the same. Australia does not have the constant changes of scenery that Europe does, and can become terribly monotonous. Pierre showed me on the map that we could have made a much shorter trip, almost across the middle, and that it would have been very different.

Did I tell you about Moe, Geelong and Warnambool? Yes, you may have guessed, my wonderful husband made love to me in each of these, too. Each orgasm has been remembered by a red circle on my Touring Atlas of Australia, and there are still many virgin pages. Later, I realised that I would be happy to go travelling again. It's a long, long drive to Perth...

⅜　⅝

Finally, we arrived in Adelaide. It was beautiful. I was a little concerned after spending two or three days exploring the city. There seemed to be a church at every crossroad, and I asked my husband if this was a city of puritans. He reassured me: there were probably more puritans in Adelaide than in any other city in Australia, but even so they would not number more than 200.

I was delighted when Pierre told me that he had found a house up in the Adelaide hills, with a magnificent view over the city, a beautiful garden, a large swimming pool, and, above all, air conditioning.

Pierre's initial work concerned helping French investors interested in the Barossa Valley wine growing region. I accompanied him often, and once met two Frenchmen, representing Pierre's clients, who were exploring potential wineries. They both wanted to flirt, apparently because they had not seen any French female flesh for a few weeks. I think that if I had been a Frenchman living in Adelaide, I would have been awfully attracted to some of those tall blonde beauties I saw on Glenelg beach, a vivid contrast to the small brunettes that France seems to produce.

But Olivier and Franck insisted that I was beautiful, and to please them I would tan my French body beside my beautiful swimming pool while Pierre burned meat on the barbecue and they drank white wine and drooled. I was just rubbing some oil around my nipples when Olivier pointed his wine glass in my direction.

"Pierre, you see there two reasons why a Frenchman can never stay too long away from his home country."

"Unless he brings his favourite toys with him," Pierre suggested.

I joined in the laughter. Pierre told me that evening that he had not realised just how important his wife's tits would be to the promotion of French investments in Australian wineries. I told him not to be vulgar, and pointed out that I could also have been just as successful in real estate and trucking.

80   G3

Over the months, I discovered the pleasures of living in what was a very special city. While Australia is far away from home, Adelaide is far from everything else in Australia. A very rude man from Sydney told me that if you looked at a map of Australia, it looked like a pair of squatting buttocks. And Adelaide was the arsehole, he added. I told him that he was vulgar and stupid.

I noticed that many people in Adelaide went to Melbourne for their holidays. Also, although Adelaide faces the Great Australian Bight and Antarctica, the people there considered themselves to be living on the East Coast. I think it was the Adelaide way of keeping as far as possible away from Perth.

Despite the distance, and the hot summers, I still love Adelaide. But perhaps this is because it was in Adelaide that I met my first lover.

As usual when opening up business in a new city, Pierre sought out the preferred local partner. The Embassy had introduced him to Jimmy Matthews, an investment adviser in one of the major banks. Jimmy had been helpful in the past to French interests. After a couple of meetings with Pierre and a dinner at our home with his sparkling wife, Shelley, Jimmy accepted Pierre's proposal to become the firm's manager for South Australia as well as a minor shareholder in the Australian operation. He gave in his notice to the bank, and never looked back.

We became good friends, and often had dinner together in one of the good restaurants of Adelaide. One evening, after an excellent Italian meal, Jimmy asked if we would like to see Shelley's favourite after-dinner haunt. At first his wife looked a little embarrassed, but then she giggled and gave in. Ten minutes later we were in the Erotic Cavern Sex Shop, the first time in my life that I entered this kind of establishment. At first, there did not appear to be much to see. The magazines were wrapped in plastic, but their front covers told all. The category offering stimulation for males proposed vulgar blondes with inflated pendulum breasts, or some delightful pictures of sweet young men sucking one another's penises.

Further on, the ladies could choose between the collection of American Negroes with penises hanging below their knees, or determined young ladies offering one another vaginal delights with appropriate tools of various colour, size and consistency.

Shelley grabbed me by the arm to drag me over to her favourite corner: a showcase of artificial penises, stimulators and vibrators of different shapes and sizes. Until now, Jimmy had refused to buy her the toy of her dreams, still proudly displayed: a black, four-speed penis around 20 centimetres long. Mike, the owner of the store, obviously knew our friends very well, as he was leading Jimmy and Pierre towards a viewing cubicle, the front door of which was a heavy black curtain.

"I'll keep the ladies entertained," he assured them as they disappeared inside.

I had been wandering around the shop, gazing at covers of R-rated videos, when Mike introduced me to Jonathan, another visitor he knew well. I must confess that I had noticed him: he had been staring at me, and I had been flattered by the attention of such a handsome man.

For the first few minutes of our encounter, he prattled and I stared. He was tall and slim, with a smile which I am sure could melt pantyhose, a thin moustache and dark, wavy hair. He was probably just under 40 and, in my opinion, ready to be consumed immediately.

"I understand that you are French?" he asked.

I admitted that I was. He waved a hand towards the videos.

"Then you will find all this boring. I believe that X-rated movies are allowed in France, even at the cinema and on television."

I murmured that I believed this was the case.

"And, of course, the films are full of those beautiful French women reputed for their sexual maturity and dexterity," he added.

Foolishly, I nodded.

"You are typically French, I suppose?"

I blushed and explained that I had not experienced all the things done in the French cinema he was referring to. In fact, I added, some of these acts were quite disgusting to me.

"You're wrong!" he declared emphatically. "I know that Mike has some educational films hidden away. Strictly illegal of course. I must arrange for you to borrow a couple."

I protested vigorously but, ten minutes later, found myself holding a brown paper bag containing two visual horrors. As I tried to push them back into the shopkeeper's hands, Shelley called out. I had not noticed that she had disappeared, and realised that she was in a small viewing cubicle, where she had probably retired with her favourite vibrator.

"For God's sake don't tell her she was being filmed," Jonathan whispered.

Then he flashed his wonderful smile, and even today I still wonder if he was joking.

Jimmy introduced Pierre to Jonathan. Shelley kissed Mike goodbye and I whispered that I would bring the videos back as quickly as possible. We all disappeared down the street to an all-night coffee shop. It was the night of miracles.

Over a cup of rich, black coffee, we discovered that Jonathan was manager of a large wine-producing property in the Barossa Valley and was looking for finance. The owners wanted to sell and retire to Spain, he wanted to buy them out, but could not raise enough cash.

Pierre and Jimmy had been looking for a small wine estate in the Barossa Valley for some French investors. While most French consumers were still making rude comments about the Australian wines they had never tasted, some of the wiser vignerons were beginning to take a serious interest in the down-under wine industry. Australia had good product, offered wines totally different because of the different climate and soil; and was surrounded by millions of potential Asian consumers. Furthermore, it used new and clever technologies. Why, Australia was even selling wine to England, Sweden, Ireland and Holland.

It was obvious that common ground could be found to bring together local and foreign interests: the French company had the money, Jonathan knew the winery and had the technology. Pierre and Jonathan agreed that they would pursue the issue further, but that Pierre would not approach the vendors himself. Jonathan was concerned that his employers would refuse an offer from an overseas buyer, simply out of sheer patriotism. Pierre thought privately that this might be true; then again perhaps Jonathan was trying to protect his own prospective interests in the business.

Meanwhile, Jimmy would continue to pursue other investment projects. I wondered whether he might find a French investor interested in a dildo manufacturing plant. Shelley would make an excellent marketing manager…

℘   ℭ

Jonathan rang me three times that week; fortunately Pierre had also given him our private number. He asked if I had looked at the video films and I confessed that I had, several times.

"What did you think?" he asked.

"I was intrigued. I thought it was something a tart did for a man to make him happy, but the girls seemed so happy, even excited. There was one …"

"The blonde?" he interrupted.

"Yes. How did you know?"

"She has made several films about oral sex. She has told the press that she enjoys it more than any other form of sexual intercourse."

"This I could see. I know that these women shout and scream and gasp because they are actors. But this woman, it was obvious, loved what she was doing. Why is this?"

Jonathan laughed.

"We all have our hobbies, our pleasures. Why try to analyse all of this?"

He was right, of course, but whether I could call that a hobby, I am not sure. Certainly, I was curious to know more. The opportunity came sooner than I thought.

Pierre needed to visit the winery, to see its vineyards, its operations and its production facilities from the inside. Like most of the wineries in the area, it encouraged visitors, but such a conducted tour was only a public relations exercise. Jonathan had a better idea. As he lived on the property in the manager's home, why could we not come to spend two or three days with him, as friends visiting the Barossa Valley? Next week would be particularly good, he announced, as the owners would be visiting relatives in Cairns.

Pierre accepted with pleasure. Over the next week, he would learn all he needed to know about the winery and could then probably work on a plan. I had a little flutter in my stomach. Something was telling me that I was also going to learn something new during that week and make a serious personal investment of my own. This was confirmed when Jonathan rang me at home to tell me that he had obtained a copy of a video made by Suzie Love (his favourite actress), explaining her professional life and her passion for *fellatio*. We would view this together one evening, and I hoped that Pierre would be happy with the idea.

I forgot to mention the phone call when my husband came home that evening, but I was very passionate that night. We made love in the swimming pool, with only the underwater lights, and he declared me even more exciting than the little virgin that he first married.

The following evening, after a quiet dinner, I warned Pierre that Jonathan had been concerned with my lack of oral skills and was hoping to provide further motivation during our stay. Pierre grinned and told me that he was aware of the proceedings and was all in favour of anything that could improve his hitherto boring sex life. I shouted in pretended anger, we threw cushions, we grappled, and I was vanquished.

Pierre had insisted that I take some attractive cocktail wear for the elegant evenings ahead of us. I challenged him, saying that what he really meant was that he wanted me to take that outrageous dress that we both loved. It was practically impossible to wear anything underneath it, but I realised that the dress could be beneficial to the business discussions which would take place. At least, I pretended that was my reasoning.

We arrived at Jonathan's house on the Thursday evening. It was absolutely beautiful, set among the vineyards in a private garden surrounded by tall trees. We had missed the 1981 grape picking, but I hoped that I would be still here in 1982. It was a typical autumn evening in South Australia: the night sky was dark blue, with millions of stars winking at us, and a breeze was swaying the branches of the eucalypts. Our host greeted us at the door in a crimson short sleeve shirt and white slacks.

He led us to our bedroom, which had a four-poster bed and French doors that opened on to a balcony overlooking the front lawns. There was a walk-in wardrobe and an ensuite with a spa.

I clapped my hands in glee and announced that I was putting the spa to the test immediately. As the water flowed, I added lavender oil and the steam climbed towards the ceiling. I began to undress. The men remained seated on the edge of the bath, deep in conversation and apparently oblivious to my preparations. I decided to put them to the test, and proved my point. As I stepped, naked, into the tub, the conversation ceased suddenly, and four eyes followed my progress. I was delighted.

"She's so much prettier than those skinny models in the magazines," Jonathan commented, and Pierre nodded in agreement. I threw bubbles in their direction and they beat a hasty retreat. Later, as I enjoyed the massage of the jets, beneath the camouflage of foam my fingers slipped casually between my legs. I closed my eyes, imagined that Jonathan was in the bath opposite me, and enjoyed a quiet and solitary climax.

It took me five minutes to get dressed: white lace panties, *that* dress and some stiletto shoes. I spent much more time, and was more meticulous, that evening with make-up, highlighting my big, innocent eyes, my faultless cheeks and my soft lips. A heavy gold necklace drew attention to the bottomless chasm that was the cocktail dress, and pendant earrings pointed in the general direction of my breasts, just in case they went unnoticed.

The men were in deep conversation in front of the large fire place in the living room, when the curved staircase delivered me for their appraisal. Their chatter ceased, and Jonathan sighed.

"I don't know how I'm going to last out the evening," he commented. "I might have to ask you to put on a raincoat at some stage."

Pierre laughed.

"She looks much sexier in a pinafore," he joked.

I ignored their banter and gazed around me. The room must have been at least 40 square metres, covered from wall to wall in thick white carpet. There were heavy armchairs and couches scattered around the room, all covered in dark green velvet. The walls were of hewn yellow stone and held several portraits, all of women.

Jonathan caught my gaze and explained.

"The ladies are all members of the family which created and developed this property: wives, sisters, cousins, daughters."

I laughed.

"Chambermaids? In Australia?"

Jonathan nodded.

"Of course. You forget the penal colony. In those days, you could get 'staff' from Melbourne with little difficulty."

"I didn't realise that there were women convicts," I told him.

"It is a sad story. Some were petty thieves; others were whores from the Port of London. They kept the sailors entertained during the voyage, and then most of them married free settlers or convicts when they got here."

"So men married these… well, these… used women?" I asked, incredulously.

Jonathan smiled and shrugged his shoulders.

"Female flesh was in short supply in the colony," he explained. "Besides, even today, how many of us marry a virgin?"

"Pierre did," I retorted.

"He was very lucky. But did your virginity make you a better wife?"

I hesitated for a few seconds, and then I shook my head.

"Probably not, you are right. In fact, a few premarital adventures might have made the early days a little easier."

Pierre clapped his hands in delight.

"Well done, Jonathan. She admits that for the first time. A couple of post-marital noggins might do her the world of good, also."

Jonathan nodded, and I felt my cheeks flush.

That night we were going to play a game, a dangerous game; there was an implicit challenge in the atmosphere. I was the prey, or perhaps 'the offering' was a better expression, because I knew deep within myself that if Jonathan was to take me sometime during the evening, I would not resist. Pierre was the master of the game; nothing could be ventured, offered or taken without his consent. Jonathan was the consumer, the privileged invitee, the man who would be allowed to take, to use, to consume, to fill, as his pleasure may dictate.

We sat at the dinner table, and a young Asian girl served our dinner. Jonathan explained that in our honour he had called in a caterer who was preparing the meal in the kitchen, and who had brought his personnel with him.

"Will the girl stay after the meal?" Pierre enquired with a wink.

The girl placed her hand before her mouth to hide her giggle.

Jonathan grinned.

"We are in Adelaide, not Bangkok. No, she is a trainee from a local catering school, I imagine."

The girl nodded.

"Such a pity," Pierre sighed. "But, then, there are so many needs to be catered for."

I had never seen my husband in such a flirtatious mood.

"I know that there are escort services in the phone book," I interjected. "Maybe we could find a lady there to satisfy your needs."

Pierre laughed.

"It was just a little innocent game. My needs are fully satisfied by my beautiful wife."

The meal was delicious. We began with enormous fresh crabs which came, according to Jonathan, from the Southern Ocean. This was followed by asparagus from the South East, crisp yet tender, served in a warm butter sauce. The rack of lamb with pureed sweet potatoes had been baked in a prune and brandy marinade, and was most unusual, but totally delightful. It was accompanied by a Coonawarra red wine which warmed my heart and sent delicious tingles up and down my thighs.

While I served the coffee at the low table in front of the fire, Jonathan went to the kitchen. He came back ten minutes or so later.

"The caterers have left," he announced. "We can now relax."

It was at that moment that the gods intervened. I took up my glass to finish the beautiful Cabernet Sauvignon, and inadvertently spilled it down the front of my dress.

"Oh dear, I must take it off immediately and soak it in warm water. Is there a bathroom downstairs?" I asked.

Jonathan pointed to a door beside the staircase, and Pierre held out his hand.

"Give it to me, I'll soak it."

I hesitated, but he approached and slipped the straps off my shoulders. The stained dress fell to the floor.

"I must find a dressing gown," I suggested, covering my breasts with my hands.

"There's no rush," Jonathan protested. "It's quite warm here. Oh, and you don't have to hide them. I have seen breasts before, you know."

I could hear Pierre running water into a basin while he whistled. I dropped my hands and offered myself for inspection. Jonathan's eyes travelled slowly, very deliberately, over my body. I swear I could feel them moving from spot to spot.

"I'll correct that statement. I have never seen breasts as beautiful as yours."

Pierre came back a few moments later, with a fluffy white bathrobe that I was happy to slip on. We drank our coffee, accompanied by a soft whisky liqueur, and the conversation wandered from topic to topic, although it often came back to the property and the investors. I pouted playfully.

"You men are all the same. Here you are sitting in front of a big fire with a woman almost naked on the carpet in front of you, and you talk business."

"Ah, and that reminds me. I have that documentary film to show you," Jonathan exclaimed. "You remember, the one made by Suzie Love."

Pierre raised an inquisitive eyebrow, and I blushed again.

"She's a porn star whom Jonathan admires greatly," I explained.

Pierre smiled and shrugged.

"I don't like porn very much. But I see that you have a billiards room, if I may?"

"Of course, please help yourself. But this is not a porn movie. It is a documentary made by this girl who became known the world over because of her, well, shall I say 'oral' expertise?"

Pierre laughed.

"I know exactly what you mean. But I prefer to receive the service rather than to watch somebody else's pleasure. I'll offer myself a little snooker challenge."

As Pierre wandered away, Jonathan asked if I wanted to play snooker or watch the film.

I smiled, embarrassed.

"They are both things that I need to learn. Let's play snooker afterwards."

Jonathan sighed. And as the door to the billiards room closed softly behind me, he used his remote control to dim the lights and lower a projection screen from the ceiling. He invited me, with a simple gesture, to move to the couch, and we sank down together. It was quite dark, and as the introduction appeared on the screen, his hand slipped over my shoulder, into the gown, and cupped my breast.

"Do you mind?" he whispered.

"I was hoping that you would," I admitted softly.

Suzie Love appeared on the screen. She was an attractive, well-dressed blonde, a little over 40, and seeing her sitting in an armchair wearing a black two-piece suit and an apricot coloured blouse, you would never have guessed that she was a porn star. But as she explained each point she wanted to make, we were shown film clips of her work from her younger years, naked and desirable, and totally devoted to providing pleasure to her male partner. I do not recall actually seeing a man's face in the film. All the extracts we were offered showed a man lying on his back, motionless, offering a very large and rigid penis to his companion.

In an hour, I discovered many things.

Firstly, I noted that while Anglo-Saxon slang refers to the act of fellatio as 'sucking' or 'blowing', in fact the lady does neither. Secondly, while the actresses in pornographic films rub the sperm over their faces or breasts, this actress explained that this was mainly, but not only, for the benefit of the spectators. Sometimes, a woman may take sperm in her mouth and, on much rarer occasions, swallow it. The latter act is often considered as a special gesture of bonding or of deep affection.

She explained the difference in taste between young, eager males and older, more experienced men. It is a question of texture and acidity. But she also insisted on the fact that while the act appears to be servile, something a whore will do to please her client or a slave to please her master, it is often the woman who derives the greater pleasure. She admitted that her mouth could water when she saw a handsome man, imagining him swelling in her mouth.

She explained how fellatio was used in many cultures as a means of birth control and how the act of offering simultaneous oral pleasure was called '69', and how popular it was in France, in Spain or in Italy, good Catholic countries where the use of other anti-natal measures was not always accepted.

Towards the end of the film, I discovered something else. This kind of film had a dramatic effect on Jonathan. Just watching Suzie earn her dollars made him swell up enormously.

I could still hear the billiard balls clicking in the other room, so taking my courage, and Jonathan himself, in both hands, I made a suggestion.

"Would you mind if I tried?"

He looked at me thoughtfully.

"You're sure that you want to?"

I nodded, eagerly, and begged.

"Please. I want to learn. I want it to be you. And if you teach me well, I could make Pierre very happy."

He accepted the sacrifice with a self-satisfied smile, placing himself on the carpet, in the same position as the actors in the film. I tried to imitate the beautiful Suzie. Within ten minutes, my hands, lips and tongue were having a party, and on occasions he would beg me to stop for fear of coming in my mouth.

"It's all right," I growled, relinquishing my dessert for a moment.

"That's not the point, I want it to last a little longer," he explained.

I went back to my task and was delighted when he placed his two hands on the top of my head. Gently, he encouraged me to be a little greedier, and I obeyed. I had feared retching, but discovered that it was even nicer when it filled my mouth totally. Finally, he surrendered. He offered a last word of warning, I grunted with my mouth full, and he came, in long, powerful spurts. I was delighted and drank hungrily.

We lay, side by side on the carpet, for about ten minutes, his finger travelling lazily around my right nipple.

"As you can see, you are a gifted French girl. It was just all there inside waiting to come out."

I giggled.

"I love your choice of words."

He laughed, too.

"I think that you had better tell Pierre that you have passed the test."

I sat up, frowning.

"I can't hear the billiard balls any more, can you?"

"Oh, he went up to his room about 20 minutes ago. He waved to me as he walked up the stairs."

I gasped with fear and anger.

"Did he see what I was doing?"

"Oh, yes. He even stopped for a moment on the staircase to watch you, and raised his thumb in approval. I think he was pleasantly surprised."

I ran up the staircase, sobbing, and bumped into Pierre halfway.

"What is all of this about?" he asked, gruffly.

I fell to my knees on the step in front of him.

"Please forgive me, I have dishonoured our marriage."

Gravely, he took me by the hand and led me back to the lounge room.

"You are a beautiful married woman who has taken a lover, with your husband's consent. The lover has taught you new arts which you will practise on your husband, and this wonderful triangle of love will remain a cherished secret between us," he explained.

I gazed at him amazed and delighted.

"And this is what you believe and accept?" I asked my husband. He nodded, with a smile.

I then turned to Jonathan.

"And you would accept to be my lover?" I asked.

He nodded enthusiastically. A few minutes later, we sat in a tight triangle on the carpet. The men talked about beauty, sex and me, and I enjoyed listening to their banter with a swollen penis in each hand. I was a goddess.

Later, I took Pierre into my mouth for the first time. Jonathan was whispering words of encouragement as my husband moaned with pleasure. I swallowed for the second time that night, with pride and delight.

"Did you notice a difference?" Jonathan asked.

"Probably the difference between pumpkin and garlic," Pierre suggested, and we all laughed.

Then Jonathan decided that I should enjoy some pleasures as well, and began to work carefully with a very agile and inquisitive tongue. Pierre did not seem concerned by the intrusion, so I relaxed and offered myself as generously as possible.

"I think that I will have to allow him to take me," I whispered to Pierre, in French.

He nodded gravely.

"I think you should. It seems a logical issue."

"Will you hold my hand while he rides me?" I asked timidly.

"Of course. If that's what you want."

Pierre then explained our conversation, in English, to Jonathan. He was delighted and slipped immediately into the appropriate position. I gasped and squeezed Pierre's fingers as my new lover entered me for the first time. It was gentle, but firm, the thrusts were rhythmic and regular, with an occasional deeper push, which would make me cry out with surprise. Somehow, during the process, I lost my husband's hand and then I was clutching Jonathan's back, begging him to go faster, deeper. I think I may have screamed with pleasure when he filled me. It took me some time to recover, and then I told him a secret.

"You are the best extramarital lover I ever had."

Both men laughed.

"And also the first!"

"That is true," Pierre agreed.

I then asked my husband to take me, and Jonathan asked if he could watch. We agreed, of course. He came too quickly, and apologised. I kissed him before he withdrew.

"I have my husband's and my lover's seeds inside me, together. Perhaps those little spermatozoids are waging war inside?"

The men laughed again, and then we all went to bed. I slept, peacefully, with my husband at my side, dreaming of Jonathan filling my mouth with his beautiful penis, coated with honey.

We were all looking a little embarrassed the next morning, over breakfast. Then I came out with a joke, which had us all roaring with laughter.

"Tonight," I suggested, "Pierre will watch the film while Jonathan and I play snooker."

It wasn't that funny. But the men added their own flavour, with a few suggestive jokes about billiard balls and cues which made me blush. Pierre explained to Jonathan that in French a billiard cue is called a 'tail', which is also a slang expression for a penis.

Jonathan looked at me gravely.

"You will show me your cue strokes this evening."

I assured him that I would.

∞   ∞

The men spent most of the day visiting the estate: the vineyards, the buildings, the cellars, the vats, the laboratory, and the presses. After a while, dragging along behind them, I found it all a little boring and Jonathan lent me a small car so that I could visit a nearby village. It was the first time that I had driven alone on the wrong side of the road.

I discovered what people meant by the 'Australian cringe'. While the people are so justifiably proud of their country, they need visitors to confirm as often as possible their own admiration for it. The locals continue to cling to their European heritage and to copy it as far as possible. The little village of Hahndorf was a typical example. I understand that there is even a local Germanic patois. It was quaint, it had quaint people, it had quaint little shops selling quaint little pots of jam, chutney and mustard.

An hour later, along another road, I decided to stop in a small service station for ten litres of petrol. The tank was far from empty, but when I first drove past I had noticed, on the forecourt, a young blond-haired athlete whose suntanned muscles and arrogant smile merited closer inspection. I was now an accomplished woman, an expert in sexual pleasures, and no longer feared approaching a strange man. I wanted to tease.

My skirt up around my thighs, my straps hanging loose, my breasts desperately looking for a little air, I pulled up to the pump.

He leaned in through the window, and I let his eyes wander.

"You're not from around here," he noted.

I grinned cheekily.

"How did you guess?"

He yawned, showing gaps where a few teeth should have been.

"Never seen those tits before. Bloody beautiful. Waddya want?"

"Ten litres of petrol, that's all."

He grinned stupidly.

"Ten litres? You're joking. Nobody pulls in for ten litres."

He let his eyes wander again, and noticed that I was not worried by his stare. Bravely, he let a finger wander to my shoulder, and pulled down the strap of my dress. I watched his eyes gleam as my breast appeared. Suddenly, he realised what was happening.

"Hey, I saw you drive by about ten minutes ago, didn't I? You came back looking for me, didn't you?"

I lowered my eyes in pretend shame and nodded. What a conceited man.

"Tell you what, if you want to come round tomorrow, I'll make you feel good. See that little wooden house behind the service station? That's my place, and I'm free on Sundays."

I pretended to gasp with girlish pleasure.

"Would you really? You're not making fun of me?"

"Course not. Girl like you needs looking after, anyone can see that."

I pretended to consider the offer of this arrogant idiot.

"I'll come round if I can. I'm staying with two guys, it might be hard to get away."

"Down at Jonathan Beecham's place?" he asked.

"How did you know that?"

"I recognised the car. I'm sure he won't mind. Tell him you met Steve, he knows me."

I winked and drove off, crunching first gear in my hurry to get away and give in to the desperate urge to laugh. What an idiot!

    ∞ ℞

I was still giggling when I told an abridged version of the encounter to my two men. Pierre looked terribly grave, and Jonathan laughed.

"That was totally stupid and dangerous," Pierre shouted angrily. "I will not have my wife acting like a tart in the street in front of everybody."

"Even worse," added Jonathan jokingly, "it was also my official mistress in one of the company's cars. But you chose well, the guy has a big... er, reputation."

I begged forgiveness. The two men considered their judgement, and then delivered their sentence.

I would spend the rest of the day in the house. In addition, I would submit totally to any desire of my lover and my husband.

I clapped my hands in glee and, to save time, threw my sun dress, shoes and panties on the kitchen bench.

Then, a thought struck me.

"What about the staff?"

"You will have to be very careful," Jonathan suggested solemnly.

"And hide very quickly," my lovely husband added.

I decided I loved my husband even more than I had before. He had given me his friend as a lover, and they shared me like two brothers. I was a woman blessed by the gods of love.

    ∞ ℞

That evening we had the same caterers. The pretty Asian girl appeared in the lounge, shortly after six, while we were enjoying a lovely white wine from the estate. I had slipped into a bathrobe just before she arrived.

The girl served us at the table, and the meal was sumptuous, once again. I lost the bathrobe just before she arrived with the roast duckling, but my nudity did not seem to concern her. In fact, she even offered a little joke.

"I think that the cook would be really happy if you went into the kitchen to congratulate him," she suggested.

I grinned.

"I think not. It might spoil the rest of the meal."

"He was hoping to see you," she said wistfully. "He will be terribly disappointed."

I shook my head, and my men laughed.

"It is amazing how having a lover has changed your attitude to life," my husband commented, when she left the room. "You laugh, you assume, you can look people in the face, instead of being shy and timid."

"Jonathan does me a lot of good," I confirmed.

He smiled.

"I am sure. Tonight, we are going to teach you synchronised orgasm. It's like synchronised swimming but it's not in the Olympics. Would you like that?"

I confessed that I was always happy to receive lessons from my two loved ones.

It was very simple. I simply crouched between Jonathan's legs and took him in my mouth, from a kneeling position. My darling husband knelt behind me, slipped himself into me, and began his work. The two men conversed freely; unfortunately I had my mouth full and could not join in. But they began to get more and more excited until Jonathan shouted, "Now!" They both filled me, at exactly the same moment.

I had to admit that few women could enjoy such ecstasy. How many of us have the luxury of making love to their husband and their lover at the same time? Over a large glass of whisky, the men continued to debate about which offered the greatest pleasure, my mouth or my sex. Finally, Jonathan had the perfect solution.

"Why not start again, but change ends?"

Pierre and I agreed that it was an excellent idea.

It was just as good. It also proved that we were a perfect trio and that I was desperately in love with the two of them.

Early on Sunday morning, the phone rang. It was Jimmy who announced that the French group from Lille had arrived and that a meeting had been organised with their prospective partners early on Monday morning. He wanted Pierre to meet him that afternoon to go over the strategy before managing the discussions.

"I'll have to go," Pierre explained, regretfully. "If you like, you can stay and Jonathan will bring you home this evening."

"You might like to try snooker?" Jonathan suggested.

"That would be nice," I agreed.

I sincerely swear that I did try to learn to play snooker that morning. I just got confused with Jonathan holding his arms around me, taking my hands to place them on the cue, bending me over the table. I found every movement in his company totally erotic and stimulating. Finally, as I leaned over the table for a third attempt at striking the white ball with my cue, I felt him stiffen behind me. After pretending to resist, I abandoned the cue, grasped the cushions of the table, and let him have his way. We must have looked funny, but it was wonderful, and I cried out my pleasure.

As I began to leave my position on the billiard table, still gasping to regain my breath, May, the Asian girl, offered me an iced tea. She seemed embarrassed and excited at the same time. I blushed.

"That was beautiful," she whispered to me.

& &

Later, that afternoon, Jonathan asked me to pack my clothes as he would be taking me home before dusk.

"Wear something light and easy to remove," he suggested.

I laughed. My lover was becoming just as passionate as my husband.

We drove off, and 20 minutes later we were at the service station I had visited the day before.

"This is the wrong way," I commented.

"Not for Steve, it isn't," he answered, pulling the car up beside the small wooden house.

"You don't expect me to give myself to that lout?" I hissed. "You must be mad."

He smiled.

"Look at your hands. You are trembling in anticipation. You wanted to tempt him; he challenged you, now you have to face the challenge."

At that moment, Steve appeared on the front veranda. The pump attendant approached the car, smiling.

"Why, it's the little lady from yesterday," he said with a grin.

Jonathan leaned across the car and opened my door.

"I'll be back in about an hour," he called as I stepped out, then I turned back towards the car. Jonathan had already slipped the gear into reverse, but he stopped as I approached his window.

"No, please, please take me home. Pierre will be furious."

Jonathan smiled mischievously.

"He'll never know. And if you don't walk through that door, you'll never know either."

"I think you should take me home," I muttered.

Steve was watching the conversation, and turned away, walking back to his house, hands in his pockets, looking dejected. Jonathan grabbed me by the arm and pulled me closer.

"You want this guy. There is something deep inside you, telling you that you want to have this guy shag you as hard as he can go, isn't there?"

I nodded, silently.

"But, please don't tell Pierre."

"Don't be silly, of course I won't. It's something you need to get out of your system. Go get yourself laid, he's hung like a donkey, you'll never forget it."

Then Jonathan called out, "Steve, come and collect her!"

The pump attendant turned around, his face lit up with a giant smile.

"Come here, darling. Come and let big Stevie make you happy."

I turned and walked towards him on trembling legs. I could hear, behind me, the car reversing away. I was committed. Steve grabbed my arm, waved in Jonathan's direction, and dragged me into the house. As soon as the door was closed, we were together, mouths glued, pulling one another's clothes from our bodies. When I saw his penis, I nearly fainted, but I dropped to my knees to try to take that monstrous pillar in my mouth.

After a few minutes, I stood up and begged him to take me. And then the world changed. Suddenly, this vulgar idiot was a wonderful partner. The service station pump attendant was a competent and sensual lover, determined but always gentle and he murmured quiet words of tenderness as he laboured inside me. Softly, I begged him never to stop, ever. We came simultaneously, with muffled cries, and then we kissed tenderly.

"Are you staying here long?"

"I'm going back now, when I leave you. Sorry."

He sighed.

"That's okay. Anyhow, if you come back, don't forget to call. Any time you like, no charge, it'll be a pleasure."

I think he was trying to joke, but I decided not to find out if I was right or wrong. Jonathan began blowing his horn outside to say that time was up. I stood up and raised myself on my toes to place a farewell kiss on his lips. He squeezed my breasts gently.

"I must tell you," he stammered, blushing. "I've had a lot of nice girls in my life, but never one like you."

I kissed him again, turned, squeezed his hand and left the house. As I approached the car, Jonathan leaned across to open the door.

"Happy?" he asked, as I climbed into the car.

I nodded. We drove away.

        −− −−

During the trip back to Adelaide, Jonathan talked. He told me that it was fine to have a lover, accepted and approved, almost chosen by my husband. It might even be acceptable to have a one night stand with a total stranger, now and again. But I should not lower myself by trying to act like a tart. Exceptionally, he had facilitated my mount, but I should not make a habit of getting myself laid by total strangers, just for the fun of it. I listened, sulked, accepted, agreed, and nodded.

When I arrived home, late that night, Jimmy was still there, working on the plan with Pierre. There was a white board in my living room and papers all over the table. Pierre smiled when he saw my face.

"Marie has been in the Barossa Valley," he explained to Jimmy. "She was taking snooker lessons."

I nodded wearily.

"It was most frustrating and tiring," I confirmed. "I think I'll go straight to bed."

I was not a depraved woman. I was still madly in love with my husband, and if Jonathan came to visit us twice over the next three months, we only had sex once, for about half an hour. We did not write, we did not phone. Pierre told me that he had heard that the little Chinese girl, May, had become a full-time accessory in Jonathan's life. I was not jealous; on the contrary I was pleased to see an opportunity for him to settle down. There was no future in our relationship, we just enjoyed sex together.

He was also a clever and witty man. I remember during one of his visits, just after dinner, he tried to explain Australian economic rationalism to me.

"The theory is very simple. If you live in a beautiful home, which is appreciating, but you have a mortgage, then that is poor management of your budget because of your external debt. But if you sell your house and your car, you pay off your mortgage and your credit card, you buy a tent and sleep in the street, then you are being economically rational. You have not tied up your capital in assets which do not generate income, and you have no debts. You are an economic genius."

I was not impressed with the theory. However, I must admit that in France the philosophies are just as ridiculous. Most people believe that major industries should belong to the State and be managed by public servants. Pierre explained to Jonathan that France had many enormous corporations which lost a lot of money or were racked by scandals.

"And, of course, being in France, the problems often begin with the mistress," I added.

"Wonderful!" Jonathan exclaimed. "When I am the Chairman of a large French company, I will ask you to become my official mistress. That is, if Pierre does not mind, of course?"

Pierre shrugged.

"It is often of great material advantage to be the husband of a powerful mistress," he explained, simply. "Also, I would insist on being on the Board of Directors."

I was constantly amazed by this cheerful banter, carried out in front of me, by my husband and my lover.

                                                                             ❧   ❧

The investment in the winery went through, the old owners retired and Jonathan was offered a 20 per cent holding and the job of General Manager. Pierre was appointed to the Board of the new company. Meanwhile, Jimmy was pursuing an important commercial real estate investment opportunity in Adelaide, which kept Pierre very busy.

Once a week I went to a meeting of genteel ladies of our neighbourhood, where we would discuss housework, children, private schools and concerts over cups of tea. Finally, it was my turn to invite. I served wine and cheese, played rock and roll music very loudly and explained how I had enjoyed triangular sex with my husband and my lover. The invitations came to an abrupt halt, but I am sure that, secretly, most of the old hags were jealous. I told Pierre of my tasteless joke, and he was not amused.

"You used to be very shy. Suddenly, you are becoming too bold. I do not like the change."

Once, to show myself how brazen I had become, I rang Steve at his little service station.

"Would you like to take me?" I asked, simply.

He admitted that he would like nothing better. He took a 'sickie' the following Wednesday afternoon and we spent three hours on a bed in a nearby motel.

To this day, I have never told Pierre about my two meetings with the service station attendant. They are not the proudest moments of my life, but they were motivated, above all, by sheer boredom. I also admit that I enjoyed being told by the regional stud that I was the most beautiful girl he had ever possessed. Such words are pleasing to the ears of any woman.

Pierre and I still made love nearly every day, and he told me often that he loved me. But I think that I was becoming slowly jealous of his business activities. He spent more time with them than with me. I confess that he talked to me often about the work he was doing and I shared his delight in the small or big success stories: the French restaurant, the soft drink manufacturer, the wine wholesaling and importing business, these were all new ventures where he had carefully brought together French and local interests, to the satisfaction of both. Pierre never did 'dirty' deals. He always acted as an honest arbitrator between both parties, and I was proud of the compliments he was receiving from his clients and from Paris.

∞   ∞

Finally, at the end of 1984, we were warned of the imminent visit of Bernard Courtot, Pierre's big boss from Paris. We never knew what new strategies he would announce, and it was important to keep him on side. As a precaution, I bought a new summer mini-dress with almost invisible straps and a neckline so low he would be able to check the colour of my nipples if he stood on his toes. He was not a tall man.

As usual with a new dress, Pierre wanted a fashion display, then, true to custom, he took me on the carpet with the dress still on, but only just. It was really just wrapped around my waist. This is what he called 'breaking in' new clothing. I did not complain, because I always like to wash and press new clothes before I wear them, and I was also able to check that it was reasonably crush proof.

At dinner, Bernard Courtot was enjoying himself and our company.

"My dear Marie," he told me, "the problem with you being in Australia is that I do not see enough of you."

"It's an old joke, Bernard. Any more and I would be completely indecent," I retorted.

He roared with laughter and turned to Pierre.

"It is hard to believe that this is the shy little lady you married in France. Life in the antipodes has favoured her."

Pierre smiled.

"Sometimes, I miss the shy girl I married," he admitted. "But I know that she is still there, hiding underneath that glorious sun tan and behind that brazen look."

Bernard Courtot stayed two days. I knew nothing of the private conversations between the two men, but when he left, he kissed me on both cheeks at the airport and promised to offer me a wonderful banquet in Paris in three years time. When we got back home, Pierre told me the news.

Jimmy was going to manage the Adelaide operations by himself. Pierre and I would be moving to Canberra shortly. I was not overly excited as I feared that I would be even more bored in the capital than in Adelaide. In the meantime, the company was paying for me to take a trip home to see the family for Christmas, while Pierre finished the formalities of handing over the local management to Jimmy.

It was wonderful to see the family and to enjoy a real winter Christmas with snow. But I shortened my stay, to the disappointment of my mother, because I could no longer survive without Pierre. On the flight back, I was heavily courted by my neighbour, an Italian businessman on his first trip to Australia, but I was very reserved. I gave him my husband's business card as we got off the plane in Melbourne, and wished him luck.

When I arrived in Adelaide it was dreadfully hot. Only two years before, terrible bushfires had severely damaged our suburb, and I hoped that there would be no more disasters this year. Luckily the packing was already under way, and we would be moving in two weeks. A few days later, we moved into a short-term serviced apartment, as our furniture was being sent to a storage depot in Canberra. Once we arrived in the capital city, we would rent a serviced apartment there too, until we found something suitable.

I asked Pierre if he had seen Jonathan.

He smiled.

"He always asks after you. Why don't you give him a call?"

I pouted.

"He should call me!" I declared.

"Now, now. You must not be so possessive. He is only your lover, not your husband," Pierre reminded me.

"A quite indifferent lover he is, too," I commented. "I would have thought that he would wish us a *bon voyage*."

Pierre smiled.

"Jonathan is a gentleman," was his enigmatic reply.

Our last evening came, and Pierre rang to say that he would be home late. He asked me not to prepare any food, he would have a surprise for me. I decided that his attention had been waning lately, and that it might be appropriate for me to offer him a little surprise, too. I had bought a transparent mini nightdress in France, it weighed nothing, it hid nothing, but it was wonderfully expensive. I knew that he was a connoisseur of such things.

When the doorbell rang, the lights were dimmed and *Bilitis* was playing softly on the stereo. I did not expect him to even make the bedroom when I threw open the door.

Jonathan was wearing a big grin and Pierre assured him, "You see, it was no surprise. She knew that you were coming."

I tried to protest, but they refused to listen. They had their arms full, and I discovered that they had bought oysters, cooked lobster and champagne. After the second glass, Jonathan asked if I would offer him a parting gift: he wanted the flimsy night dress I was wearing.

I glanced at Pierre, who nodded, and I agreed.

"Now," he added.

I obeyed. The damned thing, well screwed up, actually fitted into his trouser pocket. I was worried that it might get damaged later on, now I was reassured. It was probably why Pierre noticed that I looked more relaxed.

We had an indoor picnic. We laid the table cloth on the carpet and sat cross-legged to eat our meal. I am inclined to dribble when I eat oysters, but that night there was always a friendly tongue to capture the elusive trickles as they slid down my body. Both men had also removed their clothing, and I noted with great pleasure their profound admiration. I could still attract a man, even at midnight and splattered with mayonnaise and white wine. Even two at once.

After coffee, I removed the plates and the table cloth. Jonathan moved the candles further back and Pierre laid out a soft duvet on the carpet. He decided to take me first.

I tried to be quiet, as I did not want Jonathan, who was to follow, to feel discouraged. He sipped his cognac, smiled, and encouraged me to climax. I could not resist such an invitation. Then Pierre kissed me and stood up.

"We have to be away early tomorrow morning, and as I will be doing all the driving, I am going to sleep. Please don't make too much noise."

He and Jonathan shook hands formally to say goodbye. It would have made such a beautiful photograph: two naked businessmen, shaking hands, one with an enormous erection, the other with a limp, dripping penis. A typical 'before and after' scene. These are the beautiful things in life that the puritans never experience.

Once Pierre had disappeared, Jonathan wanted to play. He explained that he was a nostalgic, and wanted to re-enact all those lessons he had provided before, those which had made me an orally competent woman. We played, like two actors, occasionally gasping or groaning like vaudeville artists. There was no orgasm, no ejaculation, just games. He queried my competence, finding that I had gained skills over the last few months. He questioned me, jealously. I told him of all the pleasures I now gave to my beloved husband, then I confessed the second trip to see Steve. He was not amused.

"If that's what you want, I can also deliver," he growled, pushing me down on to my back. He was inside me, taking vigorous possession, within a few seconds.

I cannot say how long all this lasted, but it must have been several hours. Pierre opened the door twice, begging for a little less noise when I climaxed, suggesting that I might like to turn in as it was getting late.

"He won't stop," I explained, giggling, over the bucking shoulder of my official lover. "It must be the oysters."

Jonathan climaxed at that very moment, filling me for a third time. Panting, he looked over his shoulder at Pierre.

"Just another half an hour, then I crawl home to die," he begged.

Pierre looked at me, questions in his eyes. For once, I answered in French.

"I may never see him again. Another hour would be marvellous."

He smiled, woefully, and replied also in French.

"Please try not to cry out so loudly when you come. You wake me every time."

Then turning to Jonathan who was trying to follow, and reverting to English, "You have one hour."

Jonathan grinned his thanks. He worked me for the full hour, enjoying every second. My arms were wrapped around his neck, my hips were lifting with each of his thrusts, and I was whispering the most dreadful encouragements in his ear. At the 59th minute, he filled me again. They were the best oysters I had ever experienced; he was performing like a 20 year old.

I crept into bed beside Pierre, hoping that he would not be awake. Generally, after my bouts with Jonathan, he liked to resume possession of the place, as he said. But, for once, I was saturated. Luckily, he was deep in sleep. I looked at the alarm clock before slipping off, it was 2.20 am.

At seven o'clock, Pierre shook me.

"It's time to get up," he warned. "We leave in an hour. Oh, and by the way, you're leaking."

I pushed back the sheets. My thighs were sticky, the sheets were damp. During the night, Jonathan's donations had succumbed to gravity. I knew that men do not like having their beds stained by other men's pleasures, unless they are homosexual, of course. And my Pierre was certainly not one of those. I begged forgiveness.

"You look exhausted," he commented. "What time did you get to bed?"

I sighed and shrugged my shoulders.

"I don't know, around one o'clock I think."

He smiled.

"It was past one when I asked you to stop shouting to the world that another orgasm was on the way. I think even the neighbours got up for a cigarette afterwards," he said, tartly. "The man's a human drilling rig."

I pouted. "He's my official lover."

"Not any more, I've just sacked him," he said.

Then, seeing the look of total horror on my face, he added a parting shot.

"That was a joke, by the way. For goodness sake, wash that man out of your body and get some clothes on."

He threw a last look at the bed.

"God knows what the chambermaid will say."

I smiled.

"She will probably ask for your phone number," I suggested sweetly.

          80   03

It was a long, straight, dusty, hot and boring ride. Pierre saw that I was tired, and hardly talked. We stopped for a snack and a drink in Bordertown, but I was not hungry. As we drove on, I tried to sleep, but I kept shifting and waking.

Finally I confessed that I was terribly irritated in a very intimate place and would love to find a suitable soothing ointment. He laughed, and then he apologised for not being sufficiently understanding.

We pulled into Horsham, realising that, if possible, February here was even hotter than in Adelaide. Luckily, we found an ice-cold air-conditioned motel and Pierre asked for directions. He wanted a doctor specialised in 'secret women's business'. He got more than he bargained for.

Doctor Patricia Welsham would have looked more at ease on a Playboy calendar. She was stunning. Pierre was still staring when she led me into her surgery. She examined, clucked, told me not to worry, and wrote out a prescription.

"No sex for two or three days," she recommended. "Now, I'd like to have a private word with your husband."

Pierre told me the rest of the story when we got back to the motel room. By the time he had closed the door of the surgery behind himself, two buttons of Pamela's blouse had slipped from their position of security, and her lipstick was gleaming. She patted his hand, sat him in the visitor's chair, perched herself on the arm rest and leaned towards him.

"Look, I know you have a stunning wife, but you must go a little easy on her. This time, you have literally worn her out."

He was about to explain.

"Now, now," she patted his shoulder. "Just two or three days, that's all. In the meantime, if you're staying in Horsham, and if you need some help, just give me a call."

Finally, Pierre was able to get a word out.

"I'm sorry, we're leaving Horsham tomorrow, but that's very kind of you."

He deliberately gazed down the front of her blouse, paused, and licked his lips.

"Maybe we can have a drink later this evening, though," he suggested.

She beamed.

"Now, there's a good idea. Once your wife has settled down for the night, of course."

"Even before. That way, I'll get her to give you Jonathan's phone number."

She looked surprised.

"Jonathan?"

"Well, he was the one who was banging her most of the time, last night. With my permission, of course."

She raised herself from the arm rest, smoothed her skirt over her thighs and gazed at him coldly.

"I'll think that will be enough. You are horribly sick people," she commented.

"That's why we came to see you doctor," Pierre explained chirpily as he closed the door.

5. Capital Frustrations

Thanks to a marvellous aloe vera based ointment recommended by a charming young pharmacist, I was able to avoid Dr Welsham's prescribed drugs. In fact, by the next afternoon I was feeling quite merry.

"Another two days, and I'll have to find myself a man," I commented cheerfully to Pierre.

"I think we'll stick to marital convention for a while," he suggested, just as brightly. "I, too, have a few things to catch up on."

"Lovely," I agreed, squeezing his thigh. "But as soon as you start feeling a little tired, just say so."

We set off for the Australian Alps, which are, I must say, a lot smaller than ours. But the scenery was pleasant and the climate a nice change from the heat of the plains. We stopped at Adaminaby to eat trout paté and crusty bread, accompanied by a crisp King Valley Chenin Blanc, sitting on our travel rug in a little park in front of the village. When the wine was finished, Pierre was feeling very 'interested', but we decided that offering a spectacle of passionate love on the village square might raise the ire of the local policeman.

As Pierre had been very self-serving with the wine, it was decided that from then on I would drive and he would navigate. A couple of hours later I asked him to warn me when we got to Canberra, as I was not yet prepared to face city traffic.

"We've been in Canberra for the last ten minutes," he replied.

I pulled up immediately.

"Either that is a silly joke, or this is a strange city," I commented.

"This is a strange city," he confirmed.

Little did I realise at that time just how unusual life in Canberra could be and what an impact this city would have on my life.

We booked in at a serviced apartment where we would hang our clothes for a few weeks. Pierre was to open an office and began discussions with the commercial counsellor at the French Embassy who would, in turn, open doors to the Federal Government and the local finance community. Meanwhile, I would spend my days looking for a suitable house to rent.

Never in my life have I felt so lost. In this crazy city, there are roundabouts and flyovers that all go in the wrong direction. You can drive around Parliament House all day without getting anywhere. If that was not complicated enough, they have hidden suburbs down small, insignificant and inoffensive side-streets. I spent half a day driving around the embassies, where there was nothing to rent, and finally I stopped in front of the US Embassy to ask the security guard how to escape. He was very, very suspicious, but when he saw that my little summer dress could not conceal anything that could represent a threat, he relaxed and decided to enjoy the weapons of feminine charm on offer.

As I pulled away, he called after me, and I slowed.

"When you bring out your first calendar, send me a copy," he suggested.

"I'll make a hand delivery," I promised.

He sighed, "I bet you do that beautifully."

I laughed and drove off. I really should stop teasing men, I thought; I could get myself into big trouble one day.

I wandered through many of the inner southern suburbs, looking for suitable accommodation, because I thought it would be practical for Pierre if we were close to his work. He had found offices on Northbourne Avenue, not far from Canberra University.

One morning, I decided to stop in a small shopping area, where there were about 12 shops facing a small street. The mix was typical: a small deli, an Indian takeaway, a florist, two real estate agents, and a lovely little café with large parasols on the footpath. It was mid-March, autumn was fast approaching, and the trees were shedding their summer fashions. I ordered a coffee, and the waiter smiled.

"I haven't seen you around here before. Do you work upstairs?" he asked.

"No, I don't. Why do you ask?"

"Because they only employ beautiful women," he replied simply.

And he pointed to the staircase which led to the first floor above the café. A small bronze plaque announced The Wanderer's Club.

"That's interesting," I commented. "I'm new to Canberra and I would like to find a job, at least part time."

"The boss is called Kevin. I'm sure he'd like to meet you. Say Mario sent you up."

"Thank you, I will."

I would be so proud to tell Pierre that I had found a new activity. I finished my coffee quietly, paid Mario and told him I was going up to see Kevin, straight away.

"Good luck," he beamed. "I'm sure Kevin will be interested. I know that he's looking for a new lady and you look just like the kind of person he wants."

I decided that Mario was an excellent judge of character and personality and climbed the staircase. The door at the top was locked, to my surprise, and I had to press a bell to gain entry to the Club.

The man who opened the door seemed a little taken back to see me, but then he smiled.

"Are you Kevin?" I asked.

"I certainly am. How can I help you?"

I decided to be positive.

"Mario, downstairs, told me that I would be exactly the kind of person you are looking for," I explained.

He grinned widely, and almost dragged me inside. Holding me by the arm, he led me past a small counter where a stunning redhead was working on a crossword, towards a small office. The walls were red, the lighting was dim, it looked a little like a Chinese takeaway.

He sat me down, almost forcefully, opposite his desk before plumping himself down on a swivel chair.

"Are you working at the moment?" he asked.

I shook my head.

"No, I've only just arrived in Canberra, from Adelaide."

"Were you working there?"

"I haven't worked full time since I left France," I explained. "I have just done odd jobs for my husband, entertaining some of his prospective clients, that's all."

He rubbed his hands in glee.

"I'm looking for a girl for the day shift, Monday to Friday, 10 am to 6 pm," he explained. "You can earn a fixed sum of $200 per day, or have 50 per cent of your gross takings."

This was an excellent opportunity, but I had to explain that I was not looking for full-time work. I really only wanted to work two days a week, three days maximum.

He frowned.

"I can't do that. It makes life too complicated for me, and it's not fair to the other girls," he explained. "Look, I'll explain the general conditions, and then you can tell me what you think. What's your name?"

"Marie. Yes, I'd like to hear about the conditions, but I don't think it will change my mind."

"We'll see."

A few minutes later, Stella, the redhead from the front counter, led me into a large room. There were two comfortable chairs, a coffee table and a spa bath, and a large bed. It was tastefully decorated, and I told Stella how impressed I was.

She nodded.

"Yes, we do have nice working conditions. Of course, you have to keep Kevin happy, and some girls find that is a bit of a pain."

I nodded.

"He is the boss, after all," I commented. "It's important to have a contented boss."

She grinned. "I like your enthusiasm. You can have my turn."

About 20 minutes later we were still sitting on the bed, chatting, as women do, about important things, when Kevin walked in. Stella sat up and smiled.

"Kevin will take over now," she said as she left the room.

Kevin sat on the bed and began to explain. If I took the job, I might have sex with him once a week. This allowed him to enjoy a good relationship with his staff and keep a check on their performance. It was a quite unusual working contract, but I let him continue. I had heard about such employment arrangements in France, but would never have thought I would discover such conditions in Australia.

"Are you married?" he asked.

I nodded.

"That's not a problem," he commented. "You decide whether you tell your husband or not. We like to be frank about our work, so all the girls here have husbands or boyfriends who know about their job and about me. We all get along fine."

Was I beginning to understand something that had not been explained at the outset? I realised he was offering me a job as a whore. His club was a luxurious brothel. Mario and I were going to have words. I told him I did not have sex for money, ever. He was disappointed.

"It's a pity. You could make good money here. You are good looking, you have talent. We need people like you."

I am sure he was right, but I never went back. I found a nice house in May, with good central heating, and we moved in. I avoided explaining to Pierre how I had experienced a special job interview.

ℬ ℭ

In July, Pierre announced the imminent arrival of Jonathan. He was, it appeared, eager to see those frostbitten Canberra mornings. I could not hide my delight, and I knew that I could keep him warm.

"You have missed him," Pierre said, jokingly.

I blushed. Unfortunately, his arrival coincided with the impromptu visit of Laura, the ex-wife of an old friend of Pierre. She had been married to an Australian diplomat who had fallen in love with an Italian undersecretary, 24 years his junior, called Loretta. It was obvious to me that Laura was sex hungry and had taken a particular liking to Pierre. As soon as we moved into our new house, only a five minute walk from hers, she became a regular evening visitor.

She was obviously surprised by the enthusiastic welcome I gave to Jonathan, who was staying just one night before going on to the Hunter Valley. She followed me into the kitchen, excited.

"What a guy," she exclaimed. "I could put him up at my place this evening, if you're cramped."

I laughed and turned towards her, dish of ice cubes in my hand.

"If he puts himself up anywhere tonight, my dear, it will be with my help and consent."

She thought that statement over carefully.

"Do you mean that he will be having sex with you tonight? That's disgusting. After all, you're married. What will your poor husband be doing?"

I smiled sweetly. "Watching, probably."

She gave up and went home, much to Pierre's surprise, who had thought of inviting her to dinner to make up a foursome. As it happened, Jonathan slipped away to bed straight after the meal, protesting fatigue. I was very intrigued.

Over the next fortnight, I was busy putting things in place in our new house, when Pierre announced that Jonathan had returned and would be calling around one evening.

"I hope he will be less tired this time," I commented. "I love you dearly, my husband. But it would be nice to make love to Jonathan again, who knows, perhaps for the last time."

He smiled wistfully.

"I think you might be right in thinking it could be the last time."

When Jonathan's car pulled into our driveway, a week later, I understood what my darling husband had feared to tell me. May was sitting in the car next to Jonathan.

He gave me a kiss and a wonderful hug, nearly cracking my ribs. May also kissed me, but more gently. I threw a quick glance to Pierre who shrugged his shoulders and smiled. I had made up a bed in the spare room for Jonathan; it was a double bed so I would have to ask the question at some time.

In a typically Australian way, we sat down together to take tea and biscuits. Pierre delighted in watching me take up new habits in this new land. We chatted about business, about old friends in Adelaide, and Jonathan asked lots of questions about Canberra. He then formally announced that he was engaged to May and that they were to marry in September.

"Are you already sleeping together?" I asked, bluntly.

Jonathan laughed.

"Of course, as often as possible. Why do you ask?"

"Because of my bed arrangements," I explained.

May suddenly looked embarrassed.

"We were expecting to stay at a hotel."

"We have a lovely room with a very comfortable double bed," I protested.

"Then we would love to stay," she assured me.

Later, May and I drove to the shops while the men talked business. At her suggestion, we actually pulled into a pub and shared a glass of wine. May needed to talk, and we both needed to clear the air.

"Nowadays, I help Jonathan market his wines. He has taught me to appreciate wine, and I can now recognise one wine from the other, because he has educated my taste-buds."

"He did the same for me," I replied, cheekily.

She laughed and blushed.

"He taught me that, too. He is an excellent tutor. But now he is mine. From tomorrow, that is. Tonight, he will make his farewells to you."

I protested, but May insisted. She had been practically a witness of our relationship, she realised how important it had been to both of us, and she wanted us to enjoy one another for a last time.

"You are a wonderful woman, and I hope we will always be friends," I told her.

She smiled and squeezed my hand affectionately.

"I might even spend a little time with you myself, this evening," she said softly, and my heart fluttered.

"I would like that very much," I whispered.

We had a beautiful candlelit dinner. The men were looking smart and I could see the excitement in their eyes. I had warned Pierre of May's program, and obviously she had also explained her arrangements to Jonathan.

I was wearing the same dress that I had first worn in Adelaide. May was looking stunning in a shimmering satin frock that clung to her slim body, and I could see that Pierre, although not a great fan of breasts that can be hidden by egg cups, found her quite attractive.

My husband had kept my wine glass well filled; he knew that this was the secret to success. During coffee, I slipped away to the bathroom to glance in the mirror. My eyes were sparkling, my cheeks were flushed. I was ready.

I wandered into the master bedroom, dropped all my clothes, and snatched the duvet from the bed to toss it over my shoulder. I am sure that I offered a splendid sight when I walked back into the living room.

"I am ready for love," I announced simply, dropping the duvet on the floor.

"Me too," replied May. Within a few seconds, we were together, enlaced, kissing, touching, caressing. The two men settled down, each in a deep arm chair, glass of cognac in hand, to enjoy the spectacle.

I have never been interested in a lesbian relationship. But I do know that I can find pleasure in exchanging caresses with another woman. I believe that most women are the same, if they want to overcome the barriers imposed by their culture or their education. With May, it was simple. She was gentle, shy, but ready to offer and exchange. We were both hesitant, and slowly became bolder as the minutes passed. I could hear the men murmuring appreciations and compliments; Pierre was even comparing the two styles of beauty: I was voluptuous, she was slim and lithe.

Gradually, May became more adventurous and I was more offering. As her mouth moved over my body, slowly travelling further and further south, she lifted her hips and lowered her bust, her breasts trailing over my stomach. Meanwhile, she lifted her hips higher, offering a magnificent view of her slim buttocks to the delighted men. I knew where she wanted to go, and began to part my thighs, slowly.

Pierre was whispering quiet encouragements to me in French. He realised that if I was to offer them a view of my most secret treasure, I would need to overcome a last barrier of shyness.

Finally, I succumbed. I spread my legs, and smiled.

"May, kiss me, please," I whispered.

As her tongue and lips began to explore, I ran my fingers through her long, silky hair. Then she found me, and I began to moan. I could hear the soft ruffling of cloth as the men began to remove their clothes. May was moving faster and faster, groaning herself with happiness. Two other mouths had now reached me, playing with my nipples. I knew that very, very soon, I was to be filled.

May's mouth disappeared and I heard her murmur to Jonathan.

"Come quickly, she is ready."

I opened my eyes and my lovely Jonathan was above me, smiling. He slipped inside me with ease, and began to slide back and forth.

I held his head and kissed him on the lips.

"Please do it slowly. I want it to last a long time. Pierre can wait."

This was the last time that I would feel my beautiful Jonathan inside me, filling me with his joy. It was a desperately important moment in my life.

It was minutes later that I realised that there was activity beside me. May's head was beside mine, and she turned and kissed me on the cheek. Then Pierre kissed me on the lips, and I realised that he was poised above May. Fear and jealousy clutched my heart. Then I reasoned. May's fiancée was inside me, I could hardly refuse her the right to use my husband. Then the excitement of this socially unacceptable moment took over. I climaxed, crying out as my wonderful Jonathan filled me.

A few minutes later, it was May's turn. I watched Pierre as he thrust himself faster and faster into the slim body, and almost feared that he would break her in two. When he filled her, he was holding himself on stiffened arms and I saw his eyes bulge.

May screamed, thrashing her head from side to side and begging him to fill her with words I would never have thought I would hear from such a sweet mouth.

Afterwards, we were all a little embarrassed. I slipped into the kitchen and May joined me a few minutes later.

She stroked my buttocks as she spoke to me softly.

"I must apologise, but I have never experienced such an orgasm as the one that I just had with Pierre, your husband. But, like you and Jonathan, Pierre and I will never have sex together again."

I smiled.

"That is good. I was having so much fun with your man, then Pierre began to make love to you and I was suddenly desperately jealous."

She nodded.

"Excellent. How about you and me?"

I turned, placed my hands behind her head, and kissed her softly on the mouth. Our nipples touched.

"That was wonderful. Perhaps if I never make love to Jonathan again, I can still enjoy some pleasures with his wife."

May laughed.

"Maybe, maybe. Meanwhile, why not serve the coffee, and then we will each look after our own man."

"What a lovely idea," I murmured.

The men were delighted. May proved to be just as clever with her mouth as I was, but we had both probably been educated by the same teacher. I forget who came first, but it was of no importance.

We dressed, finished our coffees and Jonathan and May went to bed while Pierre and I sat and talked for a few minutes.

Our guests left the next morning with apologies, claiming other urgent commitments. Jonathan kissed me on both cheeks, very formally, in the French way, while May kissed me on the mouth, both hands on my buttocks, and promised that we would meet again soon.

We waved farewell from the driveway, Pierre's arm around my waist. As we turned and entered the house, he pinched me gently.

"That little Chinese tongue was doing wonders last night, I think?"

I nodded.

"Oh, Pierre, why is it that I seem to enjoy sex so much at the moment?"

"It's probably got something to do with your hormones. Perhaps a lively French tongue might help you settle down, what do you think?"

I laughed.

"I think that would be wonderful."

I do believe that Jonathan and May could have perhaps just reached the next suburb by the time I was holding Pierre by the ears and begging him to go deeper, deeper. Nobody makes love to me like my husband, although several have tried.

Later that same week, thinking back over our evening together, I changed my mind. Knowing that I would never make love to Jonathan again, I decided that if May attempted to develop a relationship, I would refuse. I did not want to give her a second opportunity with my husband. Pierre is emotionally fragile and does not need that kind of temptation. I shouldn't have worried. I did not see either of them for a long time.

৪০   ৫৪

We were in the middle of spring, and Canberra was truly beautiful. In a few days, early in September, we would celebrate my husband's fortieth birthday. Pierre was busy in diplomatic circles. His job in Canberra was quite different to his activities in the other cities. Here, he was to establish a quiet office which would lobby the Federal Government on behalf of French companies that developed and sold new technologies. His operations would be subject to 'offset' programs, whereby Australian companies would become local manufacturing partners to the French companies, producing and selling their technology into Australia. He would intervene where the role of the diplomat ended: Pierre could negotiate, barter, entice or use all sorts of shrewd tactics to get his way.

I was invited to accompany him on some of his official functions, generally luncheons or cocktail parties hosted by the French Embassy. I did not enjoy the pomp and ceremony, and the wives of the diplomats I met appeared to be all suffering from chronic social constipation. I discovered, with surprise, that living in Canberra was considered as a 'hardship posting' by the ladies who missed the cafés, the theatres and the big shops of Paris. I was always seeking excuses not to attend these functions, but Pierre knew only too well that I was unoccupied and dreadfully bored. I could not claim a conflict with other activities: there were none.

We had been in Canberra for a year, and had celebrated my birthday with an intimate dinner for two at home. It was October 1986, I was 34 and, according to my favourite man, at the peak of my beauty. At the end of the meal I was relaxed and quite merry, and he chose that moment to announce my special birthday present. He told me that it would cure my boredom.

I raised an inquisitive eyebrow.

"He works for an escort agency, his name is Andrew, and he is coming at ten o'clock to be your slave for an hour."

It took a little time for me to focus on the announcement and to digest what he meant. Of course, I understood that an escort was a person who came to somebody's house or hotel room for sexual intercourse, and that in this case the escort was a handsome young male devoted to my pleasure.

I finished my glass of wine in one gulp, trying to absorb the announcement at the same time, and then I challenged my husband.

"Did you say you wanted a man to screw your wife?" I asked, angrily.

He smiled, sheepishly.

"As a matter of fact I said that you were my sister-in-law, over here on holidays from France, and that your name was Brigitte. I explained that you had been here for two weeks and, being French, could not last any longer without a man."

I could not help laughing.

"I think that if Brigitte was here, in Canberra, for a fortnight, she would certainly be pretty desperate."

"That's what gave me the idea in the first place," he admitted.

"This is totally stupid. At what time is he coming? At 10? My God, it's already 9.30."

I think my husband had rarely seen me get organised so quickly. In 30 minutes I had showered, slipped into my disgraceful peach cocktail dress, and nothing else, added a touch of mascara and rouge, sprayed a little perfume and brushed my hair.

"How do I look?" I asked, excitedly.

"Very excited," he replied.

Andrew was about 25, a child, dark haired with a lovely smile. Pierre introduced me as Brigitte, his sex-starved sister-in-law, and paid the fee with his credit card. He then withdrew discreetly, but not before shaking Andrew's hand vigorously.

"My wife is already asleep, and does not approve of my little present. However, she has insisted that she does not want a stranger in any of her beds," Pierre said.

Andrew looked a little worried, but I squeezed his arm to reassure him.

"Don't worry, I've organised something nice. A doona in the living room."

We lost about 20 minutes in shy chatter before I decided that I could not waste any more time. I helped him undress, led him to the doona and then helped him lie down. His penis was beautiful and a wonderful barometer of his happiness. I swear that when I removed my cocktail dress, it grew another centimetre.

He was wonderfully docile, and lent himself to my wishes. Basically, he stretched out on his back and stayed in that position all the time. There were a few attempts to take over proceedings, probably motivated by a professional conscience, but each time I pushed him down, and continued to show him the art of the French kiss. I only stopped when he announced a potential explosion, leaving him to deflate a little, and then I resumed oral operations. He told me that I was an angel. Finally, I lowered myself onto his erect penis, squatting vertically, and began to canter. He stroked my breasts with extreme care, told me I was beautiful, then, with a little cry, he filled me.

"I'm not supposed to do that," he explained, afterwards. "Ejaculation is not on the everyday menu. I should charge you extra."

I told him that he was not funny. He laughed.

"I was kidding! As for you, I reckon you need to get out and about a little."

He told me about a nice club, not far from where we lived, devoted to several sports.

"You should get your brother-in-law to take you there; you will meet lots of people."

"I'm not terribly interested in sport," I muttered.

He laughed again.

"What I mean is that rather than paying an escort agency you will find lots of beautiful young cricket players or tennis men who would be happy to play with you."

I sighed.

"You mean I could fine some willing sexual partners there," I said.

"Of course, there is plenty of choice for a girl as beautiful as you."

He winked heavily.

"I often go there myself."

Once I had waved Andrew goodbye and closed the front door, Pierre was with me. My darling, marvellous husband and soul-mate filled me in a few seconds and I cried out in delight.

"Just resuming possession," he explained afterwards, between gasps.

ℬ ℭ

In February 1987, racked with boredom, I decided to attend a technical institute to follow an advanced course in the English language, as it is spoken in Australia. I met people from all over the world. I learned slang and funny expressions which made Pierre laugh when I tried them on him of an evening. I organised a couple of tea parties, inviting other students from my class, but soon got bored with the chatter of the housewives from the

Philippines, Sri Lanka and Turkey. Most of the conversation was concerned with bringing up children (an occupation I had decided to avoid), or how to keep their husbands happy and satisfied (an art in which I was not prepared to share my secrets).

Pierre went to Sydney to meet the French commercial attaché there. For once, I did not accompany him, pleading that I needed some private time to look for a job. That evening, I dropped in to the club, pretending it was by accident. At the bar, I met Andrew himself.

"So, you've taken my advice?" he asked.

I shrugged my shoulders.

"It's more curiosity than anything else," I pleaded.

He laughed.

"Where's your brother-in-law?"

I hesitated, and then remembered the story. But it was too late. He smiled.

"Don't worry, I understand. He wanted his wife to have some fun."

I nodded dumbly. He slid from his barstool and took me by the hand.

"I'll introduce you to Donald. He's the best squash player in the club but his girlfriend left him about four months ago. He's feeling quite lonely."

I don't know who the girlfriend was, but she must have been mad. Donald was tall, handsome and exciting. An hour and two whiskies later I was invited to visit his flat. Andrew had already disappeared, called away for a service, so I accepted.

I discovered that squash players were gentlemen with enormous stamina, and I was quite exhausted by the time he had overcome four months of hunger. We were very well suited, and I enjoyed every minute. He then asked if I would like to meet a close friend, another squash player with emotional problems. I was still considering his suggestion when he rang David and invited him over. I had not realised that when he had said 'meet' he meant 'meet now'.

David was delightful, and Donald was so pleased with our evening that he came back for seconds. They took me back to the club car park at close to four o'clock in the morning. They hugged and kissed me before packing me into my car, and begging me to call the next time I was feeling lonely. There were many, many unhappy bachelors in the squash club, they assured me, and they were all Francophiles.

I woke up the next morning wondering whether I had gone mad and feeling depressed. Was I not capable of restraining these terrible urges which a couple of glasses of alcohol seem to release? Pierre arrived home that afternoon and found me tired and depressed. I told him, blushing, about my foray into the game of squash, and he frowned angrily. He was quite concerned that I should find myself a job, urgently. He thought it would be a more licit way of overcoming boredom.

He went away again, by himself, in March 1987, making strong recommendations as he crossed the threshold of our love nest. Laura was most disappointed when she turned up unexpectedly at my house to find the cupboard bare, so to speak. We had a glass of wine together while she explained the sexual desert she was crossing at that time.

"Why don't you try an escort agency?" I suggested. "It's clean, prompt and efficient."

She glared.

"That's a strange idea, paying for sex," she commented.

"It's been going on for a few thousand years," I suggested, grinning.

"I'm sure I could have some fun if only I knew where to look," she wailed.

The idea came to me suddenly.

"Let's go down to the club for dinner."

She didn't know 'the club' and I explained. She was very surprised by my intimate knowledge of Canberra, but accepted immediately. She raced off home to slip into something 'comfortable' and designed to leave little to the imagination.

Dinner was quiet, the food good, and the wine excellent. I then dragged her to the bar, renowned for after-dinner drinks and strange encounters. Laura's eyes lit up when she saw the abundance of beautiful male flesh. It was a nymphomaniac's paradise.

Within ten minutes, I was approached by a trio of young males, hunting in a pack. The leader remembered that he had met me briefly one evening, introduced by his friend, Andrew. They offered us drinks, and we accepted.

"How do you know all these people?" Laura hissed.

"Shut up." I hissed back. "If you want to get laid, leave it to me, and stop asking silly questions."

I explained to Trevor, Andrew's friend, that Laura was a little starved of male friendship and that she thought that his friend Steve looked nice. He explained that the other friend, Brian, was pretty good, too. I looked them over and realised that they were all under 30, so at least ten years younger than Laura, and were built like rugby players.

Ten minutes later we left the club in Trevor's Kingswood. It was not really a car, but a utility of which the rear section had been equipped with a double mattress and fancy interior lights, for 'camping' he explained. We drove out to a quiet spot near Cotter's Dam, Laura in the back with Steve and Brian. Trevor pulled up under some trees and he and I shared a joint while his friends began to service the divorcee. The vehicle began to bounce charmingly, but I found the whole event rather boring. Laura announced loudly that she had decided not to resist the violation of her innocence, and that the invader was of the highest calibre, or words to that effect. Five minutes later, the vehicle began to bounce again.

"That'll be Brian," Trevor explained, while enjoying the hand job I had just begun, to pass the time. "Slower rhythm but better service, so they say. Bigger equipment, probably."

"Bet it's not as nice as this one," I muttered as I worked away.

A few minutes later, Laura announced loudly that Brian had met all expectations, and Trevor lost his control at the same time. There was at least five minutes of silence, and then Laura called out from behind.

"Would you like to pop in the back, Trevor?" she suggested.

Trevor, who had just filled my Kleenex, was adamant.

"Not tonight, love, thanks all the same. But another evening we can catch up at the club, if you like."

He then drove us back, and we went straight to Laura's car.

"How could you just sit there?" she asked. "Didn't you feel like a good screw this evening?"

I smiled. "Not really. It's the wrong time in the month. How did it go?"

She blushed. I never thought I would see Laura blush.

"Wonderful. I feel nice and relaxed. No more cobwebs. Oh, you won't mention this to Pierre, will you?"

I swore I would not, but I guessed that this was because she was hoping to continue to pass for an innocent, unsullied temptation in my husband's eyes. Nevertheless, over the following weeks, she visited us less frequently, then one evening, at the beginning of June, she appeared with a young man in tow.

"This is my friend, Stan," she explained. "I met him at the club."

Stan looked very capable of keeping Laura satisfied. He had a promising hump in the groin region, goat-like eyes and knuckles that scraped the ground. While she talked, he gazed at her in silent admiration. Reading the shadows under her eyes, I decided that I would no longer need to protect my darling husband from her hungry advances. At least for a few weeks.

👻 ℃

I would soon celebrate my second birthday in Canberra. I had suffered two years of frustrated ambitions. Surely, I must be able to find something to do? Finally, I decided to apply for a position as a marketing representative, which was advertised in the newspaper. Three days later, I received a phone call and an appointment was made to meet me, in my home.

The senior sales representative was a beautiful young lady, neatly dressed and a little over-groomed. Everything was visible and in large doses, and there was enough lipstick to fill a raspberry pavlova. It took her a long, long time to come out with even the business name, but, in the end, she admitted it was a popular pyramid business, selling a wide range of household products.

She was offering me three options: I could buy products for my own use; I could go out and sell, sell, sell; or else (nudge-nudge, wink-wink), I could simply get other idiots to join and to go out to do these things, while I sat back, painted my toenails and collected the money.

She had a lovely album of colour photos showing all those who had succeeded. I remember a picture of a happy couple leaning on their pink Cadillac convertible, pointing to their eight-bedroom, two swimming pool Miami mansion in the background, and wishing me all the best. If I did well, I would meet them at the next congress in Hong Kong. Maybe, in a few years, I would have all these trappings too.

I went for the hard option. I went out knocking on doors, offering miraculous washing detergents and dog shampoos. The consumers were recalcitrant. They did NOT believe in direct marketing, and they HATED people ringing their front door bells when they were loading the washing machine. It seemed they actually WANTED to drag screaming kids around the supermarket aisles, it was one of their greatest pleasures in life.

I stuck at it for five months. I went to motivation classes and met scores of wonderful ladies or couples who had earned extra stars, better commissions, nicer ties or brooches, even trips to Fiji, for God's sake. I was the smiling, eager, attentive loser.

Pierre was very supportive and he never said "I told you so". In fact, he told me how proud he was to share his bed with a super salesgirl. When I gave up, he approved, he told me that I had done my best, and confirmed that even after this dismal failure, he still loved me. I am so lucky to have a husband who is caring, hard-working, handsome, passionate, and a lion between the bed sheets.

৩০   ৫৪

I continued to hunt through the employment opportunities in the *Canberra Times*, and found an advertisement assuring me that there were women earning good money selling cosmetics and fragrances. Despite my previous experience in Adelaide, I was so desperate that I decided to join their ranks.

The company had training offices not far from where we lived, so I attended a series of open seminars. I was immediately adopted by a senior consultant, a lady of Greek origin called Maria, who took me under her wing and told me that with my natural beauty I would make a fortune.

It was the same 'pyramid' story. I could join up just to buy products for myself, or because I felt that I was capable of selling products to other women, or, preferably, because I believed I could persuade other women to become my sales representatives. I started door knocking, with different products, but still without success. I must say that Pierre was very supportive and even expressed admiration for my courage. I think that he knew, secretly, that I would not succeed.

I met many people. It confirmed my experience in household products. There were a couple of angry ladies who slammed their doors in my face, but most people were polite and kind. There were those who shook their heads with a sad smile or others who even invited me in for a cup of tea. There were a surprising number of men at home during the daytime: some laughed, some told me their wife was out, and a few even wanted me to come in for a private demonstration.

I attended regular briefing sessions in the training office and announced my failures. Maria just smiled and offered me a new batch of brochures after each defeat.

The business operated from the first floor of a commercial building, stuck between a shopping centre and a service station. Apart from Nature's Cosmetics there was a solicitor, a tax agent, a chiropractor and an establishment called the Coquette Club. The latter seemed to take up almost half of that floor of the building but it had no windows along the corridor. The single door looked massive, and the name of the establishment was indicated by an elegant brass plate, accompanied by a discreet door bell. There was no suggestion of what activity might be exercised inside.

Strangely, on several of my visits to the great cosmetics distributor, I would meet the same lady either opening the Club door with her key, or emerging. Each time, she tossed me a lovely smile. She was terribly blonde, probably around 40, attractive and always immaculately dressed. On one such warm Wednesday afternoon, we met again. She held out her hand, and changed my life. We were a few weeks from my birthday and she was about to offer me a wonderful present.

"Hello, I'm Michelle."

I shook her hand and introduced myself as Marie. Exchanging simply first names is a common practice in Australia.

"Do you work in one of the offices here?" she asked.

"No, I'm afraid not. I'm trying to become a cosmetics consultant," I explained.

"Oh dear," she smiled, wistfully. "I have seen quite a few of those coming up and down the corridor. They never seem to last more than a few months."

I nodded.

"It's difficult."

"Perhaps almost impossible," she suggested. "I was going down to the café in the shopping centre to have a coffee. Why don't you join me?"

I accepted with pleasure. It would be nice to have a female shoulder to cry on, as I had not had the courage to admit my frustrations to Pierre. Although I loved my husband dearly, I did not always wish to be the weaker partner. He recognised that I had no choice but to follow him from place to place, as his career dictated, and he readily admitted that in such circumstances it was difficult for me to establish myself in a stable career. Nevertheless, I found my inactivity frustrating and my life totally boring.

I explained most of this to Michelle, with some hesitation. She was obviously a good listener, and she asked the right questions at the right time. Then she explained that she was the owner of the Coquette Club, and about its activity. I was not surprised about its trade as I had suspected as much, and I told her about my previous encounter with Kevin. She pressed for more details, and I succumbed.

Then she began to talk about offering me a job. She knew Kevin, and did not like his operation. She was a different type of boss, as she had been herself a sex worker for 20 years, before setting up her own business. She treated her staff as if they were her daughters. If I wanted, I could go to the Coquette Club for a few hours every week, at my convenience, with no pressures on me to perform or to provide.

She looked me in the face and said, very gravely, "I think you're going through that strange but exciting period in your life when you want to experiment with your sexuality. You are lucky; so many women never reach that stage. With me, you can come and satisfy your curiosity and earn a little pocket money at the same time."

I was terribly embarrassed by her understanding of my secret, but she was so gentle and so perceptive, I could only nod in agreement.

"What about my husband?" I asked.

She smiled, patting my arm.

"Look, I don't generally recommend deception, but in your case I would suggest that you don't tell him about this for two or three weeks. In that way, if it doesn't work out, you won't have caused any unnecessary stress."

I liked the idea.

"Are you free on Friday morning of next week?" she asked.

I frowned.

"I thought there was to be no pressure."

She grinned, reassuringly.

"It's okay. It's just that every Friday morning a good friend of mine comes to the Club. He helped me get started financially. He is very handsome, and was my lover for a few years. Nowadays, we are still good friends and he comes to see if all is well. He could talk to you about what men expect; he could test your talents and give you some advice."

I nodded, blushing with embarrassment.

"That's good. But I think that it will be difficult to talk about those sorts of things with a stranger."

She laughed.

"I promise you that you will survive."

She gave me her card.

"Ring me on Friday morning. I'll talk to him in the meantime."

I spent two days wondering whether I would talk to Pierre or remain silent. I knew that Michelle's advice was sound, but at the same time I hated the idea of keeping secrets from the man I adored. I washed my hair twice, hoping that it would help me clear my mind. I paid a brief visit to the beautician, changed the colour of my nail varnish, and then I decided to drastically trim my pubic hair.

I prepared *escalopes de veau à la crème* for Pierre that Thursday evening, which I served with fluffy rice and baby beans in garlic butter. It was accompanied by a delightful little Merlot from a small vineyard in Tasmania, a surprise I discovered in our local bottle shop.

While he enjoyed his food, he found me extraordinarily tantalising that evening. He liked the new hairstyle, the fresh flush to my cheeks (almost totally natural) and was eager to explore, as soon as possible, the work I had undertaken with the safety razor and trimming scissors. He buried his face between my legs and began to do those things in which he has great expertise, simply to demonstrate how access to my secret spots had been improved. He nearly drove me crazy with pleasure.

I slept peacefully, totally satisfied. In fact, the next morning, which was Friday, after kissing my husband on the doorstep to wish him a lovely day, I was close to believing that I was totally happy and would not be tempted to explore other avenues of pleasure.

I called Michelle, trying to persuade myself that it was probably with the intention of cancelling. She was delightful, cheerful, encouraging, and told me that I was expected at midday, and that Karl was looking forward to meeting me. I promised I would be there, and my hand was shaking so badly I made three attempts at putting the telephone back on its cradle.

I took a hot bath, adding lavender salts to the water, then washed and fluffed my hair. I slipped into a low-cut red and orange summer dress with thin shoulder straps, and decided to wear only a brief pair of panties underneath. I added a little extra flush to my cheeks, and a little more eye shadow than usual. When I looked in the mirror, I knew that Karl would not be disappointed.

I arrived ten minutes early and Michelle answered the bell herself. She took a step back when she saw it was me, then took me in her arms and hugged me. She then held me at arms length, eyes wandering and examining me from head to toe.

"You look absolutely stunning," she admitted. "Karl will be very surprised. I think you will have an enjoyable afternoon."

I blushed.

"I'm still not sure why I'm here," I confessed.

"Today? Today is for training, information, maybe even for a little shared pleasure, nothing more. Today, we will see if the man I respect finds you beautiful, sensual and capable of giving and receiving pleasure."

I smiled.

"I can make men happy, that I do know. I have a husband, I used to have a lover, and I have had sex with two or three men since my marriage, just for pleasure. This is different. You are asking me to have sex with a total stranger, just for money."

"No, not today," she assured me. "Today, it will be as if you had just discovered a new lover, nothing more."

I followed her into her office and she offered me tea or coffee. I whispered that a glass of cool white wine would have a far more soothing effect on my nerves. She smiled understandingly and, without a word, opened a refrigerator cunningly hidden in her bookcase. She served us a glass of wine each and offered a toast. We drank to pleasure.

We chatted for a few minutes about Pierre's work, and then she stood up.

"Okay, let's go. There's no point in keeping him waiting."

I followed her into a beautiful room. It was quietly air-conditioned and the walls were clothed in red tapestry. There was a king size bed in the middle of the room, dressed with satin sheets, and soft music was playing in the background. There was a large mirror on the ceiling and on the wall facing the foot of the bed.

I saw no lover. But Michelle herself took me in her arms, slipped the straps from my shoulders and helped my light dress sink to the floor. She began to stroke my nipples very softly, murmuring that I was beautiful, and then we kissed. As we exchanged caresses, I heard a door open and close. Michelle was now running her tongue across my navel, making me shiver with delight. I could hear the rustling of clothing behind me, and realised that my lover had appeared and was preparing himself.

Suddenly, a tall, handsome, dark-haired man appeared beside us. Softly, he broke our grip and kissed Michelle on the lips. During their embrace, I allowed my eyes to make a quick inspection, and I knew instantly that I would be very happy that afternoon. He was handsome, well proportioned, and obviously ready for the foray.

Michelle took my hand and guided it towards his swollen penis.

"You won't need a condom today," she whispered. "Just enjoy."

She obviously assumed that I was here for the pleasure, rather than for a job interview. I must admit that she was right.

As she slipped quietly from the room, I turned and kissed him on the mouth.

"Good afternoon, Karl. My name is Marie, and I want to make love to you."

He was surprised, and smiled.

"Then show me how the French ladies tend to mankind," he suggested.

I sank to my knees and took his magnificent erection in both hands to guide it carefully between my lips. He uttered a great sigh of satisfaction as I began to move my head backwards and forwards, very slowly. It was not easy; my new lover would put any service station attendant to shame.

"Now I know that you are truly French," he groaned.

If only you knew, my good friend, that this famous French art had, in fact, been taught to me by an Australian winemaker in Adelaide. The world is full of misconceptions.

I spent in all more than two hours with Karl. He was in amazing health and climaxed three times during our frolics: once in my mouth, once on my breasts, and once in the classical way recommended by the Church. He was also seriously attentive to my needs, even those I ignored. When he was about to leave, he told me that if I came to work for Michelle he would be a permanent fixture on my diary. I told him, laughing, that I hoped that this would not be every day, as I would be totally exhausted.

"Are you happily married?" he asked, suddenly.

I hesitated, and then nodded.

"Excellent. Married women or women in long-standing, solid relationships work so much better."

We exchanged an almost chaste kiss before Michelle came to fetch me. I slipped into my dress and shoes, but could not find my panties. Michelle smiled.

"When Karl steals a souvenir, it means he is happy," she assured me. "Now, come, I want to show you something."

I followed her into a smaller room, next door, filled with boxes, old mattresses and chairs. She pulled back the curtain which would normally cover a window, and I discovered that I was looking into the room I had just left, through part of the wall mirror. I was quite angry, but she hushed my protests with a finger to my lips.

"This was your first day. I needed to know if you were capable of satisfying a demanding man, without being afraid. Once I saw you and Karl enjoying such great pleasure together, I closed the curtain."

"But this means that there is no privacy," I protested.

"Not at all. Only I have the key to this room. If ever you are using that room and I have clients who want to watch, they can only do that with your permission."

"Do they pay to watch?" I asked.

She laughed.

"That is the right question. Yes. And the woman who acts in front of the mirror earns a lot of extra money. But I only have one lady here who does that, for the moment. The others are too shy."

"I understand," I murmured.

She stood up and took me to the door.

"Today, you would have theoretically earned about $150. But you do not yet work for me. So there is no money."

I nodded. It seemed reasonable in the circumstances.

She almost pushed me towards the front door.

"You are beautiful and talented. I really want to see you work here. You come when it suits you, but please warn me the day before. For the moment, I think you should stick to daytime and weekdays, in other words, when your husband is at work. Later, we may change, if you want."

I was terribly embarrassed to slip out through the door of this unusual club, frightened that I would be seen and identified as a professional prostitute. I told myself, at that moment, that I would never walk through that door again.

6. My Initiation into a Very Private Profession

I did not mention my fiery afternoon to Pierre. Although he loves me dearly, he may not have liked the idea. He has on several occasions acknowledged my sudden surges in temperament, but every private initiative has always annoyed him. When the occasion is right, such as with Jonathan or Andrew, he likes to organise things himself. He is overly possessive, but that is what love is all about.

Every morning drew me closer to the moment when I would have to ring Michelle, thank her, and say that I could not consider having sex with total strangers for a few hundred dollars a week. I realised, deep within my soul, that this was a silly argument. It had nothing to do with money.

I could try to train as a salesperson on a perfume counter, as a hairdresser, as a pharmacist assistant or as a dog washer. In any of these jobs, I would eventually find employment and earn money. This was not about fighting poverty, but boredom.

Secondly, I had to admit to myself that there was a period during each month when I was in need of greater sexual activity.

It was probably due to hormones, everything else is. But I knew that I had really enjoyed sex with Jonathan, with Karl, with Andrew, with Steve, and with a couple of squash players, without these events having any detrimental effect on my married life and my love for my husband. In fact, and I am ashamed to admit this, what I really enjoyed was having sex with Jonathan under the admiring gaze of my darling husband. I was happy, he was happy. I rang Michelle on Tuesday afternoon and asked if I could work on Wednesday. She was delighted.

"Come in around nine o'clock, so that I can show you around and find you a dress. We are all on deck at ten, and some of our visitors like to come in early, so be prepared. For the first day, I suggest you only stay until about three o'clock."

"Will that be enough?" I asked, shyly.

She laughed.

"I would hope that you would have had at least three men and earned more than $200 in that time. There is competition, there are other pretty and eager girls working here."

I smiled into the phone.

"Would that be good for a first day?" I asked.

"Let's say it would be a nice start. But don't worry about all of that. Let's see what you want to do. If you put your mind to it, you can earn a lot of money."

"I don't need a lot of money," I protested.

She laughed.

"I know, darling. Just come relaxed and enjoy yourself. We'll talk this over in a week or two when you have a better feel for the job."

I liked her expression.

I arrived Wednesday morning, a little early, and finely dressed. Michelle smiled when she opened the door.

"You won't need clothes like that here. Just come in jeans and t-shirt. I'll lend you a couple of dresses to get started, and let's hope that most of the day you won't be wearing anything at all."

My first pleasant surprise was to meet Fabienne, the receptionist. She was also French. We promised to chat later, as she was busy making sure that all the rooms were ready for the first visitors. Michelle explained that after each visit the bed linen was changed, and that the club had two large industrial washing machines in the back of the building.

I met the other three girls working with me. Sandy was a tall blonde studying political sciences at university, who came in two days a week to pay for her food and rent. Suzie, another blonde, was a housewife who worked four days a week to put her daughters through a private school. Maisie was a redhead with skin like fresh cream. She was 19 and from Ireland, visiting Australia on a working visa. She would be working for the next four months, every weekday, before moving on to Queensland.

I was told that I should give myself a name for the profession, different to my real one. Instinctively, and to give myself more courage, I decided to call myself Brigitte. I have always associated my sister with sexual popularity.

Michelle took me to her private wardrobe and produced a beautiful, red lace mini-dress. She explained that there were shops in Fyshwick which sold clothing for the business, and that if I decided to become a professional, I would have to go there to select my garments. She warned me that I was not allowed to show my vagina or my nipples in the reception area, but that the dresses were designed to show off everything else. I tried on the red dress, and she clapped her hands in delight.

"If you walked across Northbourne Avenue dressed like that you would create a multiple pile-up. Now don't forget, when the client comes in, let him have a good look and offer a smile which promises wonders."

The routine was simple. When the door bell rang, we, the four lovely ladies, would take our places on the couches in the lounge. Fabienne would then explain the fees for services to the visitor, and then introduce him. After a few kind words with each of us, he would then retire to tell Fabienne which one he wanted and for how long.

The first client was at 10:15 am. I had my first booking ten minutes later. I led the Asian visitor into Room 3, asked him to undress and take a shower, and promised that I would be back in ten minutes. Michelle was behind the door, rubbing her hands in glee.

"I knew it, I knew it! If you can learn to relax and give them what they want, you are going to be a wonderful success," she assured me. "Remember one important thing. Nobody can explain why, but a guy always prefers to have sex with a pretty woman rather than an ugly one."

I promised that I would remember something which seemed perfectly logical.

"Oh, and grab this. It's a lubricant you might need with the first client early in the morning. After two or three, you will be fine."

I nodded and went back to join my guest. He was lying on his back and gently stroking himself to ensure rigidity.

"You don't have to do that," I assured him, slipping out of my dress. "That's my job."

I tried to look assured, but my voice was wobbly. He smiled.

"This is your first day, isn't it?"

I nodded.

"Excellent. I am very proud to be the first, and I know I will not be the last. I like to come early in the morning so the lady is nice and fresh. I will be very gentle."

He patted the bed, inviting me to sit next to him. He explained that he was originally from Sri Lanka and that his compatriots are reputed to be excellent lovers. He was an accountant, married, with three children, and his wife had decided that all sexual activities should cease as the family had achieved the right size. As he talked, he softly traced circles around my nipples with an inquisitive finger. I was holding him firmly and delighted in seeing just how interested he was becoming. Suddenly, I leaned forward and slipped him into my mouth. He gasped with pleasure.

I completely overlooked the fact that I should be using a condom, and, strangely, none of my visitors on that first day seemed to notice. I think they were all too happy to meet the new girl. I was amazed to hear Fabienne rap on the door and announce that we had only ten minutes left. I panicked.

"You must take me now, quickly."

He laughed.

"Don't worry."

We did not need a lubricant, and he was delighted to find his 'little virgin' so wet and ready.

"Not too fast?" he suggested.

"Not too fast," I agreed.

He was a master in the art. At the end, I cried out loudly, begging him to fill me, and he whispered his delighted acceptance before releasing his load.

Before lunch, he was replaced by Bill, a fitter from Queanbeyan, and then by Robert, who was a local employee in one of the embassies. After nice foreplay, they both delivered,

Bill on my breasts, Robert in my hand. Like Brian, they promised to become regular visitors if I decided to stay on.

I had a quick lunch and then succumbed to the charm of Charles, a magnificent Fijian. His penis was quite thick, but I was totally relaxed and everything went perfectly. He booked me for an hour, and I climaxed twice with this magnificent airline pilot.

"You have a splendid joystick," I told him as we were leaving the room. "I would fly anywhere with you in total confidence."

His laughter shook the dust from the corridor walls. As I was walking back to the lounge, Michelle grabbed me by the arm and pulled me into her office.

"Okay, that's good for today. Are you happy?"

I smiled. "I'm delighted, it was fantastic."

She frowned.

"I have a few questions. We didn't find any condoms in the waste basket."

"That's all right," I assured her. "I never use them, I have a coil."

She shook her head.

"That may be okay if you are having sex with people you know, don't forget, here they are strangers and probably having sex with several women. It's best to be safe."

I nodded.

"Okay, but somebody will have to show me how to fit them…"

She laughed. "That's not a problem. Another thing is when you're faking those orgasms, be a little quieter. The guy screwing you might be delighted, but the clients with girls in other rooms get a little stressed."

I smiled gently.

"I'm sorry, but I wasn't faking."

She stared at me for a moment.

"You're not joking, are you? That Fijian stud made you really come twice?"

I grinned happily.

"And he's coming back next Wednesday."

She looked at me with a lopsided grin.

"Which means that you are coming back, too?"

I stared at her.

"Of course. I would like to come Friday, then Tuesday and Wednesday of next week."

She nodded.

"Of course. But today, you go home and have a hot bath. The other girls are getting a little worried, you're stealing their business."

"Fabienne said that there was a young uni student asking to see me before he made his choice."

"I like your enthusiasm," she assured me. "He is now firmly embedded in the green fields of Ireland. Go home."

I took her advice, and went home to take a hot bath, $280 richer. Then I prepared a rare pepper steak with green beans and French fries (what else?) accompanied by a wonderful Pinot Noir, and Pierre was surprised and delighted.

"Does the pepper steak mean what I think it means?" he asked afterwards.

It did. It was nearly one o'clock in the morning when he begged me to let him sleep, swearing on his honour that I was the most exciting and beautiful woman he had ever met, but that he needed his sleep and that, if necessary, I should go and ring that nice young man from the escort agency. My poor little darling, I thought to myself as he began to snore softly. I no longer pay, now I sell my skills to others.

80   03

Thursday was Pierre's birthday. I had been at a loss to choose an interesting present, but he told me not to worry. He was staying home that day, and wanted me to guarantee that I would stay with him.

The visitor who appeared at 11 o'clock was a handsome young man, but his arms were full of photographic equipment. He was going to offer Pierre the basis for his birthday present. He took a series of classic photos of me, nude, under Pierre's close supervision. The photographer was sweating profusely, a sure sign that things were going well. Later, Pierre had to decide which of the photographs would be used for the oil painting of me he wanted in his study. This would be his birthday gift. I decided that visitors to that room would be subjected to strong scrutiny.

The following day, I was at work at ten o'clock. Friday was always a busy day, so Michelle let me work through until five in the afternoon. I gave immense joy to two Italians, masturbated a Chinaman, offered a first oral experience to a New Zealander called Chris, and allowed the last visitor, from Brisbane, to mount me from behind, as I knelt on a chair. Before the final act, I had slowly and orally fitted him with a ribbed condom, and his moans of pleasure had not gone unnoticed. As I left, I apologised to the other girls for the noise, and took home $280.

The following Monday, Pierre proudly brought home a leather-bound album containing 28 photographs of his beautiful wife.

"Did you get the negatives?" I asked, breathlessly, after seeing the collection.

He brandished them proudly.

"You want a series for somebody?" he asked, impishly.

"No," I laughed. "I just wanted to make sure the photographer would not be making any other copies."

"Oh, is that all? No, that's fine, he just has a set of 'masters' for his personal records."

He was grinning, and I was not happy with the reply. Hopefully, he was just making fun of me.

☜   ☞

Three weeks later, Michelle and I went out to lunch. In four weeks I had worked ten days and earned more than a $2,000. I was desperately looking for a place to hide the money. More importantly, people like Chris, Karl, Charles my black beauty, the deliriously happy Chinaman and the accountant from Sri Lanka were all hoping to renew friendships. I could also not overlook the fact that Pierre was becoming curious about my own happiness and insatiable appetite in bed. Also, as we sat down at the table, Michelle reminded me that four of my lovely men were already booked for the following Tuesday, and it was time I made a decision.

I told her that the decision was made. I enjoyed the job, I loved bringing comfort and happiness to others, and I was no longer bored. The experience had already told me much about my own sexual needs and those of others, and I was giving even more pleasure to my husband than before. I added, with a grin, that I had gone to Fyshwick the previous day and bought two dresses: one in black lace and one in orange satin.

"Do they fit you well?" she asked, with a smile.

"They fit, but they hardly cover much at all," I boasted. "I will be a walking menu of desire."

She smiled wistfully.

"We still need to talk about other matters in the business. But first of all, you need to talk to your husband."

"I was thinking that I could just carry on like this, and he would not need to know."

She shook her head and frowned.

"I will not take you on professionally unless he agrees or you leave him. Also, if you become a full member of my staff you will have a fixed program, but you might get a call now and again for an escort job or for weekend or night duty."

I gazed at her thoughtfully.

"Would this extra business happen often?" I asked.

"Not really," she assured me. "But there can always be an emergency and I might have to call you in. But in your case, as a married woman, it would be very rarely."

We then worked on a strategy, or rather, I listened as she outlined hers. Michelle had a lot of experience in announcing to husbands that their wives were offering themselves to a wide community of hungry males. She had started by announcing to her own lover, at the age of 21, that she wanted to dabble in prostitution. He had refused, threatened, begged and finally accepted. Then, 20 years later, Karl helped her set up her current business. Generally, it is not a suggestion that a man takes to easily. Man is a jealous, possessive animal, and likes to believe that he can more than satisfy the needs of his partner. Often, he also believes that his partner lacks the necessary talent.

She explained that she thought that all would go well with Pierre, because I was to take up a part-time career, not for money, but to overcome boredom, to meet people and to offer happiness and comfort. It was almost like joining the Red Cross. Also, my passionate description of my husband led her to think that he would understand.

She assured me that it was far more difficult when the couple was in desperate need of money. In this case, invariably the male saw a challenge, not only to his own sexual capabilities, but also to his role as head of the family and principal breadwinner. Whatever his skills and motivations, he would soon discover that his wife could earn far more money lying on her back, moaning and assuring complete strangers that she had never been so happy. She warned me that, even in the case of Pierre, there would always be a latent jealousy and a fear that a complete stranger might make love to me better than him. All men have the same fears.

"You may find that when you come home from work he will want to take you immediately. This is very male. He will believe that when he penetrates you he resumes possession of your body, and that he will chase away all the other memories of the day. He may even ask you to show him how you work, and to make love to him as a street whore would take a passing client. Give in to all of his desires, within reason. Remember, despite all the men who may give you pleasure during a day, or all the men to whom you have brought happiness or relief, no man is more worthy of your attention than him."

Years later, I realised just how lucky I was to have been led into the profession by a woman as outstanding as Michelle. For a start, her strategy was simple: I would tell Pierre that she was offering me a job, and that we should discuss it together over dinner. I announced the important news to Pierre that evening. I had been offered a part-time job, and my future employer believed that I would prove to be very successful and talented in the career she offered. Because it was an unusual and innovative form of leisure activity, she thought that it would be good to talk it over together, preferably while enjoying a pleasant meal, before making any decision. He immediately noted the 'she'.

"And what would be the qualities you would bring to the job she is offering?" he asked, almost petulantly.

"Beauty and passion," I replied, simply.

He smiled.

"I'm glad you didn't add 'modesty', it would have sounded odd. Well, you certainly have a lot of both. I hope you will be using them carefully."

He then resumed his surgical attack on the rack of lamb in front of him. I was really annoyed that he did not want to ask anything more, and to see that he was apparently quite content with my short explanation and the promise of an intimate and refined dinner on Thursday evening. I was expecting more curiosity, more opposition, or even, quite simply, a greater interest. Deep down, I had a nagging suspicion that he had a small idea of what we were going to talk about.

The next morning, as he passed through the door, he shot me a parting glance and commented, "I do hope that you're not proposing to be a table-top dancer."

I ran into the garden behind him.

"And why not?" I asked angrily.

"Because you are not tall enough. Also, I'm told that it gives you varicose veins."

I could see that he was making fun of me and I threw the tea towel in his direction, as he ducked into the car.

That evening, I was, however, allowed to wear an apron as I prepared a stir-fry in the kitchen.

"I must look after your assets," he muttered. "I don't want to start off by picking a fight with the beautiful Michelle."

"How do you know she is beautiful, you have not seen her?" I threw at him, angrily.

He smiled.

"Because you rave about her all the time. Anyhow, you only mix with beautiful women. It is a well-known fact that beauty attracts beauty."

"That must be why I married you," I added, sweetly.

"Probably," he admitted, a little pompously. "I'm more interested in the 'passion' bit. Could you give me a demonstration?"

I did.

          ℬ   ℭ

Michelle was wearing a low-cut, black cocktail dress, and her hair was in a tight bun at the nape of her neck, held by a large gold comb. She wore long gold ear chains and a gold necklace studded with tiny brilliants.

Pierre kissed her hand and told her she was stunningly beautiful. She told him that he was even more handsome than I had described. She then led us to a private room which she had reserved for our meal. As we sat at the table, I picked up the menu card and showed it to Pierre.

"Oysters, avocados stuffed with fresh prawns, hare stew, gratin of silver beet, raspberry meringue... this is a fine menu," he commented. "You must be very eager to employ my wife."

She nodded.

"In its field, mine is one of the most reputed businesses in Canberra. With two or three people like Marie, it could be one of the best in Australia."

Pierre nodded as he slid his first oyster from the shell.

"Tell me more."

Michelle began to speak. We ate quietly, and Pierre asked no questions. I was too frightened to interrupt, but her explanation stopped each time a member of the restaurant staff entered our private room.

As we began the hare stew, Michelle stopped. She had described the business, the premises, the hours I would work, the money I could earn, and why my contribution would be so important.

"So, it's not just a simple whore house you're running?" my husband asked, crudely, dabbing the corner of his mouth with his napkin.

She smiled.

"No, it's not. It is a place where people come to relax, to talk, to seek advice, to find comfort and understanding. I don't employ hags who lie on their backs with their legs apart moaning about the cost of living. I employ people who can offer beauty, kindness, sensuality, and understanding."

Pierre nodded. "A place of pleasure, nevertheless?"

"Of course," she replied. "Pleasure is always at the end of the menu, but it can come in different ways. Sometimes, there is no penetration, no 'straight sex' as you might like to call it."

Pierre was thoughtful.

"The hare is delicious, by the way. But how do you know that Marie will be the kind of 'consultant' you would want?"

I blushed deeply as she explained my 'trial period'. Pierre looked at me sternly, then, seeing my embarrassment, was forced to laugh.

"I think I can almost guess what days you passed your exams," he commented. "There were evenings when you were terribly hot."

Michelle nodded.

"This is often the case. The job will stimulate the wife's sexuality, and make the marriage even more wonderful."

Pierre grinned. "Believe me, my wife needs little stimulation."

Michelle laughed.

"I think you may be right, although she can be a little shy."

"Only for the first ten minutes," Pierre assured her.

We stopped as the waiters served the raspberry meringue.

"What is the proposal?" Pierre asked when the staff had left.

Michelle explained the offer of three days a week from ten in the morning until five or six in the afternoon. Other employment might be offered occasionally but could be refused. I was paid one half of the gross income I earned.

"What would that represent?" he asked.

Michelle shrugged.

"It's variable. With Marie, I would guess that we could hope to see her earn about $800 dollars a week."

Pierre whistled softly. "That's good money for a half-week. Are there any male jobs going?"

She laughed, knowing that the battle was won.

"Not at the moment. But if there are, I'll give you a ring."

"Don't forget the trial period," he said with a heavy wink.

"I always interview my male escorts personally," she promised.

Pierre looked at me with great concern.

"I am going to agree to you taking up this job, for a trial period of three months. This is on the understanding that Michelle ensures your comfort and safety at all times. Your job will remain a secret, known only to the three of us."

I nodded, sighing with relief.

"You will not be disappointed," I assured him. "And I will give you all the money."

He shook his head.

"No, the money is yours. But it's not for the money, is it?"

I shook my head and lowered my eyes. "No, it's not. I can't really explain."

He patted my hand on the tablecloth.

"Don't even try. You will bring joy and comfort to many, I know that."

Michelle was delighted, and we agreed that I would start next week, working Tuesday, Thursday and Friday.

"I'll warn Karl and Fabienne," she promised. "And I think that we will arrange for Pierre to visit our premises in the close future."

"I don't know if he would like that," I protested.

"I think he'll love it," he countered.

We finished our desserts and Michelle gave the head waiter her credit card.

"We'll have coffee at my place," she suggested.

We accepted with pleasure, both eager to see where such a lady lived. Her house was, in fact, in one of the more modest suburbs of South Canberra, but, once inside, it was obvious that she had both money and good taste. She was eager to show us 'the boudoir', a bedroom beautifully decorated as if it were straight out of 19th century France.

"This is my illegal operation. It is here, on occasions, that very beautiful women meet Very Important Persons for an hour or two. By that I mean people in the public view, whose faces are known and who cannot be seen in a brothel."

"Do you use it yourself, sometimes?" Pierre enquired.

She laughed.

"You want to know if I sometimes entertain them myself? Why do you ask?"

"Because you said it was reserved only for beautiful women," he explained glibly.

There are actually times when Pierre angers me.

She smiled, nodding understandingly.

"Ah, the Frenchman. The mouth is always full of compliments. I do hope that one day your darling wife might meet a foreign Prince or Prime Minister in this room. Who knows?"

"If she does, I know that it will be the most memorable part of his official visit," Pierre commented.

There are other times when he makes me so happy.

Michelle smiled and changed the subject.

"Do you know that a few years ago I went to a brothel owners' congress in Sydney. I had been invited to speak on an issue of my choice, and my subject was sex workers who should not be on the job."

I was interested.

"So you explained why some ladies should not be prostitutes? It must have been highly interesting."

Michelle nodded. "It was taped. Do you want to see it?"

We both nodded and accepted a second cup of coffee. She dimmed the lights, switched on the TV, and slid a video cassette into the player. I think it must be one of the funniest videos I have ever seen. She just stood at the microphone and delivered this monologue of a bad worker looking after a client. She later gave me the transcript, and I cannot resist the opportunity of including it for its insightfulness.

"Hello, love, what's yer name? Roger? Oh, that's nice. I've actually fucked quite a few Rogers. Always nice, polite, gentle, clean, real gentlemen. Now, I'll just slip out of this and stretch out on the bed to get myself ready while yer get yer gear off.

"This? Oh, it's a lubricant we use, just to make sure the gentleman can get it in nice and easy. Don't want anything getting stuck halfway, do we?

"Now, be a good boy and hang yer pants up nicely, no creasing, don't want the missus getting suspicious, do we? Well, well, we are excited, aren't we? Let's have a look at Little Johnny. How are we? Looks nice and clean to me, smells all right too. Now, just slip on a little rubber for me, there in a box on the bedside table. Look, we've just got some blue ones in, they look nice. There... well, you know something? Blue suits yer.

"Right, you can slip it in now... whoops, not too much of a hurry, take it easy! Got it? Well, there we are. All nice and snug. Does that feel good? Yer know there are lots of gentlemen who go up there regularly, they reckon I'm nice and comfortable and warm.

"Now, don't get too excited, yer booked for half an hour, didn't you? Eh? No, I don't do blow jobs, hate the taste of rubber. No, we're not allowed to do that, in any case last time I got an infection. I didn't know that I had a tooth cavity, did I?

"Have yer seen that latest film with Sharon Stone? They reckon that she doesn't pretend, she really does it with the actor, can yer believe that? Yer wouldn't catch me doin' that sort of thing. After five or six blokes a day here, I'd rather do some knitting. Bloody nympho, I reckon. Here, slow down a bit, you're not building a bloody Falcon."

KNOCK ON THE DOOR, A VOICE FROM OUTSIDE SHOUTS "Five minutes!"

"Hey, Sally, is George there?"

"Yeah, he's waiting."

"Tell him I'll be out in five. Oh, and if he wants to arse fuck, he pays an extra 50, up front, right now. No do it now and pay after shit, okay?

"Whoops... sorry, I've lost yer. Why are yer giggling? 'Up front', yeah, that's what I said. What's funny about paying 50 up front to stick it up the back door? The guys love it. Not many housewives let their husbands do any of that stuff. Here, let me rub it up for yer. Wanna finish by hand?

"Okay, tell yer what I'll take the rubber off. No, yer can't touch me tits, they're a bit painful at the moment. No, I don't kiss, it's not allowed. Hey. There she goes. There's a nice big load for Mummy. Well, well... I reckon yer haven't been using it too often lately, right? Now go and wash up and we'll be off."

KNOCK ON THE DOOR. A VOICE OUTSIDE SHOUTS "You right, there?"

"No problems. Just finished jerking him off. Has George paid up?"

THE VOICE 'OFF' CONFIRMS THE EXTRA $50 HAS BEEN PAID.

"Lovely. Tell him it'll be really good.

"How are we going love? Good, I'll just slip into this skirt... Fuck! Look at that bloody zip, will yer? Completely ruined. Nicked it from Kmart only last week. Next time I'll hit Target... better quality.

"Come on, gotta go. Yer get back to Mum and the kids, eh? Tell yer what, give me an extra 20 next time, on the quiet, and I might give you a quiet little blow job. But, careful, no talking, all right? That's just between us. Ever had a blow job? Never? Yer kidding! Ah, well, see yer next week..."

The sketch was wonderful, and, of course, we saw all the gestures which went with it. I have never seen Pierre laugh so much in his life. Then, it was suddenly all very serious. As she ushered us towards the door, Michelle explained to Pierre that the sketch described the kind of people she did not want to employ. She added that I was a special person and, as such, I would only meet the best type of client. She patted his shoulder gently.

"Do not worry; she will come to no harm. She might get some chocolates or some flowers now and again. She will be happy, she will be respected, and she will always love you."

As we were through the door and turned to wave for the last time, she added, "Don't forget my invitation, Pierre. If you ever want to come and visit, please give me a call. If it's on one of Marie's working days, I am sure she won't mind. You might even be able to see her at work, who knows?"

She caught my worried frown, and laughed. "With her permission, of course. And if you want personal attention, I will ensure you have the best … mine."

On the way home, I made Pierre swear that he would never come to spy on me and that if he ever visited Michelle's establishment, it would be with my prior knowledge and consent. When we made love, I was careful to make sure that he kept his eyes open and that they were glued to mine. I know about these men who make love to their wife while fantasising that they are with another. I have cheated myself, having a lovely orgasm with an enthusiastic visitor labouring away as I knelt on the bed, in front of him, imagining that I was being taken by my darling husband, Pierre. My darling husband came, called my name as he filled me, and told me he loved me before rolling over, exhausted.

"And what do you think of Michelle," I asked, several minutes later.

As I asked the question, I felt him swell suddenly in my hand, and I knew the answer.

"Only with my permission," I reminded him.

Then I took him in my mouth and exhausted him. He would not be seeing other women tonight, even in his dreams. The thought alone would make his empty balls ache. Thanks to Michelle, I have learned how to master the male of the species.

7. Life as a Private Servant in Canberra

Pierre talked little of my new career after that dinner. He simply wished me luck as he left Tuesday morning for work. It was the 12th of January 1988, a milestone in my life: my first day as a professional prostitute. I think that for any woman, it would be an important moment, and I knew that while my darling was being flippant as he walked out the door, he, too, knew that it was a moment neither of us would forget.

"First day in the office," he remarked cheerfully. "Hope it goes well."

Even in those early days, I kept a diary and record of my work, because in the back of my mind I thought I might eventually offer my stories and diary notes for publication. I had an interesting story to tell, and a few preconceived ideas to redress. But I decided that the daily routine would only show initials for the client's name, a number representing the sexual service provided and, at the bottom of the page, the net amount I had earned.

For example, 'JA 2' meant simply that I had relieved my darling client Jeremy manually, as was usually the case, after a long period of kiss and cuddle. But I had decided that as I was carrying out the same acts, often with the same people every time, this would be boring to the reader and simply become a pornographic outcry. I wanted to talk about despair, friendship, dignity and affection.

Looking back over the 18 months I spent working for Michelle in Canberra, it quickly became obvious that I was popular, sought after, and that after a few months I had a large club of regular visitors. I actually became excited when I was able to lead a total stranger into my room of pleasure and quietly fantasise about what was going to happen with this new man. Regular clients, like lovers, become predictable. Two or three of my regulars even admitted (or boasted) that they had sex with me more frequently than with their wives. I found this most distressing.

My average daily net earnings went from $150 to $240; my record day was a Friday, when I earned $310. Pierre was amazed as he saw my income grow. He claimed concern about the physical strains I was placing on myself, but he was obliged to admit that his sex life at home had, if anything, improved, and that I was slimmer, more confident and more outgoing. For the first few weeks, I was obliged to announce, as soon as I got home, how many gentlemen I had entertained and how I had relieved them. We would then have sex in the bedroom, before dinner, in an act which he called 'resumption of ownership'. I must confess this regular submission to my husband and master became a wonderful ritual, and he was always delighted with my frenzied orgasms.

After a few weeks, he was forced to acknowledge that I was not working for the money but for the pleasure and the joy I gave to others. Naturally, sometimes that joy was shared. Finally, and this was an additional asset, I was no longer complaining about being bored, living in a city-park full of public servants.

There were, however, days when events were funnier, more exciting, and more unusual. These were often those 'exceptional' days which Michelle had warned might occur. There was one famous Saturday morning when Michelle called and begged me to help her out. The full-time sex consultants who worked for her during the week often went up to Sydney to make a little extra money on the weekends. She had a roster, but this time, somebody had let her down. I accepted her request to be on deck (or on the bed) from midday to six in the evening. Pierre sighed, shrugged and murmured his agreement.

Saturdays were usually terribly quiet. Married gentlemen visit brothels at night (after a business dinner or convention) or during working hours. There are few who have the courage to tell their wives that this Saturday they can go to Coles New World with the kids, because he, the master, is off to get a blow job.

This Saturday was dramatic. When I arrived, I found that not only was the business short-staffed, but I was, in fact, the only 'lady' on duty. This, in itself, was not necessarily dramatic, because when push came to shove our receptionist would often step into the breech to keep the customers moving. However, on this particular Saturday my receptionist was Jane, an outright lesbian who claimed that just the sight of a penis made her throw up.

Usually, if we were rushed off our feet, Michelle would often step in herself. I may have forgotten to say that although Michelle was retired, she was still partial to a little crumpet, particularly if the client was young and handsome. In fact, I have seen days when some of the girls were quite annoyed to see Michelle step in and declare, in her husky voice, that she was going to give the 'little darling' her personal attention. On this particular day,

Michelle's personal attention was focused on an auction near Bateman's Bay, which would reach its climax (pardon the pun) when she became the proud owner of a lovely holiday cottage with a view.

That Saturday, just after two o'clock, we were invaded. Jane told me afterwards that she had heard the visitors talking among themselves about a cancelled volleyball tournament and the plane they were catching back to Auckland the following day.

The eight moustached young gentlemen from New Zealand fell silent when I clapped my hands and begged their attention. I announced that they would have half an hour of oral sex each for $80, starting in ten minutes time. They would choose their order of appearance between themselves. I would remain in the room when I had provided the service, wash my face and hands, and await the next on the list. One of them asked what I would be wearing and I replied nothing but my earrings. They were so delighted, they clapped.

"Be wary of the clappers," hissed Jane, who also had a warped sense of humour.

Jake was the first to appear, followed by Donald, Murray, Phil, Terry, Stan, Eddie and Horace. Out of the eight, I had three who had never experienced oral sex before. The success rate was 100 per cent, all delivered on time and on target. What I did not realise was that those who had been serviced did not leave. They stayed in the lounge, drinking tea, chatting to each other, encouraging those still waiting and complimenting Jane on the quality of the house. They also talked about me and what a wonderful time they had each had. When I finally joined the reception desk, exhausted but happy, at nearly seven o'clock, Pierre was on the phone, worried that I was not home. I promised to see him within 15 minutes.

When I had been applauded, again, invited to visit the Bay of Islands and offered an honorary club supporter's card, they finally all left. As I was moving towards the door, Jane called me back to say that Michelle had phoned in to check if we were okay and that she was delighted with my initiative. Jane herself insisted on offering me a very long congratulatory kiss before I left.

On the way home, I decided that I would simply tell Pierre that I had been obliged to take a client who had arrived late, when the other girls had left early.

∞   ∞

It was a Thursday afternoon in March when an unexpected call came for an escort service. For once all the other girls were busy and I was alone reading *Cleo*. Michelle begged, Fabienne prayed, finally I gave in. But I warned them that I did not know my way around the client's local area very well so the client, a Mr Webster, should be told to be patient.

I went round Capital Circle, State Circle, National Circuit, Empire Circuit and Dominion Circuit until I was dizzy. About 40 minutes later I drew up in the car park of a motel in Deakin, hoping it was the right one. I rushed into the reception office, where the manager was talking to two male visitors.

"Do you have a Mr Webster here?" I panted.

The manager stared at me.

"Are you the tart from the escort agency? My word, things are looking up. Are those tits real?"

"Please, please," I begged him. "Mr Webster?"

"Room three," he grunted.

"Can we see you afterwards?" asked one of the other men, with a vile smile, as I reached the door.

I hesitated, turned round and blushed.

"I don't know. You'll have to ring Fabienne and ask. It's fine by me."

They all laughed at my candour.

I found Mr Webster and we rang Fabienne together to say that I had finally arrived. She was very relieved. He had booked me for an hour, and I zapped his credit card for the appropriate amount while he undressed.

※   ※

Pierre was negotiating the opening of a branch operation in Sydney. It was to be a franchise, using an existing partnership between two French business consultants who had worked in that city for many years. When he went to Sydney for a day or two, I generally accompanied him, just to browse around the shops. This time, he would be away for a week, and I pleaded job commitments to be able to stay.

In fact, there was another reason. I wanted the opportunity to try night work, and Michelle had reluctantly agreed, although she had warned me that I would probably not enjoy it. So I waved Pierre farewell, and set down impatiently waiting to take my seven o'clock shift, which went through to two o'clock in the morning.

I must admit that it was quite different. Many of the visitors were there for a 'quickie', and foreplay was not on the menu. Most of my clients wanted me to crouch on the bed while they banged away from behind, proudly watching their possession in the wall-mounted mirror. A couple of them even slapped me on the buttocks afterwards to tell me I was a good ride. After all, most Australians are proud of their rural background. Some of the visitors were drunk, and told to leave, with the receptionist threatening to call the police, if necessary.

I had to admit that by two o'clock I was tired. Being possessed masterfully can be invigorating and, sometimes, satisfying, but I was not sure I'd be able to continue non-stop for four nights. My compensation came with the taxi Michelle had promised to book each evening, at her expense, to take me home.

The taxi driver, Mario, was a young Italian migrant, 28 years old, who had been living in Canberra for four years. He could not believe that such a beautiful woman was working in a whore-house. I took him home, gave him a glass of red wine and showed him Pierre's favourite photo album. I was 36 and proud of my body. He was very complimentary, found some poses quite artistic, and stayed on for a couple of hours to study them more carefully.

Before he left, exhausted but delighted, we agreed that he would act as my sponsor and bring new clients to the brothel. He was often asked by visitors collected at the airport where the best place in Canberra would be. For every client he brought, I would be very, very kind, at home, in the afternoon.

Michelle laughed when I told her of the arrangement.

"You are getting a feeling for the business, but I already have an arrangement with Mario. For every two clients who turn up in his taxi, he gets a free ride with a lady of his choice, but here, on site. Believe me, it is better and more discreet than having his taxi parked in front of your house every week."

I was annoyed. I should have realised that my taxi driver had been hand-picked by Michelle. But I did ask if I could be added to the list of his ladies of his choice. Michelle nodded.

"Yes," she murmured, eyes half-closed as if recalling past memories. "He is rather nice, isn't he?"

I only did two more nights. It was boring and tiring. Michelle smiled and let me go. I did return to night duty, once or twice, on special occasions, but reluctantly.

Meanwhile, and from then onwards, every time Pierre flew to Brisbane or Adelaide, I rang Mario to take him to the airport. Pierre found him to be a good driver, and he told me with pride that Mario found his wife to be very beautiful.

"Have you noticed that when you book him he always comes on time?" I asked.

"So I'm told," he laughed.

I blushed and then pretended to be angry at his misreading of my words. He patted me on the rump.

"Have fun, darling," he whispered.

Damn it. He knows.

Sometimes, if he is not too busy, Mario will come back to let me know that Pierre has taken the plane safely. Because of Michelle's warning, I always leave the garage door open, and he likes the idea as the car stays cool instead of sitting in the sun for an hour or so. I think it is probably only in Canberra that you can get such wonderfully personalised service from a taxi driver, but I do hate it when his beeper goes off – always at a crucial moment.

⊗   ⟶

I did have one really strange client. He would often book me early on Saturday afternoons, for an hour. It always made Pierre grumble, but as he lived in a nice townhouse near our favourite shopping centre, it did not interfere too badly with our weekly routine. Pierre did the shopping while I got laid. He would always place me, crouching, on his favourite couch, and I could watch the traffic through the lace curtains while he laboured away. He hated foreplay and would not have any other girl but me, and only on Saturday afternoons, and only on that couch. After a few weeks he explained his problem. He used to make love with his girlfriend there, every Saturday afternoon, until she finally decided that she would not leave her husband, and their relationship ended. Our position was the one they adopted for their final meeting, as it allowed her to see her husband's car when he came to pick her up!

&⌒ ⌒⅋

My most impressive client was a very important politician. Our liaison started one day when Michelle called me at home, one evening, to ask if I could look after a 'special gentleman' at her place, in the boudoir. I passed on the message to Pierre who agreed and I accepted. That client would be a friend for life.

When I arrived, she took me into her kitchen.

"You are going to meet a man you may recognise. I must ask you never to mention his name at work and never to mention your meetings here. This is most important. You will be paid double the usual rate."

I patted her arm.

"You know I am discreet. And you know that the money is not important. I like to make people happy."

She smiled.

"You will. He wants the most beautiful, the classiest, the sexiest. I told him that was you. Oh, and, if you don't mind, no condoms. You're both clean, so please enjoy one another without restraint."

I did not recognise him, and he asked me to call him Nigel. He was about 50, handsome and elegant. He was slim, tanned, good-looking, and was a wonderful sexual partner. Michelle called me the next evening to say that he had been absolutely delighted and wanted to meet me every time he came to Canberra.

I remember sitting with Pierre watching ABC news one evening, and, suddenly, I saw Nigel walk off a plane. He was then interviewed about some international political matters.

"Michelle will call me tomorrow, I'm sure," I told Pierre, still watching the screen.

"You're not telling me that he is your 'Nigel'?" he asked.

"You're right. I'm not."

An hour later, the phone rang. Michelle was very embarrassed. I turned to Pierre, confused, distressed.

"He wants me now," I whispered.

Pierre nodded.

"Yes, he'll be involved in that international conference over the next three days. He probably needs to unwind."

I stared at Pierre.

"You don't understand. He wants me for the night. It will be $1,000."

My darling husband gazed at me solemnly.

"Then you must go. Not for the $1,000, but because he is a good politician and he will one day serve this country well."

I passed on the message and Michelle sighed with relief. An hour later, a large black limousine with driver whisked me away, and Pierre admitted later that he watched me leave, through a chink in the curtains, with great pride.

We watched the news the next evening, and Nigel was debating vigorously.

"I don't know where he finds the energy," I muttered aloud. "I'm exhausted."

Pierre laughed.

"That's how you recognise great men," he suggested.

"How?" I asked.

"They spend a night keeping you happy and survive," he said jokingly.

I stood up and pulled my dress over my head.

"Come, great man. Come satisfy me."

৪০ ৫৪

I had five meetings with Nigel while we lived in Canberra, but all the others were daytime events. He was quite sad when I told him that I would be leaving soon.

"I thought that might be the case. I have friends who know your husband well. He is a good man."

Pierre was not surprised when I reported the conversation, although he was flattered.

৪০ ৫৪

My last memorable adventure in Canberra was Phil the Greek. This particular Phil was a builder in Queanbeyan. In June, Michelle had taken the decision to move her operations to Fyshwick, and to build a special quarters there to act as a haven for sexual satisfactions. I could understand the need to change as there were days when our waiting room was severely cramped, and it was sometimes embarrassing to exit from the chamber of love, still damp and exhausted, to escort the satisfied client to the door, draped in a small towel, when the next in the queue was waiting, feasting on the show with hungry eyes. The negative side of the eventual move was that my future workplace would be a long way from home, at least 20 minutes in the car.

Phil was a regular visitor and was, I fear, a little in love with me. I was not terribly surprised when he was given the contract to build and fit out the new building, nor did the special clause really surprise me. As each room destined to be a nest of love was fitted out, Phil and I would try out the installation and, in particular, the bed. Michelle would pay for my time. There were, in all, ten rooms, and I got to know the building quite well before we actually moved in, particularly the ceilings. There was nothing refined about our Phil.

My work initiating the new premises was interrupted by my commitment to official duties. It was in June 1988 that Nigel offered me a wonderful present: a trip on Sydney harbour on one of the beautiful sailing ships which had come to celebrate the bicentenary of the settlement of the First Colony in Australia. Pierre was very proud to accompany me as my 'boyfriend'. The ship had arrived with several others in a friendly race from Hobart. Little did we know at that time that we would be celebrating another bicentenary with Nigel a year later.

৪০   ৫৪

Throughout my career in Canberra, I had two special clients. Donald and Wayne were both postgraduate students and had been quite regular visitors to the house of pleasure before my arrival. After I joined the illustrious team there, they both became my loyal and regular lovers.

Donald, who was 12 years younger than me, fell in love when we first met. It was a complicated relationship, because he was not very rich. After the first few weeks, I would actually give him the money to cover the visit, once we were in the room, alone. After a few months, Michelle realised that if Donald was spending an hour with me every week, somebody was giving him the money. That 'somebody' could only be me. She told me it had to stop. For the rest of my stay in Canberra, I met Donald regularly in a small flat near Civic, which a friend lent him for the purpose. No money changed hands.

Wayne was not in love, and his problem was physical. The first time that Fabienne announced that Wayne had arrived, there was a loud groan in the lounge. By popular opinion, it was decided that the newcomer should 'handle him', so to speak.

When we got to the room, I realised the problem. Poor Wayne had an enormous penis, one which would put fear into the heart of the bravest English maiden. But I was French.

I explained to him how we would undertake the task of providing him with sexual pleasure, all he had to do was to relax. I began the arduous task of performing oral sex on an object about the size of a policeman's truncheon, but was relieved and delighted to discover that, in the meantime, he had decided on a little exploration himself. This man's tongue was also exceptional, and he reached areas within me rarely visited by other explorers. When he made me come, I was literally shaking with pleasure.

His fine work had made me very wet and beautifully lubricated. It was the moment to offer Wayne some more joy. I decided to lie on my side and to encourage him to slip himself inside me from behind, very carefully. He was only halfway there when I began to shudder again. He took me gently, with a soft rhythm, gradually improving his possession. We came together, and then I remembered that we had forgotten the condom.

My colleagues were surprised by the affectionate relationship which developed between Wayne and myself.

ℰ   ℭ

I shall never forget José. He was an immigrant from Brazil, close to 60 years old, and a magnificent lover. Unfortunately, young men think that the greatest gift they can offer a mature woman is a good hammering with a swollen penis. José knew the fine art of lovemaking, offering joy and delight to a woman. He was a regular visitor, but one day he came to me with a strange request. He wanted me to teach his son, Carlos, a 23-year-old virgin, closely protected by his Catholic mother. Carlos was to marry an Italian beauty in three months time. Of course, I agreed.

José left $800 with Michelle for a training program of four one-hour sessions. We were not to say that we knew his father, it was understood that I had been recommended by a friend. Carlos was stunningly handsome, tall, with dark hair and dark eyes, his perfect skin a soft and sweet light brown, and it was no hardship to give myself totally to him. I envied the future bride, and thought that she would have to learn to handle competition, including mine.

I decided that we would not use a condom, as he was a virgin and thus totally pure. He found me wonderfully beautiful, and found my breasts much nicer than any he had seen in specialised publications. He played with them often, and I taught him how to explore every inch of a woman's body and to give pleasure with gentleness but determination. He was amazed to know that a woman could be so happy to take a man's penis into her mouth.

Before we departed, I made him promise that he would never talk about me or this house of pleasure. He begged to be allowed to come back and visit me, and I told him that I would love that very much, but suggested that he should spend at least six months devoting himself solely to his new wife.

I saw José, the father, over a month later. He brought with him a special gift for me, a lovely gold bracelet, and some photos of the marriage.

"The bride looks absolutely beautiful. What a lovely face. Carlos will be so happy," I commented.

José laughed in delight.

"Don't worry about the groom; you should have seen the bride when they came back from their honeymoon. She had lost a little weight, her eyes were ringed with happiness, and she was hanging desperately to her husband's arm, as if she was frightened to lose him. I can see babies on the horizon."

The delighted father was so happy I gave him a special blow job to help celebrate.

৪০   ୦୪

Strangely, I only worked in the new premises for a few months, as the call came for Pierre to return to Paris.

We had lived for three years in Canberra, and my professional life had settled into a pattern, almost a routine. After a few months, Pierre became more relaxed and overcame his need to resume possession of my body as soon as I returned home. After 12 months, he no longer needed the routine report: How many clients, how much each, did you enjoy it?

That was the most difficult part. Obviously, there were many men who left me quite indifferent. But there were others who aroused me sexually, and they were often my regular partners. I can only acknowledge that I have enjoyed sex with them. Moreover, I must also confess that I delighted in seeing a strong penis grow in my company, I loved sculpting it with my hands and mouth, I rejoiced and often cried out my joy when the fountain of sperm would burst through my fingers or over my breasts. I cannot deny this, but I could not admit it to Pierre.

Most men believe that sex is love. Luckily Pierre knows the difference. He says that his wife is beautiful and that if she wants to make other men happy, she should be allowed to do so. As far as I am concerned, I can have an orgasm with other partners, but this does not mean that I am in love with them. I do admit, however, that when two people enjoy orgasms together, a wonderful bond of friendship is built.

This is why I cried when I had my last sexual encounter with Nigel, and I cherished the emerald studded bracelet he gave me as a farewell gift. This is why I stole a photo from Pierre's private album, one of the most beautiful, and had it enlarged and framed in Woden Plaza. It was my farewell present to Nigel, and I was as red as a beetroot when I collected the finished work from the framing shop.

ὀ ὃ

It was also thanks to my work in Canberra that I discovered something about my own body. My sexuality was at its most ardent after my periods. It was still quite vigorous two weeks later, but during the last week, before the new period, my sexual hunger died. Michelle kept records of our financial performance, for taxation reasons, and was the first to show me the pattern. She also knew that I would not work during ovulation, and she admitted that not all workers could. Towards the end of my time in Canberra, I began to cheat. I enlisted the help of Fabienne, and she would knowingly give me days off just before my periods.

Then, as soon as I could announce that the period was clearing, she would invent urgent replacement shifts for me, even on Sundays (if Pierre was away in Sydney). With my sexual clock now firmly accepted, I had no further hesitations. During my period of sexual hunger, I would be assured, provocative and do anything to get my man. The other girls would back off and sometimes make rude comments about 'French tarts'.

Once or twice during these times, I volunteered for night duty. Pierre was away and I did not bother to tell Michelle I had volunteered for the roster. It was a different world. On one such night, I was eager to please when in walked two beefy truck drivers, chests popping out of their good old King Gee singlets. They had slipped in for a quickie before picking up their rigs in Dandenong, and I was wet as soon as I saw them.

The following Thursday, on arrival, I was called into Michelle's office.

"I heard about your night work," she shouted, angrily. "I thought I was employing you as a lady for my special clients. Not as a truckie's whore."

I tried to protest.

"I can put you on permanent night duty, if you really need it that badly. It won't be dreadfully refined, but you'll get plenty of cock, if that's want you want. They like a bit of anal too, now and again, that should make you happy."

I was crying.

"I don't do anal, you know that," I answered, stupidly.

"That's not a problem. I can get a specialist to work you over for two or three days, and you'll be ready to roll."

"Please, please, don't do that to me," I cried.

Angrily she slapped my face, very hard, twice. Then she took me in her arms and hugged me.

"You are prohibited from night duty," she announced, kissing the tears from my cheeks. "When you get horny, just come in for an extra day that week."

I nodded my agreement.

  ⁎ ⁎

Learning that night duty was now off the menu, and seeing my red-rimmed eyes, my husband sighed with relief.

"I'll ring Michelle to thank her personally for knocking some sense into you. I was beginning to wonder if I was going to have to slip down there myself to see my little wife."

I laughed and decided that in the future my hormones would stick to day duties and that Pierre would simply have to try to meet my nocturnal needs. He was wonderfully successful.

But his comment had given me an idea, and I talked to Michelle about my plan. I wanted to make him really happy before we went back to Paris, and I thought that maybe our little house of pleasure could do the job. Michelle had a different idea, a rather selfish one, but I liked it, too. We decided to propose both.

The first gift was an evening at Michelle's home. I knew that Pierre found her attractive, and that she was finding me stimulating. For my part, I wanted to make my darling husband happy, and I was interested in exploring Michelle's ideas.

Two weeks before our departure, she invited us to dinner. We ate well, and drank happily. After the cheese, cheeks flushed and eyes sparkling, Michelle asked Pierre if he would allow her to carry out an experiment on me. She believed that many women are, unknowingly, bisexual, and that she believed that she could make me as happy as any man.

Pierre giggled and served himself another glass of wine.

"I think you are very capable of making any man or woman happy," he admitted. "And I know that there are caresses that Marie enjoys and which can be delivered by the hands or the mouth of a woman."

"So, you will allow me to try?"

He waved his arm in a generous gesture.

"Be my guest. Truck drivers, Ministers, taxi drivers, diplomats, why not a beautiful woman. But on one condition."

We looked at one another and smiled, both guessing the condition.

"You might be tempted to cheat," he added. "I want to be sure that she actually enjoys it."

"Perhaps you should watch?" suggested Michelle cunningly.

"I was about to make the same suggestion," Pierre answered. Then he fell silent.

Michelle and I stood up and undressed slowly at the table. Naked, hand-in-hand, we walked to the bedroom, and Pierre followed. Michelle stretched me out on the bed and I sighed and closed my eyes as she began to caress me. Pierre was sitting on a small chair, watching avidly, occasionally sipping from the glass of wine he had brought with him.

When Michelle's tongue finally worked my clitoris into its climax, I called out and writhed in pleasure. She looked up at my husband.

"Was that real?" she whispered.

"Absolutely," he confirmed. "Now, what about making you happy, too?"

Michelle smiled knowingly.

"I will try to teach her. Do you not find it is a little hot in here?"

Pierre agreed and began to remove his clothes while I licked Michelle's nipples. Within a few minutes, Pierre was sitting on a corner of the bed, with a lovely erection. Michelle raised her head and saw his pleasure.

"Ah, now that would be really nice. After a while, a girl needs something more than a kind tongue."

Pierre was hesitant.

"I beg you, please do it," I ordered.

"But you are my wife," he protested. "It is difficult, I love you so much."

I laughed.

"Think of all the men who have used me in Canberra, with her benediction. Wouldn't you like a little revenge?"

He lowered himself slowly and I guided his throbbing penis into place. Michelle sighed with delight.

"Take it slowly," I recommended. "Make her happy, she needs to be loved."

He was still a little shy, but Michelle offered the magic words. "Pierre, for God's sake, please."

He was magnificent.

"You are a wonderful lover," she told him, afterwards. "One of the best."

I was proud of the weary warrior I had to drive home.

80   CB

Staff from the Commercial Attaché at the French Embassy, who had worked closely and often confidentially with Pierre, threw a little cocktail party for our departure. I was embarrassed to meet several clients, including two diplomats and my favourite Fijian pilot.

The tensest moment was when Pierre introduced me to the Minister, and I shook Nigel's hand most formally, watching the twinkle in his eye. We did catch a private moment.

"The last time we met, it was not my hand you were shaking," he whispered.

I nearly choked on my champagne. That was an unexpectedly rude joke from such an important gentleman.

"I will be in Paris in December," he added. "Your husband said that I may call on you."

I decided to be cheeky in turn.

"I would love to have you in Paris, dear Minister," I assured him.

"Then you will. In this government, we aim to satisfy," he murmured.

"And you, personally, aim very well," I added.

He smiled, moving away to a group gesturing for his attention. Suddenly Pierre was beside me.

"And how is my little courtesan?" he bantered. "I think that you are beginning to enjoy this secret life."

"I think you might be right," I admitted, "and perhaps it is time to move to new horizons."

8. In the Footsteps of La Perouse

It was decided that we would fly out of Sydney in June 1989. I was sad to leave Australia. Although many would have said that I had spent most of my time in the most boring places in the country, Adelaide and Canberra, nobody could guess just how happy I had been, how much I had learned, how many pleasures I had enjoyed and shared. My disappointment had been such that Michelle had offered to Pierre to keep me with her until he returned, in two years' time. He was quite surprised by the proposal.

"Would you like to stay?" he asked me, with an unknown roughness in his voice.

"I love my job," I pleaded. "The next two years will probably be my best, professionally. I know that Michelle would look after me. But I cannot leave you, I love you too dearly. Also, I want to write a book about prostitution. I will need your help and advice."

He smiled.

"That's an interesting idea. You could start your research in Sydney; I'm told that it's the 'sin city' of Australia. You know, I'm very proud of you. I saw you swapping jokes with the Minister the other evening, and smiled at what an accomplished woman you had become. Is it strange that the husband of a high class sex worker can be proud of his wife? If I was out of work, I would stay in Canberra, encourage you to continue, maybe become a partner in the business. But if I left you alone, I would be afraid of losing you to Michelle or to one of those favourite clients."

Of course, I would accompany him to Paris and we would come back to Australia within two years, together. He expected that Bernard Courtot would now set Melbourne as a target, and he was sure that I would love that city. We hugged, kissed and made love.

◯ ◯

We flew from Canberra to Sydney, where we spent three weeks, before spending another month in Nouméa. My previous visit, to enjoy the cruise on the tall sailing ship, had not really allowed me to see much of the city. This time, I saw quite enough. It was obviously a far cry from what the explorer La Perouse, my compatriot, had seen 200 years before.

My husband was right. Sydney was the ideal place to start a study of the various forms of prostitution around the world. Nevertheless, Pierre was a little apprehensive of my lack of timidity. He begged me to wait until he came home in the evening from his discussions with the Sydney partners, so that he would be by my side when I roamed the streets.

We stayed in a Hotel in Kings Cross for a few days and we saw the mad world of commercial sex in that part of this pseudo-American city. It was frightening and probably a taste of what I was going to see in Paris.

Despite his warning, I did undertake a little exploration without his help. I was approached several times with lucrative propositions, and I could only conclude that my work in Canberra had given me an attitude of physical assurance which the regular consumers of female flesh could immediately detect.

I realised that Kings Cross, while frightening, was a pale copy of what I would discover in Paris. Teenage girls were offering their bodies in the grey side streets in exchange for money to buy their next fix. At four o'clock in the evening, I saw a young, thin, pale girl being possessed while standing in a doorway, shouting coarse words of encouragement to her client. She must have been nearly 16. One evening, in a similar side street, Pierre and I watched while two others, unperturbed by our presence, did a 'hand-job' on a tourist in a red convertible. The make-up, the gestures and the crude words of mock admiration made these young teenagers look old, worn and vulgar. We were told by our hotel staff that some of them came from good families, were attending private schools, and were simply earning money, two or three times a week, for their next fix. Others were full-time self-employed workers who had given up school.

The porter, to whom I had talked of my research, told me that in some of the best hotels, high school girls would visit the cocktail bars in the evening to offer themselves to visiting Japanese businessmen or tourists, and that he had heard that a virgin could earn thousands of dollars.

I told Pierre of our conversation. He told me that he had met an Australian couple, in the course of his current negotiations, who were experts in doing business with Japan, where they had lived for several years. They could also tell me a lot about prostitution in Asia. I told him that I would be delighted to meet them, and he organised a quiet dinner.

Most of the meal was devoted to mundane chatter and gentle jokes about the French and the Australians, but afterwards, our friends suggested after-dinner drinks in a five star hotel, where we could see the development of Australian-Japanese relationships in the cocktail bar. We watched the action.

Ted, our host, who visited Japan regularly on business, explained that Japan played an important role in the international sex industry.

We watched Japanese businessmen in deep conversations with what I perceived to be extremely young ladies, and our host, also familiar with the Sydney scene, explained that these were students from secondary schools operating as part-time sex workers to make pocket money. In those days, an hour of pleasantries with an underage girl would be rewarded with $400.

Ted also explained that during the Vietnam War, Bangkok and Sydney were used as 'relaxation centres' for American troops between rounds of duty on the front. Each boat was greeted in Woolloomooloo by eager ladies hopeful of finding a husband or of making a quick dollar, but, towards the end of the campaign, the troops preferred the professional services offered in Kings Cross. It was said that there were even a few deserters settled in Sydney, who organised the sexual entertainment of their compatriots. Irene, Ted's wife, added that the sex industry in Kings Cross had been less obtrusive before the Vietnam conflict.

I thought that Kings Cross was typical of the environment created by the development of uncontrolled commercial sex. It was the Pigalle of Sydney. I was told that until the Vietnam War, it was quite tame, but when the American soldiers on 'R & R' made their needs known, the revolution began. Street prostitution, managed by pimps or policemen, was the sex industry at its worst. The neighbourhood was naturally full of 'support services', strip joints, peep shows and sex shops. Taxis and police cars cruised the main streets, delivering and supervising potential consumers, and the crowds jostled for room on the footpaths, eager for excitement or scandal. This was the organised, illicit sex, which competed with the more formal escort services so popular in Sydney.

It was a different industry to the clean, courteous and hygienic services offered by the nice houses of Canberra. Michelle's palace of pleasure was a haven of calm and tranquillity compared with this. Obviously there were more refined and private services offered in other parts of Sydney, particularly on the North Shore and in the Eastern Suburbs. My porter, who saw the escort service ladies arrive in our hotel in the evening, told me that some were fit to be models or beauty queens. At his invitation, I sat for a couple of hours in the foyer of the hotel, and he would wink when a known 'service provider' walked in. I must admit that some of them were stunning and looked like people out of Hollywood soapies. I did wonder just how well these beauties performed when it came to delivering the goods.

৪০   ৫৪

I was glad to leave Sydney. The city frightened me, with its noise, its pollution and its overbearing arrogance. On the footpaths, I was pushed, shoved, trod on and I inhaled diesel fumes, fast food fats and body odour.

The difference between the people of the nice suburbs (one taxi driver called them the 'bay watchers') and the millions of working class in the south and west was quite startling. Few Sydney-siders actually saw, every day, those stereotypical symbols of their city's success; the Harbour Bridge and the Opera House.

9. Paris, City of Noise, Beauty and Madness

We flew from Sydney to New Caledonia and spent a glorious weekend on the Isle of Pines before flying from Nouméa to Paris on a DC 10 operated by the now extinct French airline, UTA. Its lack of reliability on services to Sydney and Auckland had encouraged Anglo-Saxon travellers to call it 'Unknown Time of Arrival'. But we had a wonderful journey as the only two passengers in First Class. French airlines have three main characteristics: they hate timetables, the food is excellent and the cabin staff is indifferent. Most of the hostesses give the impression that they are models or film stars, filling in between two *Claude Chabrol* contracts, just to pass the time. They HATE serving foreign passengers.

However, with only two passengers to service, and neither of them being dreaded Anglo-Saxons, our hostess, Nicole, become really friendly between Jakarta and Paris. She was very curious about our stay in Australia, as she had only been in Sydney a few times on overnight stopovers. She actually sat down and chatted with us before dinner, asking many questions, most of which concerned the more exotic destinations we had never seen. She finally offered to meet with me in Paris, where she would be taking a few days off within two or three weeks, to show me around. I accepted with pleasure and Pierre gave her the office phone number.

After the quiet life of Canberra, Paris was a huge change of pace. At the arrivals lounge in *Roissy*, people shoved and jostled, grabbing trolleys and snarling insults. Our taxi driver greeted us with a grunt, threw our suitcases into the boot, and took off at great speed before we even had time to fasten our safety belts. The speedometer hovered around 130 kilometres an hour until the density of traffic in the city forced him to slow down, a little.

We spent a few days in a stately hotel where porters and grooms expected tips at every turn. Our room was magnificent, with a high ceiling decorated with little naked angels blowing trumpets. The bed was a four-poster with a deep mattress and a fluffy duvet. Perfectly French, and designed for sex, as Pierre announced. He thought that *Sophie Marceau* should be on line for other services as required, and I proceeded to show him that I was far, far more experienced than that little actress. He was forced to admit, afterwards, that I was probably right, although he would have to meet the famous film star himself to make an honest comparison. I assured him that it would never happen.

It was difficult to sleep. People drive around Paris at high speed 24 hours a day. During the night, they knock over garbage bins, sing drinking songs, fight, make love, scream abuse at one another and kick dogs. The bars and restaurants close around one in the morning, at two o'clock trucks collect the garbage and at four the butchers and delicatessen owners roll up their shutters and switch on their cool-room compressors. Paris was not designed for sleep.

Nor was the city designed for pedestrians. The most dangerous thing you can do is to cross the street on what is commonly known, in other countries, as a pedestrian crossing. As far as the Parisian motorist is concerned, those stripes are simply a perfectly useless decoration. Pedestrians are strictly confined to the parts of the footpath not normally used for parking cars. I can't remember seeing a wheelchair in Paris, and Pierre suggested that the physically handicapped had probably fled to the country.

It was as if Paris were designed for the motor car. The wide avenues allow vehicles to travel in several lanes at high speed. Traffic lights are a hindrance, and at most crossroads the priority goes to the brave and the callous, or to those with the oldest and most battered cars. Parisians do not have garages or parking stations. They just leave their cars wherever they might be when they decide they no longer need them: in front of entrances, on the footpaths, on your feet, in the middle of the roads, in taxi zones or bus stops.

There are also people on two wheels. The cyclists are all quite young, probably because of the poor survival rate; messengers on motorised bikes or scooters who would put a Japanese suicide fighter pilot to shame; and a few crazy motor cyclists with studded jackets and long red beards, who always ride in the express lane reserved for buses.

Most Parisians live in rented accommodation. Buying your home is considered a poor investment and a waste of money. It is better to pay rent and use your income to eat out, to see shows, to drink and to be happy. It is during the holiday periods that the hypocrites can be identified. These are the ones who have held on to the family manor in the country where they can sleep, talk about politics, play *pétanque* and enjoy the local gastronomy. They all take their holidays either on the 1st of July or the 1st of August. The best traffic jams are on the 1st of August when those coming home meet those leaving.

I realised just how much Bernard Courtot appreciated all the work Pierre had done in Australia when I saw the furnished apartment the company had rented for us to use for the next two years. It was in the 16th 'arrondissement' of Paris, the nicest, overlooking a narrow pedestrian market street and close to several parks. I was in heaven. Bernard Courtot invited us to dinner, and spent the evening admiring my suntan, my shapely body, my sparkling eyes and my new personality.

Pierre explained how I had found a casual job in the 'public relations' area, and how it had helped me to develop so much self-confidence.

"She even dresses quite provocatively," his boss commented, eyes wandering over my white embroidered mini-dress.

I smiled.

"Only when I know that I am going to meet a connoisseur," I assured him.

He grinned at Pierre.

"I see what you mean. She has probably been a wonderful asset."

Pierre nodded.

"Marie has always been available to entertain some of our future clients, so your investment in pocket money for her in Australia was not wasted."

"Wonderful, wonderful," Bernard Courtot murmured. "She may be a good ambassador for us here in Paris, during your stay."

I smiled approvingly.

"I would enjoy that. But I should warn you that I am doing a little research at the same time, a personal project."

"On what subject?" he asked.

"Sex."

He nearly choked on his oyster. Once he had recovered with a large sip of white wine, he could not avoid the obvious Frenchman's reply.

"If I can be of any help..." he offered, eyes twinkling.

I laughed.

"That's not what I'm researching. Besides, I doubt if I'd have much to learn there."

Pierre interrupted at that point, fearing an embarrassing question.

"Marie is studying prostitution around the world and across the ages," he explained. "It's something she feels strongly about."

Bernard frowned, a little surprised, and then nodded.

"You should be careful in Paris. It is a highly protected activity."

I promised that I would.

☼   ☙

After a few months in Paris, I realised why so many of my Australian friends, and my clients, used to say that I was not the usual, arrogant, abusive French person they had met before: either they had only met Parisians, or they had only visited Paris when in France on holidays. While I hated the atmosphere of the city and the rude manners of its inhabitants, I also began to realise the enormous pressures and tension of living in such a huge city where noise, traffic jams and pollution seemed to last 24 hours of every day. It is certainly the most beautiful city in the world to visit. But it is also one of the most stressful to live in.

The two years I spent in Paris with Pierre were devoted to three streams of activity: my research into prostitution; catching up with the family; and helping my husband with his job.

Catching up with the family had its frustrating moments. I was dreadfully out of date with the local gossip, and the overseas experience had dissolved my interest in the private lives or public scandals of distant cousins or close neighbours. I tried to explain some of the aspects of my life in Australia, but there was little interest from a family which had never travelled and only visited Paris twice. We were washing dishes one afternoon in my mother's kitchen when Brigitte told me about her latest conquests, and I asked her if she was using ribbed or plain condoms. She actually stopped talking and gazed at me, speechless for a few seconds, a dripping plate in her hand.

"What do you prefer?" she asked, finally, placing the plate carefully on the drying rack.

I pretended to think that question over, and then I sighed.

"It depends on the guy, I guess. Most of the time I like it raw, but if I have some doubts, I'll use plain or ribbed, depends what I have in my handbag on the day. Oh, and I love the new ones with the mango flavour."

"I've never heard of them," she pouted. "And what guys are you talking about?"

"Oh, you know. People you meet. French girls are very popular in Australia, they have a sort of reputation, I guess. There's plenty of fun on offer."

My poor sister had begun to swab the next dish, muttering something about mangoes under her breath.

"I think I still have a dozen or so in my make up bag. I'll bring you some, next visit," I promised.

She was thoughtful for a few minutes.

"I think I'd like to come to Australia with you," she suggested.

I laughed.

"My darling sister, if only you knew."

My mother reprimanded me a few days later.

"You really must stop teasing Brigitte. She thinks that you had dozens of boyfriends in Australia. You know what she's like; she must always be the best. And what would your husband think of all of this?"

I squeezed her arm affectionately.

"Don't worry. I had a wonderful time, I had a little fun, and everything is perfect between Pierre and myself."

She frowned.

"I'm not quite sure what that means," she commented.

I laughed.

"You probably do know. But I will say no more."

As the months went by, my family began to realise that their shy young country girl had become a confident young woman and that she had learned many things in foreign lands. On occasions, eyebrows were raised, but no awkward questions were asked.

Brigitte came to Paris to spend a week with us and discovered that in the clubs the roving males were giving a lot more attention to her sister. One evening, Pierre took us to a lovely club on the banks of the Seine, near the Latin Quarter.

"Where did you get clothes like that?" she asked, as we were leaving. "Everyone can see your tits."

"Only those who want to," I corrected. "I just like showing off my suntan."

"I wish I had a tan like that," she moaned.

"It's those long Australian summers," I lied.

The club was great: good music, but not too loud; good drinks, but not too dear; nice people, but not too invasive. Brigitte was surprised by the number of people we seemed to know, without realising that it was all very much a show, and I would be greeted with a peck on each cheek by guys who ignored even my name. I was just a familiar face.

I refused an offer from Julio to go home and listen to some of his flamenco records, while Brigitte watched, fuming. Later, I asked Sebastian, who was playing with the left shoulder strap of my dress and getting close to a revealing situation, if he would like to be 'kind' to my little sister, visiting Paris from the country.

He turned towards her with a lovely smile, placing a friendly hand on her thigh.

"Are you enjoying Paris?" he asked.

"Go away. I don't want my sister's leftovers," she snarled, slapping his hand away from her thigh. Pierre laughed loudly, which made her even angrier.

Brigitte went back to her little village in Beaujolais without a conquest, which proved that Paris clubs were a little more sophisticated than the ones she was used to frequenting. I cannot imagine the stories she must have told my mother. She never came to see us in Paris again, and on my next visit to the family, she staunchly refused to take me to her local haunts.

Pierre was disappointed not to see her back in Paris, because he enjoyed teasing Brigitte himself, and complained that I had taken all the fun out of the sport.

"If only she knew the number of gentlemen you have favoured in Canberra," he laughed. "She would be terribly jealous. And you even used her name!"

"But she'll never, never know," I warned him.

"Of course, of course."

৪০ ৫৪

I did not really start my research into prostitution in the early days we spent in Paris. I was to discover, first of all, that there was a particular subculture of the city which led a quite raunchy life. My first lesson was from our neighbour, a strange young woman with raven black hair who used to sit in the front garden, in the evening, singing to her cat. She wore the long dresses which were so popular with the hippies in the '60s, reminding me of Marianne Faithfull. She was watering the plants on her balcony, one Saturday morning, when we were coming back with our shopping. She appeared to be wearing just a t-shirt, and looked as if she had just fallen out of bed.

"Hi," shouted Pierre. "We're your new neighbours. Come round and have a drink."

She simply stared at him for a moment, and then shook her head.

"You forget, this is Paris not Canberra," I reminded him as we were unpacking the shopping bags in the kitchen. "People don't invite total strangers into their home in this city."

At that moment, there was a timid knock on our kitchen door. Pierre opened, to discover our neighbour, wearing a white lace blouse, a long full black skirt, gold earrings and a lot of make-up.

"I've come for the drink," she explained. "My name is Amandine."

She talked incessantly. She believed that, coming from Australia, we were totally ignorant about life in Paris, and it was her duty to educate us. The following evening, she packed us into her little Renault 4 to take us to a little square near the Bois de Boulogne, well known for its unusual evening visitors. As we began to wander through the crowd, we noticed that most people seemed to be watching the parked cars. As we approached, we understood why. Inside the vehicles were couples, sometimes of the same sex, undertaking various sexual activities for the visual pleasure of the passing admirers. Amandine squeezed Pierre's arm and asked him if he was enjoying himself.

"I think I'm just surprised, for the moment."

Laughing, she dragged him toward a Peugeot convertible.

"Look, look, that's Jacques and Lise, they're fantastic."

Jacques was sitting on the back of the seat, and Lise was doing her orals. A tall blonde guy was standing on the footpath, masturbating as he watched, and I reached his side just in time to see him empty himself all over Lise's shoulders. She did not seem the least concerned, and continued her job, heedless of the shouts of encouragement coming from the crowd as Jacques reached the point of no return. As we walked back towards Amandine's car, I noticed that several stationary vehicles had traces of ejaculation on windows and windscreens.

"I can't believe that this is happening in a public square in Paris," I exclaimed.

She giggled.

"Paris is the most marvellous city in the world."

A few weeks later she asked if we would like to go out with her, and her good friend Henri, to a restaurant club. We were a little concerned but decided to accept.

The four of us climbed into a taxi, and Amandine directed the driver to a small street in the 15th arrondissement. On the way, she explained that Henri was not her boyfriend, but simply a male partner she had brought along for that evening.

The place was beautifully furnished, but when we saw the hostess, we knew that this was no ordinary restaurant. She led us, smiling, to a gold and white bar, where several bartenders of both sexes were busy with cocktail shakers.

"You know how the club works?" the hostess asked.

Pierre and I shook our heads, but Amandine told the hostess that she would explain. Meanwhile, we were asked our names and provided with name tags.

"It helps the atmosphere when people can call you by your first names," the hostess explained.

We ordered our drinks, and were shown the menus. It seemed very good, and I was delighted with the idea of sitting quietly at the bar and ordering my meal while sipping a refreshing *kir royal*. As soon as the first dishes were ready, we were told, we would be called to a table.

I had noticed that several gentlemen around the bar were trying to catch my eye and were throwing inviting smiles in my direction, and I was relieved when we were led to our table. I could have sworn that a few hands slid across my buttocks as I made my way past one small group.

"If you want to talk to somebody at another table, please feel free to move around," the waiter suggested as we sat down. "I have already had several enquiries for you," he added in my ear as he pushed in my chair.

As we began our fresh oysters, I asked Amandine to explain. It was then that she confessed, just when escape was almost impossible. We were in a two-plus-two club, quite popular in Paris, and heavily publicised in the tourist brochures. Basically, couples would go to the club for drinks and a meal, and during the evening each would withdraw with a stranger to one of the private little salons. It was, basically, a wife or husband swapping club.

"The facilities are excellent," Amandine explained. "This is why the food and the drinks are rather expensive. But the great thing is that you know why you are here, and everyone else knows too."

Pierre and I exchanged glances and decided to stay glued to our chairs. Just after the oysters a black gentleman came to fetch Amandine, and she came back just in time for the roast veal, dishevelled but delighted.

"Black cocks are definitely the best," she declared proudly.

I told her that this was not always the case, and that I had met some white ones which were unbeatable. She stared at me thoughtfully. Henry had left us and Amandine did not think he would be coming back.

"I hardly know him," she explained. "We just pretend to be a couple to come here, now and again, as they won't let you in alone. That's why they call it 'two-plus-two.'"

His absence went unnoticed, as a small blonde with a thick Slav accent was now sitting in his chair and taking a strong interest in Pierre.

"She's from Bosnia," he told me, blushing. "And she's terribly inquisitive about Frenchmen."

"If that hand is where I think it is, she will know everything very soon," I suggested.

At that moment, somebody grasped my shoulder. I looked up and could have sworn that I had just seen Alain Delon's cousin.

"Would you like to come and play with me?" he asked.

I had just finished my third glass of wine and was feeling particularly relaxed. A handsome guy like that was hardly a challenge to a lady who knocked over four or five paying customers a day in Canberra. I looked at Pierre who nodded, and I saw that Amandine was watching curiously.

"I love games," I told the stranger. "I hope you're a good player."

Courteously, he pulled out my chair as I stood up.

"For you, I will be unbeatable," he boasted.

As I left, the little blonde was offering to initiate Pierre in some unusual Bosnian customs, and Amandine was leaving on the arm of a tall man with a shaven head. The evening was getting into full swing.

My suitor, who introduced himself as Charles, took me down to a small room which was already quite busy. There were four other couples actively exchanging ideas, caresses and fluids. He introduced Anne and Naomi (obviously intimate friends), Christian and Rachel (too busy to shake hands), Denis who was exploring Belinda, Georges and Julien who were looking frustrated. It was helpful as none of them were wearing name tags (there was nowhere to pin them) and I realised immediately just how pleased the two lonely guys were to see me. Very, very pleased. I was offered another glass of wine, which I drank eagerly, before throwing my clothes on to the common pile in the corner. There was a murmur of appreciation when they saw my suntan.

Charles wasted no time in getting down to business, and I am ashamed to admit that I rediscovered the French lover with delight. They seem to pay so much attention to the small details of lovemaking, and are so eager to see a lady enjoy herself. He completed his task, and then Georges and Julien continued to encourage my favourable impression and unrestrained deep admiration for the French male. When Pierre finally found me, I was exhausted.

"It's nearly three, darling, we should be getting home."

A loud groan went round the little room.

"How was Croatia?" I asked Pierre in the taxi.

"Balkanic," he moaned. "But I did have my first taste of Denmark."

"I think we will try to forget Amandine," I suggested. "If we want to have a little fun, now and again, we don't need her help."

He agreed. My husband seems to agree with me most of the time, and when we got home and I suggested that sex with a legal partner seemed appropriate to chase away the memories of the past few hours, he approved of my suggestion.

He is a wonderful lover, and my husband, and the man I love, and because of all this I offer him more than any of my clients has ever received from me.

"How was Denmark, compared with that?" I asked, just before five.

"*Vive la France!*" he whispered before falling asleep.

ಙ ೞ

We went for an early walk in the Bois de Boulogne, one morning in winter. This is the largest and most popular park in Paris, and it includes a small lake and, as its name suggests, woods and thickets. I was intrigued by the popping noises under our feet as we walked through the crusty ground, but we realised after a moment what we were doing. We were crushing frozen condoms underfoot, souvenirs from the previous night's chance encounters.

The Bois was a popular meeting place for people in search of sexual diversions. Heterosexual and homosexual sex was undertaken every evening in various parts of the park, and we decided one night to come and watch the activities. As we joined the queue of cars, slowly cruising down one avenue after another, we were offered peep shows of every form of copulation imaginable, as well as shouted invitations to come and join the fun.

One car stopped suddenly in front of us, and the passenger door opened. We saw the driver lean over and frantically try to pull his wife or girlfriend back into the car, but it was too late. She ran towards a group of semi-naked men where she was greeted with shouts of pleasure. The driver of the small car blew his horn and shouted for her to come back, but she was already shedding her clothes. Several other cars pulled over to watch as the men stretched her out on a travel rug and began their friendly relationship.

                                             ℬ   ℧

I read in a weekly magazine the confessions of Madame X, a notary public solicitor who visited the Bois two evenings a week, on the way home from work. Her husband would leave her for a couple of hours, always in the same spot, near a large oak tree which was her territory. Here, she would be sexually possessed by perfect strangers, night after night. She had become popular and known, and received homage from old friends and complete strangers. I could not believe that so many people in this city enjoyed such sexual freedom, apparently with little care for their own security. It made me wonder how the real profession could survive, and I began to ask myself whether even the real street prostitute did not offer, in many ways, a certain level of security.

Nevertheless, I decided that I would do a little research into prostitution in my homeland, but without going 'into the field'.

I discovered that for many centuries the French Army was followed by its female warriors who dispensed stress-relieving services in the back of horse-drawn carts, just a few hundred yards behind the front lines. This was called the *bordel militaire de campagne*, or field military brothel. It is said that it was good for morale and, although, after a salutary visit to the ladies, the soldiers may have sallied forth with empty 'cartridges', they were ready for a good fight.

Yet while the French nation is obviously promiscuous, and terribly interested in sexual relations, it has been living under a long-term hypocrisy concerning prostitution. Every day, thousands of girls walk the streets in Paris: the French, German and English around Pigalle, the illegal African migrants around Rue Saint-Denis, the ladies from Eastern Europe anywhere and everywhere. Occasionally, a group of street workers is collected, dumped in a police cell overnight and released the next morning. It is a tradition which both police and prostitutes find totally boring.

Prostitution is an important element of the tourist industry in Paris. There are coaches which take their male foreign passengers to Pigalle every evening. As the pneumatic doors slide open, each disembarking passenger is met by a young lady offering a precise service at a specified price.

The current hypocrisy was created by a certain Marthe Richard, who proposed a law in 1946 to close all brothels. The lady was herself a local councillor and retired sex worker. Some 1,400 brothels were forced to close in Paris itself, including two famous establishments, the Sphinx and the One-Two-Two. In reality, the industry brothels were converted into hotels and the prostitutes left the comfort, safety and discretion of their parlours to offer their wares on the footpaths, in front of their places of work.

The winds of change were ruffling the French wings of Puritanism. Even Bernard Kouchner, doctor, ex-Minister of Health and founder of *Médecins Sans Frontières*, believed that the profession should have been legalised and subject to strict medical controls.

There were some picturesque slang words used in Paris to describe the various forms of prostitution: the 'amazons' drive snappy cars and toss suggestive looks at the passing punters. Call girls were the expensive ones who were reached by phone. The 'caravel' works at airports and railway stations, looking for the passing tourist trade. The 'mug-chasers' work from café terraces, and the 'shooting star' is the non-professional doing a one-night job to pay a few unpaid bills. The 'zoner' works in the woods and parklands, while the 'candle' stands immobile on the edge of the footpath. The 'walker' also operates from the footpath, but walks up and down a particular strip. The 'dragger' works in a bar, as do the 'spindle shanks', who were generally found sitting on very high stools in very short skirts.

In some country hotels, there are still two categories of chambermaids: those who do, and those who don't. The official classification of the former category is the 'maid who goes up' (you would have expected the opposite, in English).

The sex industry has to compete with the 'free agents', those whom I have already described, and the promiscuity and sexual liberties accepted by French society, such as the two-plus-two club which Pierre and I visited.

It would be impossible for me to ever tell my closest friend, my mother, or Brigitte, that was employed as a sex worker. They would not understand, because the trade is so different in my home country. They would not understand because in France the girls work on the streets and each has her own pimp.

There is much discussion in the French press about prostitution, and several books of limited interest. Generally, they all express the belief that the sex workers are slaves, and that this form of slavery is another example of women being dominated by men. My experience was exactly the opposite. I was a free woman and I could make those silly men eat out of my hand.

I enjoyed my work in Canberra and never considered myself a slave. My research in France showed me how much better the whole activity is in Australia, because I could always decide where and when I worked, what I accepted and did not accept, and the client always knew the rules concerning hygiene and decorum. I worked in a modern service industry, whereas a sex worker in France still works according to a medieval system, aggravated by legislators unwilling to look at modern options.

Pierre accompanied me on some of my evening explorations. Near the *Boulevard Haussmann* we discovered what looked like a little Irish pub, but which turned out to be one of the rare real brothels operating in Paris. The owner called it an 'American Bar' and said that her ladies were quite happy to entertain married couples. There was a lovely redhead casting languorous looks in Pierre's direction, but I dragged him away, explaining to her that he was impotent.

We also saw a beautiful blonde in a magnificent fur coat, not far from *La Place Pigalle*. We stopped to ask the price, which Pierre found expensive. Opening her coat, she showed why the price was high. I hope that coat was warm. When she discovered that she was not dealing with a serious punter she jumped into her car and sped off. The BMW looked safe and comfortable.

We walked up the dangerous rue Saint Denis and saw the African prostitutes. They get a free ticket to France, offered by a local 'consultant', and are offered the hope of becoming permanent French residents. But, first of all, they must pay off their debts. Because they work in a poor area, fees are low, interests are high. I understand that many will work for more than 20 years to pay off an imaginary debt, and will be thrown out of the doss room where they are kept when they get too old or too sick. At the end of their careers, they are often still illegal migrants.

My research was over and the results were depressing. I told Pierre that I was in danger of becoming bored, once again. He suggested jokingly that I could work for him or, true to good French tradition, take a lover. I actually did both.

10. The French Consultant

Paris is a lovely city to live in, if you have a high income and lots of activities. I found myself wandering around and, inevitably, spending. We were walking in one of the nicer shopping areas in the 16th arrondissement one Saturday morning, when we both stopped to look at a dress in a shop window. It was a lightweight, strapless white mini dress with an opaque bodice, and it fitted the mannequin beautifully.

"A woman would need to be a shameless hussy to walk around Paris with a dress like that," I commented.

"You're right," agreed Pierre. "Would you like to try it on?"

It was made for me. When I walked out of the changing room, the sales girl clapped her hands in delight and Pierre declared that I was truly beautiful. We decided that whatever I was to do during our stay in Paris, buying that dress would be a first step towards ensuring permanent marital happiness.

We had been on the way to the bank to collect a new cheque book, because in Paris everybody pays everything by cheque, even the smallest amounts. It was agreed that Pierre would go to collect the cheque book while I changed and looked around the shop for a pair of matching shoes.

I believe that the sales girl may have been Lebanese. I couldn't help noticing her dark, dark eyes as she watched me remove the dress in the small changing room. There was little space, and her hands were constantly touching parts of my body as she drew the dress over my head. I should not have moaned, it must have encouraged her. Soon, she was sucking my nipples and I was stroking her hair as I held her close to me. Later, I heard Pierre's voice.

"Marie, are you there?"

"Yes, I'm in the cubicle. I was just trying some other things while I was waiting for you. I won't be long."

My new friend and I exchanged a tender kiss, and she helped me back into my old dress.

"Did you look for some shoes?" Pierre asked, as we emerged from the cubicle.

Yes, I am not joking. My husband does actually say things like that.

"No, I have all I need," I answered.

I swear that was my answer and I do not care if you do not believe me. He filled out the cheque while Sarah folded the dress in tissue paper before slipping it carefully into a bag.

"You will come and see me again?" she asked, as we left.

"I promise," I replied.

"But next time, lock the shop door," Pierre whispered. "I didn't know that you were interested in beautiful girls."

I tossed my head and laughed.

"She was so pretty and so eager to please. Maybe next time you could try on a shirt?"

"Now, that would be interesting," he agreed. "And you can go and fetch the cheque book."

"I'd rather help with the shirt. Men are so clumsy."

                                         ℬ   ℘

Three weeks later, Pierre announced that Bernard Courtot wanted to see me. As my husband had explained that I was feeling bored in Paris, Bernard had a proposal for offering me some casual work, helping the company with its Australian clients. He suggested an appointment, at his office, the following Tuesday, just before lunch. Pierre offered to come to pick me up, but I told him that I was both French and an adult, quite capable of going to an appointment by myself. On Tuesday morning, Pierre reminded me of the meeting but cancelled the tentative luncheon date we had planned. He was going to Lille on business for the day.

The first male to see me in the streets of Paris with that little white dress was the taxi driver. I could see that he was impressed but I was terribly worried about his lack of attention to small things like traffic lights and pedestrians. The first female to see me with the dress was Madeleine, Bernard Courtot's secretary, and I could see that she was not impressed at all. She was adamant that I did not have an appointment with her boss; he was expecting a lady called Marie Duval, wife of one of his closest collaborators. When I told her that I was Marie she was reluctant to believe me.

Bernard Courtot stood at the door of his office looking a little stunned for a moment, and I could see that Madeleine was ready to throw me out.

"Marie, you look beautiful!" he exclaimed, holding out his arms and infuriating his loyal secretary at the same time.

Just to teach the possessive little executive assistant a lesson, I let him hold me, place a wet kiss on each cheek, and I pushed my breasts hard up against his chest. He was delighted. As he led me into the office, he warned the fuming Madeleine that he did not want to be disturbed. As I went through the door, I turned and offered her a heavy wink and ran my tongue across my lips.

"We'll be at least an hour," I added.

Once the door was closed, he laughed and gestured towards a chair facing his desk.

"Obviously you were not impressed with Madeleine," he commented as he slipped behind his desk. "She is a little old fashioned, but an excellent assistant. Now, let me have a good look at you."

His eyes did a lot of wandering, and I could see that he was pleased with the messages they were sending back to his hungry mind.

"I seem to remember a rather shy young lady. Although you did give a hand with a Malaysian client, I believe."

I laughed.

"That's a naughty play on words. You should be ashamed of yourself. It was not really my fault. But I am a married woman, so I know what is needed to help a man find happiness."

"And Pierre looks very happy, I must admit. Your suntan is impressive. Is that Australian?"

"No, I'm afraid not," I replied, crossing my legs slowly. "Getting a tan like this would have created a scandal in Canberra. No this comes from Nouméa, where it is quite acceptable for a lady to wear just a little string on the beach or on a boat."

"Wonderful," he breathed. "And the dress is obviously from Paris. Delightful."

"I'm glad that you're pleased," I commented. "Your visual inspection has been meticulous, to say the least."

His face flushed, and his eyes dropped.

"No, please don't be embarrassed. In fact, I find it flattering."

"You are rather, how can I say… tantalising?"

I smiled.

"If I'm wearing a dress like this, it's because it suits me and I like people to enjoy my company."

He laughed. "I'm enjoying your company very much."

"Excellent. I'm sure that Madeleine will not approve, but I actually like to please. It's the new 'me' I'm afraid, and that's the way it is."

"Don't apologise. Look, can I explain what I have to offer?"

"Please do," I said encouragingly.

It was simple. Bernard Courtot was proposing to employ me as a consultant with his company to assist with projects concerning investment in Australia. When necessary, I would be called in to assist and advise executives and their wives who might have concerns about moving to a strange country. My job would be to inform them of the quality of life in Australia, housing, education, entertainment and health being some of the subjects we would discuss. To ensure my availability when required, he was offering a retainer of 10,000 francs per month.

"Let's make it 14," I suggested, with a smile.

"Pardon?" he asked.

I rang a finger across the top of my dress, and sighed. "It is rather warm in here. I really do think I'm worth 14."

He nodded his agreement and mopped his brow with a handkerchief.

"How about lunch?" he suggested. "To seal the pact?"

I smiled.

"That would be lovely. What a pity Pierre cannot join us."

"Yes, indeed. He had a little unexpected business."

I began to think that the business which kept Pierre away today was terribly unexpected.

Madeleine booked the table, her eyes throwing daggers in my direction. We climbed into Bernard's Jaguar, and the driver whisked us off to a lovely restaurant. It was small, exclusive, and Bernard was obviously well known.

"I have to watch my figure," I apologised as I slipped on to my chair.

"I'll do that," he offered. "If I note any serious developments during the meal, I'll let you know."

My husband's boss seemed to be a professional woman chaser. We had a light lunch during which he explained how busy he was, how much he appreciated Pierre, how difficult life was in Paris, and how his wife did not understand him.

"You must get away more often to escape it all and relax," I suggested.

He watched a fat white asparagus slip into my mouth with unrestrained delight.

"Perhaps we should organise a company seminar in the Loire Valley, just to talk about Australia," he suggested.

"Could I come?" I asked, looking as if my future happiness hung from his lips.

Mopping his forehead with his table napkin, he assured me that a weekend seminar of that type could hardly exist without me.

"So you will assist Pierre with the clients for our Australian operations while you are in Paris. It is agreed?"

"Of course, Bernard, of course. And if Pierre gets called away, for example to Lille, and the business is urgent, I would deal with you directly?"

He knew that I knew what he had done to Pierre that day, but he loved it. He hardly batted an eyelid when he agreed, but I could see a little vein twitching above his left eyebrow.

"And for special occasions, such as dinners or weekend seminars, you would consider offering me a clothing bonus, I would imagine? For a little dress, like this one, for example?"

He hesitated.

"What would a dress like that cost?" he asked, allowing his eyes to travel very slowly.

I pushed out my bust a little to allow him to enjoy the trip.

"About 3,000 francs," I lied.

"Really?" he asked.

"Yes, really. I mean, it is silly, there is so little to it. When I take it off, it is no more than a few hundred grams of light cotton."

"I'd love to see that," he panted.

I laughed and patted his hand.

"Now, Bernard behave yourself, or I'll tell Madeleine. But, who knows, before I leave Paris, I might show you just how light it is. Or, better still, we can buy my next official dress together."

His hand fluttered to his chest. The suggestion had obviously provoked a little cardiac tremor.

"I think that 3,000 francs for a dress is quite reasonable," he decided, mopping his brow again. "That would mean a new dress for each function, of course."

I beamed. "But, of course!"

The Jaguar took me home, after dropping Bernard at his office. The wine had been invigorating, and my skirt had slipped upwards during the short trip to the office. I left it there for the return trip. The driver was delighted and seemed just as careless as the taxi driver had been. But I was pleased for him. He was probably earning about 8,000 a month, and he would not have many opportunities to see the golden tanned thighs of an expensive consultant.

By the time that Pierre came home that evening I had a delightful candlelit supper waiting for him. Unfortunately, when he walked through the door and dropped his briefcase in the entrance hall, I could see that he was annoyed.

"I can't understand why Bernard wanted me to deal with that business in *Lille*. It had absolutely nothing to do with our Australian projects, and it should have been left to Claude Mestier."

"Don't worry," I suggested, dragging him to a couch. Then I popped the cork on the bottle of champagne. He accepted the flute and sighed with embarrassment.

"I'm so sorry, I forgot to ask you about your interview. How did it go? No wait, don't tell me, I know that he was offering you a job, and I knew that you would accept. I even suggested to Bernard that he should pay you a retainer of 7,000 a month, which was a little cheeky."

I smiled as he took his first gulp of champagne.

"He actually offered me 10,000."

He nearly choked.

"Wow! You must have been most persuasive."

"I was, afterwards, when I asked for 14."

"You're joking – 14,000 francs a month!?"

He stared at me, almost angrily.

"You don't think I'm worth it? You think your wife is cheap?"

He blushed.

"I'm sorry, darling, that's not what I meant. How did you do that?"

"The little white dress was greatly appreciated. He found me so lovely he invited me to his favourite restaurant for lunch."

Pierre gaped, and took another gulp of champagne.

"Did Madeleine see the dress?"

"She hated it," I announced, and we were both overcome with laughter.

As I served a second flute of champagne, he smiled.

"That little white dress, eh? It was a good investment for 1,800 francs."

"It was 3,000," I corrected.

"Don't be silly darling. There is no way I would pay 3,000 francs for a dress. Even for you. Honestly, I could not afford 3,000 for a dress. I remember very well, wait I can fetch my cheque book."

I shook my head.

"Bernard Courtot believes that it cost 3,000 francs, and that's what is important. You see, every time I attend an official function for your Australian projects, he will invest another 3,000 francs in a nice little dress."

"You're joking?"

"No, darling. I sit at home getting bored for 14,000 francs a month, and every time he wants to see me, he pays an extra 3,000 for the dress."

"I'll let you negotiate my next contract," Pierre decided.

"Certainly. Now, do you want to make love before or after dinner?"

"Both," he replied as he threw me over his shoulder and headed for the bedroom. "Where's that little white dress?"

သ လ

When I was not making love to my husband, shopping or looking after tedious housework, I was thinking about my first job for Bernard Courtot. Two things appeared absolutely certain: one of my seminars would coincide with Bernard finding an urgent need to send Pierre to Marseille or Bordeaux; also, once a seminar was scheduled, my anecdotal evidence would have to be good. I rang the Australian Embassy and explained that I was a consultant helping businesses invest in Australia, and that I needed background and statistical information.

I was given an appointment the next day with a Trade Commissioner called Raymond Forbes. I decided not to wear the white dress but a little two piece pseudo-Chanel outfit we had found on a different shopping spree.

The Australian Embassy is an enormous, half-empty monstrosity built on old railway yards, now one of the most expensive pieces of real estate in Paris. It was the idea and passion of Gough Whitlam, which proves that even socialists can enjoy unrestrained financial pleasures.

Meeting Raymond was a shock. He gulped, stared, then shouted "Brigitte!" and literally ran from behind his desk to hug me. Tall, dark, handsome Raymond had been one of my more inspiring clients in Canberra, and the moments we had spent together had always been to our mutual satisfaction. When I succeeded in getting unwrapped from his investigative clutches, I explained that my name was Marie Duval, and gave him a business card to prove it. He sank into his chair and invited me to do the same with a weak gesture of the hand.

"What a waste. Consulting? This is crazy. You were excellent in your previous job."

I explained that it had been just a pleasurable pastime (he nodded enthusiastically) and then we got down to business. He was delighted with the fact that my job coincided with some of his current functions in France, and he was able to offer me a bag full of statistics, year books and pamphlets. Then the conversation wandered back to my past profession. Was I doing anything naughty in Paris? I told him no, not professionally, but that we could still meet socially. He tried to remain enthusiastic.

I told Pierre about our meeting that evening. He was delighted.

"We already had a Minister, now we have a diplomat eating out of your hand," he commented.

True. I had forgotten darling Nigel.

"It wasn't my hand they were eating out of you know."

He snorted.

"Don't be sordid. It doesn't suit you."

৪০ ෩

An opportunity to exercise my new duties appeared about three weeks later. Luckily, Pierre was not sent elsewhere on an urgent mission, as the function was to be a private dinner at our apartment. We were to invite Marc and Sophie Bayes home for dinner. Marc was a senior but young executive with a French company specialising in electronics and communications equipment. Bernard and Pierre had successfully demonstrated the opportunities awaiting them in Australia, particularly in sales of specialised equipment for government. Local assembly and production would be an added asset. Pierre had enjoyed several meetings with Marc and liked him, but, from little hints in their social conversations, he had come to the conclusion that Sophie might not be as pleasant.

"No little white dress for dinner," he suggested. "I have the impression that Madame Baye is a little conservative."

Pierre's forecast had been correct. Marc was charming, good looking and a bright conversationalist. Sophie was quite reserved and did not have a great sense of humour. But she enjoyed my cooking, and asked me many practical questions about life in Australia. Slowly she began to relax, and I thought that by the end of the evening she was feeling more peaceful and positive about their potential departure.

Pierre was delighted, and told me that I had done an excellent job. Bernard Courtot rang personally to say how impressed he had been with the results of our evening. Not surprisingly, Marc also rang, asking if we could meet privately to discuss some 'finer points'. I rang Pierre and told him that Marc was coming round Friday afternoon.

"I think the little white dress would be appropriate," was his only comment.

He rang me later the same afternoon.

"Bernard Courtot is delighted with your meeting with Marc. He thinks this could be good tactics."

"I'm sure he does. I'm not quite sure what he thinks I'm offering, but tell him the little white dress will do for this time, but the next meeting will need something new."

At the beginning, Marc's visit was official, although the little white dress threw him a little off balance. He announced that he needed my help and support to persuade Sophie that she would enjoy three years in Sydney and that their two sons would be delighted with school, the beach and the lifestyle. He then confessed that Sophie needed a little stimulating, and that life at home was not always hilarious. He hoped that the move would inspire her. I explained that I had been a rather shy provincial girl before I left, and that my social activities in Australia had allowed me to develop self-confidence.

"Of course, I can see that," he agreed. "For example, that dress is absolutely magnificent, and it needs a lot of self-esteem to wear it. Sophie would never buy anything like that."

"Who knows? I can tell you that being a French woman in Australia can be quite pleasant. Many foreign men have fantasies about French women, and I used to get a few cheeky questions, now and again."

He looked at me thoughtfully.

"You were, how should I say... popular?"

I pretended to be coy.

"Yes, several times. But please don't mention this to Pierre."

"Of course I won't. Please, you may have confidence in me. Sophie will have the same problems, maybe?"

I smiled. I doubted that she would have a lot of success unless she decided to dress differently and to smile a little more often.

"She'll just do what comes naturally. We French girls do have a reputation as lovers, you know. The French kiss, for example."

He looked a little blank, and I served him a second glass of wine.

"You know what I mean?"

"Perhaps. I'm not sure. Not really."

"Would you like me to show you?"

His hand was shaking as he put down the glass; so badly that some wine slopped on to the coffee table.

"Well, yes. But then, Pierre, Sophie, I mean, we are married, if you know what I mean."

I laughed as I knelt down in front of him, placing my hand firmly over the obvious erection.

"I find that it's the married men who like it the best."

I pulled the zip.

At first he was shy, but when I told him how much I admired his beautiful erection, he was very co-operative. He moaned, gasped and sighed. This was like the good old days in Canberra. He pleaded, begged and then came generously. He decided that this was the ultimate pleasure and suggested that Sophie needed a little training. Would I help? I laughed.

"Could you imagine Sophie and me sharing the work?" I asked.

"My God, yes!" he exclaimed.

He then became quite amorous, and the little white dress was seriously crushed and dishevelled as he explored. He was concerned that I had not been honoured as custom requires, and he was so sincere, I let him do his little duty. He was, in fact, very good and he made me happy. He was obviously delighted with his performance. He left, begging me to let him visit again. I was non-committal.

I was still under the shower when Pierre arrived, and he found the little white dress where it had been abandoned by the coffee table. Five minutes later, he was under the shower with me, resuming possession of his most cherished asset. It is wonderful to be loved by such a handsome, virile and generous husband, and my orgasm was much better than with Marc.

As we took a quiet glass of wine together, he assured me that I was not expected to have sex with every candidate for his Australian projects. I agreed, although I suspected that Bernard Courtot might think otherwise. Then I had a brilliant idea.

"Perhaps I should organise a few more meetings with Marc to discuss life in contemporary Australia," I suggested, tongue in cheek.

Pierre thought the idea over for a few seconds.

"I have no objections, but I can't see what it will change. Marc is already absolutely committed to going to Australia, the problem is Sophie."

"You mean I should court Sophie?"

He laughed and hugged me.

"No, that would not serve any purpose either. She might become homosexual, fall in love with you and leave her husband."

"There is another possibility," I suggested thoughtfully. "Perhaps I should show Marc how to be a wonderful lover, so good that his darling wife would follow him everywhere. You know, often in Canberra I taught some of my clients how to be more loving and affectionate."

He stared at me in wonder.

"Darling, that is a wonderful idea. Wait until I tell Bernard."

"Don't you dare!" I shouted at him, and then laughed, realising that he was joking.

The next day I rang Marc and asked if we could meet in a little *brasserie*, near our flat, for lunch. He accepted immediately. Over the grilled fish and French fries, I explained that I had decided to offer him my help in adding a little spice into his marriage. He lost most of his French fries on the floor.

"You mean you and me, making love together, on a regular basis?" he stammered.

"Not exactly. Look, I don't need a lover who would buy me lavish gifts. Pierre is always generous, and Bernard Courtot offers me a clothing allowance."

He was beginning to calm down.

"Your husband is, well, lacking in attention?"

I laughed.

"Not at all, Pierre is a good lover. I just thought it would be nice for you to learn how to add a little more zest into your marriage. But if you're not interested …"

He became dreadfully embarrassed.

"No, no, look, please, I would be so honoured."

I smiled sweetly.

"That's wonderful. I thought that physically we were well matched."

He blushed.

"I was over the moon. I have never enjoyed sex so much. But I will learn to do better things for you."

I laughed happily.

"You certainly will. But not for me. For Sophie, and I'm going to teach you. How about two sessions a week?"

I do believe that at certain moments during that luncheon he was quite close to having a heart attack. He told me later that it was probably one of the greatest moments in his life. However, he made one dreadful faux-pas.

"You're sure you don't want any money?"

I nearly slapped him. What an idiot. If I had wanted money, I would have told him that from the outset.

"Marc, all I want is to teach you. Twice a week. And for nothing. Get it?"

He stammered an apology.

We settled for an hour around lunchtime every Wednesday, and a longer session every Friday, for the second half of the afternoon. I told him that I would allow him to say to his employers that he was being briefed on Australia, if necessary. I also warned him that our 'lessons' must remain a secret.

Then I had my second idea: Raymond Forbes. I knew that the Trade Commissioner considered himself to be God's gift to women. I also knew that he was a good performer. I rang Pierre and explained.

The following Thursday, Raymond, Marc and Sophie came to dinner. I announced that Pierre had been called away on urgent business. We talked about settling in Australia, the life style, the beaches, the mountains. Raymond explained how I had settled well, and how we had been good friends in Canberra. He told some wonderful stories about picnics and race meetings we had never attended, and I saw Sophie relax, and even smile.

"I love your accent when you talk in French," she told Raymond. "I'm sure the French girls love it."

"I don't know. I've been so busy, I haven't even had time to look around Paris, let alone meet many of its lovely residents."

"Then, when you have a few days free, I will be your guide," she offered.

I could hardly believe my ears, and was delighted to ring Pierre, later, with the good news.

"Will he screw her?" my husband asked with an unusual lack of decorum.

"I can guarantee that he will try. I can also guarantee that if she gives in, she'll enjoy the trip."

Pierre sighed.

"I won't ask for a second opinion."

⋈

Friday was exhausting. Marc wanted 'that oral thing' and then mounted me twice.

"I hope Sophie is not expecting anything special tonight," I commented as he was getting dressed.

"No," he assured me. "We only do it on Sundays."

I sighed.

"Marc, over the next few weeks, I'm going to teach you to do really nice things to Sophie, to make her happy, and any day of the week."

He grinned.

"I'll enjoy that. What about that lovely thing you do with your mouth?"

"We'll leave that to Raymond," I said softly.

He was trying to slip his foot into his shoe, standing up, and my comment shocked him so much that he fell on to the bed.

"You mean that you think that Raymond might try to have sex with Sophie, my wife?" he asked. "That's ridiculous!"

I laughed.

"Sometimes a woman's purity and reserve can be overcome by a challenge from a stranger. Besides, what are you doing here?"

"Oh, don't get me wrong," he pleaded. "I have no right to be jealous. In fact, I have no right to dictate her life. I just do not believe that she would give in to another man."

"Believe me, he is an excellent lover," I assured him. "She may need that kind of experience to overcome her inhibitions."

He gazed at me.

"You were, um… popular with him, in Canberra?"

I smiled.

"Yes, I was. And he was dreadfully popular with me."

    ℘ ℃

On the third Wednesday, I sat Marc on a chair at the end of the dining room table, on which I had placed a large fluffy bathrobe. I then placed myself, naked, on the table, offering him a direct view of my intimacy. I then told him to lift my buttocks gently with his hands, and to begin to explore me, with his tongue.

"Pretend it's an apricot and you are searching for the kernel with your tongue."

He was a little shy, but when I promised him his favourite service if he worked well, he put his heart and tongue into the task.

"I think I've found a petal," he whispered, about half an hour later.

"I think you have. That is the secret you had to discover."

He played softly, and I cried out and shuddered. He was delighted, and I gave him the compensation he loved.

The following Friday, it was he who asked if he could practice again. This time, he made me scream with pleasure and I do believe that I was shuddering for a full five minutes after he had finished. He then mounted me, carefully but decisively, and I had another glorious orgasm when he filled me. He was so happy, and so pleased with himself, that it was dreadful telling him that this was our last sexual meeting. He asked why, and I said it was for Sophie.

"You are now an accomplished lover, and are capable of making any woman very happy. You must now demonstrate your passion to your wife."

We kissed and parted, and I told Pierre that evening of my decision, explaining everything. He was delighted with what I had done for Marc, and we did a little apricot kernelling and banana peeling that evening ourselves.

ℝ   ℞

It was important that Pierre's activities were understood and supported by the Australian Embassy, and for this reason, Raymond invited us to attend a modest little ceremony on the banks of the Seine. To commemorate the bicentenary of the French Revolution, the Australian government had offered the people of France a bust of La Perouse. It was on a cool morning of spring, 1989, that we joined a small crowd to witness an event which did not cause a ripple on national television. But, it appeared, the two governments of the time were most eager to see France and Australia celebrate such events together. I was surprised to learn that the Australian government had such a warm affection for Paris, but Raymond assured me that our Ministers' travel and hotel bills proved just how much they enjoyed the ambience! It was our second bicentenary celebration in 12 months. We shook hands with ambassadors, chargés d'affaires, Ministers, and counsellors until our wrists ached.

Marc rang me two or three times over the following month, but I gently refused his proposals. He told me that he and Sophie were now having sex three times a week, and that she was becoming terribly brazen, once the lights were turned off.

Bernard Courtot accompanied me to buy a new dress, of pale yellow chiffon, with a three quarter length skirt, which hugged my breasts very firmly. He was delighted to be the sugar daddy, and was so proud when I came out of the cubicle and twirled in front of him.

The lovely girl in the shop was most curious, even a little jealous, and asked if he was a relative.

"No," I whispered. "He's my boss."

"But he buys you dresses?" she asked. "This is not the sort of dress you would wear in an office."

"We have other relationships," I explained.

She nodded, guessing wrong and pouting with displeasure. The new dress was to please Raymond, my favourite Trade Commissioner. Bernard Courtot was planning a weekend seminar for a group of businessmen and their wives, all representing companies interested in business activities in Australia. My boss believed that if an Australian diplomat was present and took an active part in the presentations, this would add a lot of credibility to the event. It was programmed for October.

I invited Raymond out to lunch and he agreed. After lunch, he invited me back to his apartment to show me a PowerPoint slide show he had prepared for me about life in Australia. Although our afternoon was strictly for business, the meeting reminded me of Canberra and I almost felt homesick.

Pierre proudly told Bernard of my plan to make a visual presentation and his delighted boss bought me an overhead projector so that I could practice. We had a one-day seminar due in May, and he was now eager to make me a member of his team. Raymond came round twice to help me train, and the second time was a more informal meeting. I was still under the shower when Pierre came home. He found the lovely little yellow dress crumpled on the floor, and came to watch me under the shower.

"Raymond?" he asked.

"Yes, sorry, darling, I didn't have time to warn you, it came on quite suddenly. But it was strictly for business reasons." I confessed, wiping some suds away from my face. "It was a strange feeling; it reminded me of my old job."

Pierre sighed, almost wistfully.

"I wonder if Bernard Courtot will ever know just how devoted you are to your duties," he commented.

Then he threw his clothes off and joined me under the spray.

We had lunch a few days later with Raymond, and Pierre shook his hand solemnly.

"This is the first time that I've met one of my wife's Canberra clients," he said, very politely.

Raymond laughed.

"We have shared secret pleasures." Then he added, more seriously, "You are a lucky man, you have a wonderful wife."

Pierre nodded his agreement, but I reminded him that what he had said was not totally true.

"You forgot Nigel."

He smiled. "Dear Nigel."

"Nigel?" Raymond asked, almost jealously.

"Highly confidential," Pierre explained, jokingly. "I can't talk. It could start a political scandal, overturn a government, or provoke a premature –"

"– ejaculation?" Raymond interrupted.

"Well, I was going to say election," Pierre explained, grinning. "But come to think of it, that, too."

I could see that they were getting on like a house on fire, and that annoyed me.

"Before we get into the crude jokes, can I remind you that we are talking about my private life?" I asked, petulantly.

They apologised and we settled down to a quiet lunch, but I noticed that they were exchanging the occasional grin over the steak and peas. Men!

∞   ∞

My literary research into my industry continued. It was lucky for me that we were in Paris in 1991 when the Berlin wall fell, allowing hundreds of girls from Romania and Bulgaria to cross the French border and work as prostitutes. I followed much of the story in the French press. In those early days they were particularly popular: young, clean and cheap. Then the industry took over, and most of them now have their own managers. There are still girls who visit France by coach, from Poland, Russia, Hungary and the Baltic States, for their annual holidays, who will spend a month earning quite good money before going home. Most of them are married, and it seems that some special 'travel agencies' are involved in the business.

In March, Raymond told us of the imminent visit of an Australian Minister. He was coming to study certain industrial innovations in France, and, like most important politicians, he was coming in July, when the factories were closed for the summer holidays. His meetings would be held in Cannes, coinciding almost exactly with the Film Festival. Raymond had been unable to identify any major industries in that region.

Pierre grinned at Raymond's sly observation.

"I do believe that you are becoming cynical," he commented. "Like a real Frenchman."

Raymond offered a wry smile.

"I will have done most of the work before he arrives, enough for him to make a few wise press statements. But the reason I told you is that he is interested in attracting French technology into Australia, and he mentioned your operation. He seems to know both of you, and he is quite eager to meet Bernard Courtot."

Pierre groaned.

"He also wants to know if Marie could accompany him to Cannes as an interpreter. He would pay a fee, of course."

"In the middle of the summer holidays?" Pierre muttered, angrily.

I am a simple girl, but I was beginning to suspect something.

"Is this a new Minister?" I asked.

"Yes," Raymond confirmed. "He's a new appointee. There was a cabinet reshuffle a few weeks ago, and I think that the trip to Cannes was part of the deal."

"What's his name?" I asked Raymond.

"Nigel Spencer."

There was a deathly silence, and then Pierre began to laugh, helplessly.

"It's not funny," I told him angrily.

Raymond looked at us, his eyes switching from one face to the other.

"What's up, guys? Can I share the joke?"

And then it hit him.

"Oh, my God. The top secret Nigel. It's him."

"Nonsense," Pierre denied. "Of course not. And if you say a word, we'll deny everything. And you can't talk about it, you're a diplomat."

❧   ☙

Bernard Courtot was over the moon. He actually hugged me and kissed me in front of his furious secretary.

"How did you meet this Minister?" he asked, excitedly. "This is an extraordinary coincidence and a wonderful stroke of luck for us. This time we will buy a whole wardrobe, as you will be accompanying him to Cannes. It is a wonderful compliment for my staff."

I did not tell him that I had met Nigel as a paid prostitute. I did not bother to remind him that I had only just joined his staff, and that my meeting with Nigel was in a previous life. But my thoughts were interrupted. The walls shook as Madeleine closed the door behind her. As I left the office, she spoke to me, almost spitting with anger.

"I'd hate to think about the things I'd have to do to be as successful as you. Would you like to make any suggestions?"

I smiled and sidled up to her desk.

"Try being more polite, more friendly, and, for God's sake, smile. Change your clothes, you hair, make him notice. And if that doesn't work, give him a blow job," I suggested, with a grin. "You won't be the first to secure your future by sucking the boss."

She gazed at me, horrified.

"You're not joking, are you?"

I shook my head.

"No. I never joke about business. And make yourself attractive. Get yourself a bra with lift, wear some heavy lipstick, and look as if you are dying to get laid. It's easy; any woman can do it, if she really wants to … and has a secret attraction to her boss."

She snorted angrily.

"I knew you were a tart, Madame Duval, the first time you came into this office."

I laughed.

"I'm a business woman. There's not always a lot of difference, you know."

I left the office, closing the door behind me, waited a couple of minutes, and then walked back in, without knocking.

She was sobbing in her handkerchief, and my arm was around her shoulder before she could push me away. She surrendered as I whispered in her ear.

"He's a lovely man, probably married to a boring old fart. I'm going to help you to become the sexiest secretary in the office, and I will not give up until he invites you out for a dirty weekend."

The small trickle became a waterfall, but I had just earned a new friend.

‽ ∾

In April, Pierre had four new companies ready to invest in Australia and Bernard Courtot decided that they would all be invited to the May seminar, to be held in Chartres. My overhead projector and presentation was were ready, and I had practised a couple of times in front of Pierre, who was very impressed.

"Raymond is obviously a good tutor," he commented dryly. "Do you point the projector at the ceiling?"

I was not amused.

Three days later, Marc rang. He wanted us to have lunch together in a quiet restaurant, as he had important news to announce. I love gossip.

We shared a delicious *cassoulet*. As we ate, he explained the revolution in his married life. He had tried 'the apricot thing' on Sophie, who had screamed with pleasure and almost crushed his skull between her knees. To thank him, she had tried, tentatively, 'the banana thing'. He was delighted. She was thrilled. They were enjoying a wonderful life on the fruit farm.

That afternoon I rang Raymond to congratulate him on his success with Sophie. He pretended not to understand, then giggled and asked if I was jealous. I assured him that I was not, but suggested that he should back away slowly, just to avoid creating any problems for the couple. He agreed, but still thought that my advice had other, personal motivations.

The May seminar in Chartres was fast approaching. Apart from the company's primary clients, we were expecting about 50 other people from all walks of business, thanks to a good PR program ordered by Bernard Courtot.

We went to my favourite dress shop. He bought me a two-piece, apricot coloured jacket and skirt with a black lace blouse, and a delicious gold evening dress for the event. The dress was gloriously provocative, clinging where necessary to remain decent, and strapless. As I was changing, the lovely sales girl, who was always there to lend a helping hand, whispered in my ear while her hands fluttered.

"You are so lucky to have a rich lover."

In the Jaguar, which was taking him home, Bernard kept telling me how beautiful I was, and I could see the driver grinning in the mirror. Finally, Bernard noticed the smiles and angrily closed the window which separated us from the front of the car.

"I must tell you that I am a little worried about Madeleine. She is acting strangely, almost provocatively, nowadays. And she's dressing differently."

I smiled.

"Secretaries do become enamoured with their bosses. You know. It has happened before."

"I'm just a little curious, that's all," he explained, but I recognised the gleam in the eye.

"Is your wife coming to the seminar?" I asked innocently.

I knew the answer, Pierre had already told me how annoyed Bernard Courtot had been when his wife refused to accompany him to that 'boring business weekend'.

"No, she's off to Greece with her mother," he replied. "Why do you ask?"

"Because, for convenience, I think you should have a partner. Madeleine would be perfect, she knows all about the business, she can help you if there are problems, and she is always discreet."

"That's an interesting idea," he said thoughtfully. "It would also be a little compensation for the work she has been doing recently."

"Is she married?" I asked. I knew the answer to that one, too.

"No, her husband died over ten years ago."

"Then there's no problem. Why not take her to our little dress shop, just to make sure she makes a good impression?"

He looked at me strangely, but the 'our little dress shop' suggested an intimacy which brought a delighted smile to his face.

"That's going a bit far, isn't it?"

I smiled.

"I'm sure she'd be most grateful."

We had just arrived in front of my apartment and he gave me a peck on the cheek. I could see the look in his eye, he was wondering just what form her gratitude would take and whether it would be gratifying for both parties.

& ∓

The seminar attracted more than 60 visitors for the activities of the first day. Bernard spoke, followed by Raymond, and then we had coffee and biscuits. The second half was devoted to a long presentation by my wonderful husband on business opportunities in Australia. My darling Pierre can stand up on his hind legs and waffle all day without looking at his notes more than three times, and still keep the audience attentive.

We then had an informal lunch. I was placed at the official table with Bernard, Madeleine, my husband, Raymond, Marc and Sophie and another couple, Gilbert and Charlotte, also planning to move shortly to Australia for business reasons. I did notice that Sophie was looking very beautiful, and had obviously devoted time and money to her appearance. Even more interesting was the attitude of Madeleine. She was wearing a delicious two-piece rather like mine, but black, and throwing beaming smiles at everyone, including me. I ate little, concerned by the fact that after the coffee I was to give my own presentation, devoted to the lifestyle the families could expect in Australia.

My wonderful Pierre found the solution, and he was right. The second glass of wine fired me up, and I swept with confidence towards the podium. On the way, I felt the eyes of the male spectators following my progress, and knew that Pierre and Bernard were probably feeling proud.

It was a success. I never faltered, I even became sincerely carried away by my subject, and during question time the curiosity of my audience was obvious. I handled each question with simplicity, and with a certain frankness, which I sensed the participants enjoying.

While Bernard took over to summarise the day and Madeleine handed out expensive coloured pamphlets, Raymond drew me aside to say that he was proud of me. Pierre was frankly amazed by my performance and Madeleine whispered that I had been beautiful.

"Those men could not take their eyes off of you," she whispered.

"You're not doing too badly yourself," I commented.

"I'm going to have to catch up with you during the evening," she added. "I'm going to need a little guidance."

Most of our guests left after Bernard's presentation, until only four couples and Raymond remained to finish the evening together. The company had arranged accommodation for all of us that night, and we were to have a final working session the next morning, before returning to Paris. Personally, I believed that this was Bernard's idea of creating an 'opportunity' for himself, and from the little glances Madeleine was throwing in my direction, she obviously thought likewise.

My only concern was that the new female addition to our group, Charlotte, seemed to be totally absorbed in contemplating my husband. She was a small redhead with green eyes and a lovely figure, and she was very talkative, even with her hands. It was a dangerous challenge for a handsome and successful businessman, but I was not in a lending mood that evening. I saw also that Sophie was casting amorous glances in Raymond's direction, and I was not sure that Marc would want to see that little relationship continue. It was going to be an interesting evening, because, if the couples were to stay put, Raymond was going to have to find himself some entertainment. Or I would have to organise things, as usual.

The gentlemen wore their dinner suits and the ladies their evening wear. Madeleine had a lovely black and silver dress which fell to her ankles and shimmered in the light. She was looking elegant, but tense. Sophie wore a pale blue dress with shoulder straps which draped over her slim figure with discretion. The men all loved my charming gown and my wonderful cleavage.

Pierre was a little annoyed when Bernard told Raymond that he had picked it himself. Unfortunately Charlotte was even more tantalising, and I whispered to Pierre that if she bent too far forward we would see her clitoris.

"My God, I hope so," he whispered back, but he only said that to make me angry.

Luckily the dinner was perfect and the accompanying wines were like pure velvet. I enjoyed a glass or two (or three) of soft burgundy, and felt at peace with the world.

We wandered off to the deep arm chairs in the lounge for coffee and brandy. This was the dangerous part of any evening in well-dined and well-wined Gallic company, because it is at this stage that all French people talk about their favourite subjects: politics and sex. I found it interesting that in Australia these were the only two subjects nobody wanted to talk about.

Not unexpectedly, Madeleine slipped on to the little two-seater couch beside me, and began to whisper her problem. It was simple. She knew what Bernard wanted and she felt like obliging, but wondered if this was wise. And, above all, she wanted to know how to do it properly.

I will not explain the diplomatic discussions I was obliged to hold with Pierre, who was eager to help. Finally, he accepted the fact that his position in the company precluded any assistance. For reasons of discretion, I turned to a talented outsider. Half an hour later she and I were in Raymond's room.

"I was hoping to see Pierre," she complained gently.

I laughed.

"I thought you might. Don't worry, this one is good. We have known one another for a long time."

"In Australia?"

"That's right. I'll explain another day."

By the time we had removed our clothing (to avoid stains) Raymond was on the bed, naked, with his manhood pointing at the ceiling. Madeleine, shyly, admitted that he was a magnificent animal. I must say that she was absolutely right, including the 'animal' qualification. His grin was unbearable.

I gave a ten-minute demonstration of fellatio, stopping now and again to explain why it was better to let the excitement die down occasionally so that the fun lasted longer. Within 20 minutes she had hand and mouth movements perfectly synchronised and Raymond warned that unless she stopped immediately he was going to express his delight in no uncertain terms.

Before leaving she kissed us both profusely and swore that Bernard would have a night he would never forget. As she wafted through the door, Raymond called after her, reminding her that if it did not go well, she would be welcome in room 208.

"She had inherent talent," he commented, when the door closed. "Are you going to stay?"

"Sorry, I can't," I apologised. "I promised Pierre I would not be too long."

I was above all concerned about young Charlotte, who appeared to be on heat, and I did not want to leave my husband unprotected. I arrived back in the lounge room, delighted to see that Charlotte was in deep discussion with a young man at the bar. I would have thought it impossible, but her cleavage had sunk even further, and her drinking partner was obviously not listening to her chatter. Pierre explained that her husband had retired, complaining of a migraine.

"Is Madeleine ready for action?" he asked, with a smile.

"She's perfect. Raymond was most impressed."

"I suppose that he got his compensation?" he asked.

"Absolutely not," I protested. "He asked me to stay on but I refused."

"If he's hungry, he might like to try Charlotte."

"He'd better hurry up."

Pierre walked over to Bernard who was draining his brandy glass.

"Why don't you get off to bed, Bernard?" he suggested. "You've had a hard day, I can handle things here."

Bernard looked at him gratefully, and Pierre gave him his hand to help him out of the deep couch. Madeleine was looking thoughtful, as Bernard slowly climbed the marble staircase.

"We still had a few things to discuss for tomorrow," she complained to Pierre.

"Let him settle down, give him 15 minutes, then take the papers up and knock on his door. Meanwhile, I'll get a bottle of champagne sent up."

Poor Madeleine blushed like a beetroot.

"Do you think that's wise?"

"I strongly recommend it," Pierre told her. "Don't forget, the right initiative at the right time can do wonders for a stagnant career, above all when the employee is most competent."

"And you and I know that you are extremely competent," I added.

It was irresistible, we all burst into laughter.

"I think I'll ask for a rise," she commented as she stood up, smoothing her skirt around her hips. And then she added, "Tomorrow morning."

"I hope you will see one tonight," Pierre commented, and there was a second round of helpless laughter.

As she was about to leave, she turned back to face me.

"Marie, I'd like to thank you, and to apologise. I accused you of acting like a whore."

Pierre was startled by my reply.

"We women sometimes have to use our beauty and our sexuality to achieve our ambitions. The feminists can complain as much as they like, as long as man is born with a penis between his legs, women will use that fragility to exploit him."

Madeleine smiled, and turned to Pierre.

"Your wife is also a great philosopher."

"She has drunk a little too much wine tonight. It drowns her shyness. But I must admit that everything she does, she does well," he assured her.

80 CB

I slipped away to the ladies room to refresh my make-up, tidy my hair and check my general appearance. It was there that Sophie caught me, coming up from behind, slipping her arms around me and placing her chin on my shoulder. I stopped moving the brush through my hair, and we gazed at one another in the mirror.

"I would like to thank you for the apricot lessons," she said, without moving her eyes from mine. "Apricot harvesting has changed our marriage."

"I'm sorry that it happened that way," I replied, softly.

"I was angry. But then I realised that you had taken a selfish man who only thought of his own pleasures, and you gave me back a competent sexual partner, and told him it was over. I don't know why you did that, but it was very kind."

"Well, I can swear that it wasn't for Bernard Courtot," I assured her.

She laughed and moved her hands softly across my breasts.

"You did it for pleasure?"

I shook my head.

"I think I was trying to dare myself to do something outlandish," I lied. "And the banana peeling is that successful?"

She blushed and laughed, letting go of me suddenly.

"Well, I don't know what cheeky activities you have organised for this evening, but I am going to bed, now, with my own husband, and I'm going to give him a wonderful climax to his day."

I grinned, turned, and pecked her on the cheek.

"That's a wonderful idea. I'll do the same with mine. Right now."

Pierre and Marc were quite surprised when we emerged from the rest rooms, bearing down on them with determined looks on our faces, then crossing over at the last minute to each take our own husband by the hand.

"We are going upstairs to make love," Sophie announced.

They both rose quickly to the challenge, although Marc asked, timidly, if there might be a half-time swap over.

"Not tonight," I assured him. "In fact, never again."

I have read, and often been warned, that sex and love are totally unrelated. This is not totally true. Obviously, I did not fall in love with the 200 or 300 men I had sex with at my job in Canberra. There were people, however, such as Raymond, or my two university students, with whom a strong affection developed. Sometimes, after sex with a regular and gentle client, we would lie in one another's arms, exchanging a few shy kisses or caresses.

However, I do believe that true love cannot survive without sex. There are many secrets to the success of our marriage: the admiration and love each has for the other; my husband's indulgence with my little fantasies and misdemeanours; the mutual support in times of crisis; the interest and commitment to one another's professional life; and the wonderful, glorious sex we have together.

That night we made love passionately. Perhaps the success of our professional venture was also stimulating, but it became a sensual competition to see who would give the most pleasure to the other. Pierre won that battle, as usual, and my shout of joy was so strong it provoked some angry banging on the bedroom wall from neighbours who obviously, and more chastely, were seeking sleep. We chatted for almost an hour, and then Pierre raised the subject of Raymond.

"He will be feeling a little lonely tonight; everyone went off to bed early."

"Except for Charlotte," I commented. "But she was looking for younger flesh."

Pierre laughed.

"So, what do we do about Raymond? Do you want to pay him a surprise visit?"

I raised myself on my elbows, and turned to look him in the eyes.

"Do you think I should?"

"Well, he's an important ally to our business. And you enjoy one another's company."

I jumped off the bed and slipped into the bathroom to grab a robe hanging behind the door.

"I'll just slip this on, in case I meet anyone in the corridor."

Pierre smiled.

"That's probably better than walking down the corridor naked. If you do that you might not get back before morning."

I bent over to kiss him.

"Thank you, darling. You are a lovely husband. What will you be doing in the meantime?"

"I'll catch up with some reading. But hang on, let me have a little joke."

He picked up the phone, asked me for Raymond's extension, and dialled the number.

"Hi there, hope I didn't wake you. I didn't? Good. Have you seen Marie? I've been looking for her everywhere."

I could hear the loud protests on the other end.

"Okay, well it doesn't matter. She's probably having fun. Good night."

There was fresh babbling, and Pierre laughed and put down the phone.

"He said if you came he'd let me know."

I kissed him goodbye, wondering how I was going to explain that I was wandering the corridors of the hotel, naked under a bathrobe. I knocked on Raymond's door and it was obvious that he had been expecting my arrival. He was obviously terribly, terribly ready.

"Your husband is looking for you," he sighed.

"That's okay, I'll give him a call to let him know I'm in safe hands. I bet Bernard is having a night to remember," I commented as we moved towards the bed. "I can't stay too long, Pierre will get worried."

He decided to mount me immediately. It was delightful. From our first encounters in Canberra, we knew that we were sexually compatible. As soon as he started, I was clinging to his shoulders, begging him to go deeper and faster, groaning constantly with pleasure.

In the circumstances, he came a little too quickly, but I joined him anyway, and we lay together for a while, both out of breath. I was about to suggest that it was time for me to go back to my husband, when somebody knocked on his bedroom door, quite loudly.

He slipped into a dressing gown and ushered in three people, leaving me just the time to hide my nudity under the duvet.

There were two young men, both in their early 20s, one of whom I recognised as Charlotte's companion in the bar. And there was Charlotte herself. She was not looking quite as neat as the last time I had seen her: she was only wearing a towel, her hair was severely messed, her lipstick was smudged, and she was holding her lovely dress in her left hand.

"I'm sorry," she said with a pale smile. "I have had a lovely evening with James and Ben, but I need to go back to my room. I thought it was 208."

The two guys laughed and the taller one explained.

"Look, she's a good lay, but we have to get some sleep. We are off to Brussels in the morning. Do you know her?"

"You can leave her here. She's a member of our group," Raymond replied.

They were obviously eager to be rid of her, and disappeared with a loud sigh of relief. Then she saw me under the duvet.

"You're not with your husband," she noted, as if accusing me of a terrible crime.

"Neither of your friends looked like Gilbert, either," I replied.

She snorted.

"They certainly performed better. How about this one?"

I slipped out of the bed and pulled on my bathrobe.

"This one is called Raymond. He's very good. A little exhausted right now, but he'll still perform well."

She dropped her towel and climbed into the bed I had just left.

"You don't mind if I stay here tonight, do you, Raymond? You see, I can't find my room."

Raymond smiled like a true gentleman. "I will be greatly flattered."

I gave him a quick kiss on the corner of the lips and he squeezed a breast gently.

"Be careful," I whispered. "You don't know where those two guys have been."

He winked to show that he understood the message, and closed the door behind me. And I found myself face-to-face with a security guard. We were both surprised, but he came to his senses before me.

"Madame Duval," he said with a note of surprise in his voice. "I was just going to your room."

He glanced at the room number over my shoulder.

"I've just spent a few moments with Raymond. He was feeling a little depressed."

"I'm sure he's feeling much better now," he commented. "But it's another member of your party who has problems. He's lost his wife."

"Would that be Gilbert Moulin?"

He smiled. "How did you guess?"

I smiled back.

"She has just taken over from me trying to console the Trade Commissioner."

He sighed.

"He must be the luckiest guy on earth. Shall I call Mr Courtot or your husband?"

I frowned.

"Nobody should disturb Mr Courtot. He has an important meeting going on right now. I'll look after this problem myself."

He smiled wickedly.

"I wish I was rich and important."

I was tired of his insinuations.

"Listen, what happens in the rooms between consenting adults is none of your business. Where is Gilbert?"

"In his room, crying. It's 238."

Firstly, we walked down a corridor, turned right, and stopped at my room.

"Wait here," I asked him. "I'll just explain to my husband."

He smiled. "Of course. I'll be here."

I explained the situation to Pierre quickly. I told him how the two guys had dumped Charlotte in Raymond's room, of my meeting with the security guard and the difficult situation that could be created if Gilbert started roaming the corridors looking for his wife. He sighed.

"And Madame Zorro will save us all?" he asked. "Not more than an hour, I'm getting tired of lending my wife to everyone on the second floor."

"Not everyone, darling. There are 38 rooms on this floor."

"And the night is young. Maybe I should go and help Raymond. I thought the poor guy was being deprived, in fact, he must be exhausted."

I wagged an admonishing finger in his direction.

"Young Charlotte is not in need. This is all about protecting the reputation of our employers. Stay where you are."

The security guard was delighted to see me come back and begged me not to close the robe on the way down the corridor. I accepted his request, for security reasons.

හ ලු

I didn't spend a great deal of time with Gilbert. He was half way through a bottle of whisky when I arrived. When I told him about the problem, he burst into tears and explained that often, when they travelled and spent a night in a hotel, Charlotte would meet people and disappear for several hours in the company of complete strangers.

"She is too bloody beautiful," he explained. "The guys pay her compliments, she loves it and then she gets herself laid."

"I know. Men love screwing beautiful women. I have the same problem."

I opened my bathrobe to make my point, and he put down his glass. He offered little resistance and ten minutes later he had a smile on his face. The little darling came, calling out his wife's name.

"You are just like her," he apologised, and I took that as a compliment.

"Don't worry. She probably loves you, but has a lot of physical needs. Try to talk it through, instead of sulking when she's gone. Do you ever ask her where she's been, who she was with?"

He shook his head, sadly.

"I never dare."

He was falling asleep when I left the room. My security guard was waiting, with a dirty smile on his face.

"All is fine," I assured him. "We have just one last visit to make. What's your name?"

"Christian," he muttered, as he followed me down the corridor. I could see he was hoping to pluck up enough courage to make me an offer.

"I'm feeling a little lonely myself…" he confided as we set off. What did he think I was?

I popped quickly down to Raymond's room and knocked on the door. When he opened, he was looking pretty exhausted.

"For God's sake, take her away," he pleaded. I pushed him aside and walked into the room. Charlotte was totally exposed, on the bed, and not the least disturbed by my arrival.

"You want a threesome, darling?"

I shook my head.

"No thanks, I'm exhausted. I've just seen Gilbert. Fantastic. I was wondering whether you needed him for the rest of the night, if not, I might pop back later on."

"You did what?" she screamed at me, hunting desperately for her dress. "How dare you, he's my husband."

I was afraid for a moment that she was going to hit me, and Raymond slipped between the two of us, just to protect me if necessary.

I opened the door, and called Christian into the room.

"Can you take this lady back to her room, please Christian. She is a little tired."

They left within a few minutes, after Christian had helped her, very slowly, back into her dress. I had a feeling that she might not get back to Gilbert straight away, but that the trip would be interesting. Maybe a body search on the way? These security people have to be so careful.

When I got back to my own room, Pierre asked no questions. He was asleep.

🉠   🉥

The next morning, we met for the breakfast briefing, as forecast on the program. The croissants were warm and flaky, the orange marmalade perfectly bitter, and the fresh coffee capable of waking a regiment. We all looked as if we had waged a nocturnal battle, and some were exhausted, some wounded, others flushed with victory.

Marc and Sophie were shining with happiness, and she appeared to find it more comfortable to sit on top of her husband and to pass him little pieces of croissant from her mouth to his. As he chewed and giggled, her hand was exploring his crotch.

"Checking the tyre pressure," Raymond whispered in my ear. "After last night, I'm glad it's not me."

It was true that he was looking tired. He had almost retched when I offered him a chocolate croissant, and he had asked the waitress to prepare him a shot of brandy to accompany his coffee.

Pierre and I were both famished, and were enjoying the excellent continental breakfast. Gilbert was looking victorious and had decided that he wanted an English breakfast of scrambled eggs. Charlotte had a nasty bruise on one cheek, but a happy, wistful look on her face. She gazed at her husband incessantly, and asked him frequently if he wanted something. His reply was becoming monotonous.

"Only you, my darling."

Bernard Courtot looked tired but happy. He was enjoying his breakfast, which he ate slowly and delicately, while Madeleine was ruffling the paperwork for the morning's briefing, acting like the perfect secretary she was. Finally, Bernard cleared his throat to call our attention.

"I have some phone calls to make, and several incoming messages to attend to. I would like us to meet for lunch, at which time I hope to be able to provide you with some satisfying news."

I think most of us sighed with relief. Raymond declared loudly that he was going back to bed, while Charlotte made an appointment with the hotel's beauty consultant. I decided to stay in the lounge and read *Vogue* while Pierre helped Bernard.

Madeleine caught up with me during the morning, and we shared a cup of coffee. She told me that she was no longer Bernard's secretary. I was shocked.

"Oh, no, it's all right," she assured me, patting my hand. "Thanks to your training in business relations, I've been offered a promotion."

Pierre caught up with me just before lunch.

"Bernard asked me if you would be interested in becoming his public relations consultant, and I told him that you would only last a few weeks in the job."

I was annoyed.

"Thanks for your confidence. You might have asked for my opinion," I snapped.

"I told him that you would prefer to come to Melbourne with your husband."

I clapped my hands in glee.

"Melbourne? That's wonderful. I believe that it has a wonderful lifestyle."

My husband smiled lovingly.

"You are going to love it."

We met over a lunch of smoked salmon, salads and crisp, chilled white wine. Bernard spoke.

"I don't really need to go over yesterday's seminar. I must admit that the attendance was better than I had expected, and I want to congratulate Pierre, Marie and Madeleine for their performances."

We smiled.

"I would like to add that these seminars will be held, from now on, three or four times a year, and that I have decided to appoint Madeleine to the position of Functions Manager. Her salary and entitlements will be those of a middle executive."

I stood up, walked across the room, and hugged Madeleine. Bernard grinned.

"Yes, I forgot that I should point out that Marie has been a great help to Madeleine over the last few days, and I want to say just how grateful I am."

I walked back to my chair, face the colour of beetroot. Raymond laughed raucously, but Bernard ignored him and continued.

"Clozet Industrie has confirmed this morning that they will be opening offices in Sydney this year, and that Marc will be their Australian manager. They will be investing up to $30 million in manufacturing facilities. I understand that the Fougerot group will be following in their footsteps within the following year, and that they hope that Gilbert will represent them over there. We have other companies showing strong interest following our seminar, and I have received three faxes only this morning asking for further assistance."

We all clapped. It was wonderful to see how well our projects were progressing. Bernard smiled with delight.

"I want to add that Marie Duval has been appointed Public Relations Officer for our company, but this is only a short term activity. She will have the specific task of improving our relationships with the Australian government, not only through the Embassy and our friend Raymond, but at Ministerial level."

I leaned towards Raymond, smiling for appearances and hissed at him.

"If you make one snide comment, I will kick you in the balls, here and now."

Bernard ignored my interruption.

"Marie's work with us will end in September, when she will be accompanying her husband back to Australia. Pierre Duval assumes responsibility for our Australian operations from September, with the title of Chief Executive – Pacific Operations and a seat on the Board of Directors."

I could not help grabbing my darling and offering him a loud, wet and vigorous kiss on the cheek. Bernard stood up.

"Thank you, everyone. You have the rest of the afternoon off. Madeleine and I are going for a walk around the park."

11. Last Days in France

Pierre and I drove home slowly, discussing our plans for the future. The evening after the seminar had offered me the opportunity to see the more futile side of life in France, and I was looking forward to our move to Melbourne. My husband assured me that Bernard would not be requiring my services unless Madeleine decided to organise one of the half-day seminars they had discussed that morning. My main job was to look after the Minister.

It was a task that worried me. The right honourable Nigel Spencer was an active politician, and no idiot. More importantly, he had a great affection for me, and I did not want to use his 'fatal attraction' to cynically serve the business ambitions of Bernard Courtot. It was also very important that the company which employed me did not know of my past relationship with the Minister, nor under what circumstances that liaison had occurred. This could destroy the respect and esteem my husband enjoyed in the business community.

In France, such matters are less important. Later, when the ex-President Mitterrand was buried, his wife and his mistress walked together behind his coffin, and his illegitimate daughter later gained some notoriety as an author. In Australia, ethics follow the Anglo-Saxon pattern. Much later, when I was in Melbourne, I laughed at the Monica Lewinsky affair, because I was sure that she was not the only girl over the years to have given a blow job in the name of national service.

Pierre saw the traps and difficulties. In a French environment, there was no particular problem if his wife spent a few nights with a visiting foreign dignitary, in fact, considering my role in public relations, it would be almost understandable. Bernard Courtot was hoping it would happen, perhaps with a twinge of jealousy. But even a Frenchman would be disturbed to know that his employee's wife had worked as a prostitute in Australia.

Above all, we had to be careful to protect the honour of the Right Honourable Nigel Spencer. The important thing was that nobody from the media saw us together or took any photos. There were a lot of inquisitive cameramen around Cannes during the Film Festival.

To think things over, the following Thursday I spent a delightful afternoon with Sophie. We harvested apricots together, compared the merits of two different models of vibrator, and drank a little too much white wine. We were gazing in the wall length mirror and comparing the merits of her delicate A cup and my magnificent B cup when Marc came home. He put us immediately at ease by saying that we were both beautiful.

I assured him immediately that I was not a lesbian, nor was his marriage in danger. He answered by reminding me that he'd enjoyed first hand experience of my divine heterosexuality, and that his happiness in marriage with the glorious Sophie could not be challenged.

I must admit that Sophie had surprised me that afternoon. I recall my first impression of that stiff, upright little prude, and had been amazed by her sensuality, as well as the passion hiding beneath that sometimes aloof attitude. Once we were both in Australia, I thought I might meet her in Canberra one weekend to show her around.

⤷ ⤶

A few weeks later, Mr and Mrs Bernard Courtot and Mr and Mrs Pierre Duval received invitations to a cocktail party, offered by the Australian Ambassador in Paris, in honour of the visiting Minister, the Right Honourable Nigel Spencer. Naturally, they accepted.

In fact, Pierre received a phone call the day before and we had a private dinner with my favourite Minister that evening, in a small restaurant near *La Madeleine*. With Pierre's permission I wore the emerald bracelet Nigel had offered me as a farewell gift in Canberra and he recognised it immediately. He wanted our conversation to be frank and it was. He set out the conditions of our visit to Cannes, both official and personal. Pierre declared that he had no problems with either and Nigel shook his hand vigorously. Bookings had been made for the Minister and his interpreter, they would have, naturally, separate rooms, and on different floors.

It was then that Pierre surprised me. I was initially concerned with his advice to the Minister, but I realised that he had taken the right decision. He explained that one of the Trade Commissioners in Paris, Raymond Forbes, had been a regular client of Michelle's establishment in Canberra and had met 'Brigitte' several times. Inadvertently, during a conversation several months ago, I had made a passing reference to a special friend I had met in Canberra, and I had called him 'Nigel'. Since that date, Nigel Spencer had been appointed Minister and had asked for Marie Duval to accompany him to Cannes to act as his interpreter. Mr Forbes had reached certain conclusions. Nigel smiled.

"That is not a problem. I will speak to Mr Forbes tomorrow, and settle the matter."

"That might not be easy," I suggested. "Raymond can be quite, well silly, on occasions."

Nigel shook his head gently.

"I will tell him that we met socially on different occasions in Canberra. I will confirm that I have never heard of this 'Brigitte' person. I will also remind him of the fragility of a career in the Trade Commissioner's service, and how a good man can be moved from Paris to Nairobi in a few weeks, when circumstances demand a reshuffling of resources."

"I wouldn't like to see him reshuffled," I said softly. "He has been very helpful to me in Paris."

"I'm sure that he shares your concerns," Nigel assured me. "Now, let's talk about Cannes."

In fact, we listened. The Minister had organised two meetings with important people in the French film industry, as he had ambitions to see some co-productions with Australian companies in the coming years. We would also be seeing two Australian films, and he would be personally hosting one of the screenings. On the way to Cannes, we would be stopping in Lyon and Marseille to meet with the Chambers of Commerce and Industry. The ambassador and the senior trade commissioner would accompany us on those two visits, but we would go on to Cannes without them.

"This is not Raymond, then?" I asked.

"No, this will be his boss. When politicians are around and free trips are in the pipeline, the senior people suddenly find themselves with time on their hands. I used to be in the public service, I know."

"So Raymond won't think that we did not want him around?" Pierre asked.

"Of course not. He is used to being walked over by his superiors when an opportunity arises to be 'noticed' in the service."

Pierre looked relieved, and I am sure that I was looking just as happy. But my husband still felt embarrassed.

"I must say, and even tell you officially, if I may, that Raymond has been a great help to Marie and myself in our ambitions to get French companies to invest in Australia, and I venture to say, has undertaken things which are probably not in the diplomatic handbook."

Nigel grinned.

"You'd be surprised. The Trade Commissioner's handbook is very thick, and some of the Trade Commissioners share that quality. But I note your appreciation, and I thank you for telling me. If Mr Forbes behaves himself during my visit, he might find that politicians can also be quite helpful."

Then he turned to me.

"The most exciting thing is the trip itself. We are going to travel all the way on the *TGV* [1] — you know, the very fast train. It's something I have wanted to do for years. Then, to come back to Paris, we will be flying in a magnificent *Mystère 20*, on loan from the French government."

He sighed.

---

1. Train a Grande Vitesse (otherwise known as the 'Very Fast Train').

"I believe that we should have a Very Fast Train linking all our capital cities in Australia. Our continent is so deserted and flat, the machine would literally fly. But it will not happen. Do you know why?"

We shook our heads.

"Because it will only work once we have a national rail system and that will not happen tomorrow."

We laughed, but both realised that he was deadly serious. We put him in a taxi, back to the Embassy where he was spending the night. Just as the vehicle was leaving, he rolled down the window, and called out to the driver.

"Attendez, attendez, ne partez pas tout de suite." [2]

And then he stuck his head out of the window.

"By the way, don't quote me on that State government comment. The worst ones at the moment are being run by our own bloody party."

Pierre stepped forward.

"Je remarque que vous parlez bien le français, Monsieur le Ministre. Vous n'avez peut-être pas besoin d'interprète?" [3]

Nigel gave him that lovely smile that used to make my heart flip.

"I can't understand a word, mate."

Then he turned to the driver.

"Allez, dépêchez-vous, mon vieux. On ne va pas passer la nuit ici." [4]

℘   ℭ

---

2. "Wait, wait, don't leave straight away."

3. "I notice that you speak very good French, Minister. Perhaps you don't need an interpreter?"

4. "Come on, hurry up old boy. We're not going to spend the night here."

Bernard Courtot had wanted to buy me a couple of see-through nighties, but I told him that I always slept in the nude. Pierre assured him that I was taking with me clothes supplied by the company, each item designed to exude grace, competence and femininity. Then he added that Bernard was not going to get a cat walk show in the afternoon, and he would be better advised to take Madeleine out for a long, long lunch. Madeleine agreed.

80   03

It was the 16th of August 1991, when I kissed Pierre goodbye. The Minister, The Ambassador and the Trade Commissioner came to pick me up in a short convoy of two black Mercedes, the first one proudly flying the Australian flag on its front bumper bar. We went through three red lights on the way to the railway station. The difference between a diplomat and a regular Parisian, the Senior Trade Commissioner explained, is that the diplomat does not get fined for this type of infraction. I told him that it was of relatively little importance as most Parisians didn't pay their fines anyway.

We were escorted to the reserved coach of the train by railway officials who looked like South American generals. Then we were off, once out of the suburbs we were travelling at over 250 kilometres an hour. The Minister was like a schoolboy, enjoying every thrill, but the two diplomats tried hard to spoil his fun.

The Senior Trade Commissioner, whose name was Charles Bolding, was tall with a shock of thick red hair. His conversation wobbled between stories about Australia's wonderful successes in exports to France (namely, scallops) and some old and very doubtful jokes. The Ambassador, Tony Hardcock, was small and bald. I guessed, as a woman of the world, that his name was badly suited. He was mostly silent.

I commented to the Minister that we would probably meet a very small group of business people in *Lyon* and *Marseille* as we were in the middle of the summer holidays. The Ambassador and the Trade Commissioner frowned in unison, but I continued. I explained that half of France took its holidays in July, and the other half in August, so that the whole country practically closed down for two months in summer.

The Minister thanked me for that excellent information, and wondered whether the briefing material prepared by the Embassy had mentioned that. The two men sitting opposite us paled, and probably contemplated early retirement. The Minister then explained that, in any case, the scheduling of his visit during the European summer was unavoidable, due to prior commitments.

"My dear Marie… oh, may I call you Marie?"

I nodded, but thought, 'Nigel, stop it!'

"Thank you. Then please call me Nigel. Not in public, of course, but when we are together, just the two of us."

I looked pointedly in the direction of the two diplomats.

"Oh, that's fine. You can call them Tony and Charles. Is that all right, gentlemen?"

They nodded glumly, obviously not enjoying my presence, which was compromising their supposed role as local experts.

"There is so much to do and so little time," the minister added, and the diplomats nodded in agreement.

"I notice that you have some understanding of French," I said to Nigel and watched the diplomats writhe in pain.

The Minister smiled.

"I do speak a little, but in high level conversations, one must be careful not to use the wrong phrase at the wrong time.

That is why I will need you by my side, 24 hours a day, over the next week."

The Minister smiled.

"Do you know that I met Madame Duval, briefly in Canberra? We met at some official function, I can't remember where, exactly. She is a lady of great talent."

The ambassador nodded grimly. I had the impression that the Trade Commissioner was wondering whether this was an opportunity for a crude joke, then I saw his eyes cloud over. He probably had another ten years of service ahead of him, and opted for caution. If our two companions were to spend the rest of the journey just nodding in unison they were in danger of developing severe neck pains.

⁎ ⁎

Nigel and I were very careful in Lyon and in Marseille. The two diplomats were glued to us during the daytime and evening, and went to bed late. We met a small group of businessmen at the Chambers of Commerce and Industry, and the conversations, in true French tradition, were heavily punctuated with title-tossing.

The two diplomats tried desperately to assist with the course of the meetings, but Nigel wanted me to translate, and I wore, on each occasion, my little white dress. No French businessman would even bother with a foreign diplomat when I was wearing that dress, and I am sure that they had all decided that the Minister had excellent taste and that my services were not only linguistic.

Business cards and promises of follow-up were exchanged, as well as a few of the usual jokes about kangaroos and politicians. My Minister was charming, and seemed to be particularly enjoying himself in a French environment. I decided that I would have to ask him why he spoke French so well.

After the *Marseille* meeting, Charles and Tony flew back to Paris, while Nigel and I took a normal train to Cannes.

"Alone, at last," he sighed.

Cannes was magnificent, but terribly crowded. The waterfront and beach was invaded by young beauties of both sexes desperately trying to get themselves photographed. Nigel was quite amused that several strangers took photos of me, and suggested that the little white dress in Riviera sunlight was particularly revealing.

"They probably take you for some foreign movie star. You know, they think they recognise the body but can't put a name to it."

"You are very flattering."

We booked into the hotel and parted, the Minister for his luxurious suite on the fifth floor, me for my adequate room on the second. The Embassy had obviously decided that I was not going to be pampered, but I guessed that I was not going to be spending a lot of time in that room, in any case. I was wrong.

Nigel called me on the phone and asked if he could come down to see me, as he wanted to discuss preparations for a meeting with a French film producer. I agreed. Ten minutes later he appeared with a bottle of champagne, two flutes and a greedy smile.

"You're still dressed?" he asked.

"I thought we were having a meeting, isn't that what you said?"

"That was for the girl on the switch. I'd like our meetings in Cannes to be absolutely informal."

I pulled off my dress while he poured the bubbly.

"Magnificent. You are still as beautiful as when I used to meet you in Canberra. Speaking of which …"

An hour later, the champagne was warm and we had not yet mentioned even the name of the French producer. Nigel was in sparkling form, attentive to my needs, proud of his workmanship, beautifully erect. Our meetings in Canberra had always been a little genteel, but here in Cannes he was probably influenced by the French environment. He mounted me energetically, and laughed with delight when I announced my satisfaction.

We then sipped some lukewarm champagne, just to get our breath back, and then he stretched out and asked for a 'Brigitte special'. He was extraordinarily big and stiff, and I suspect that he had been preparing himself for this meeting with some medical supplements. I worked him well, bringing him two or three times to the verge of ecstasy, and then slowing him down. The fourth time, I took him all the way, and he came with a shout of delight.

Afterwards, I asked him about his knowledge of the French language and he told me that he had done a year of secondary studies in Lyon, as an exchange student. He laughed.

"I was only 16, and a lovely little blonde in my class took me out to the country and taught me how to make love. French girls are amazing."

"And you are still enjoying French girls," I noted.

"Only one," he corrected.

We did see a French producer or two, even a 'promoter' who asked if I would be interested in some secondary roles in a few small productions. I asked him whether it would entail wearing costume clothing, and he confirmed my suspicions by saying that if I accepted I would be wearing very little at all. Nigel was pretending not to understand and laughing inwardly.

We went to see a couple of films, one of which was Italian and very erotic. In the dark, I slipped an inquisitive hand across my neighbour's lap, and sighed with pleasure.

"I think I'd better get you back to the hotel," I whispered.

"Hang on a second," he begged. "That looks interesting."

"We'll do it tonight," I promised.

„’† ››

One evening after dinner, we retired to his bedroom and he raised the question of money. I had anticipated this, as he had always paid generously for my services in Canberra. I explained that in Paris I was not working as a call girl, but as a public relations consultant. In this case, it was my husband's employer who was paying me to look after his happiness. Poor Nigel found that a little discomforting.

"I know that your husband is an understanding man, but it embarrasses me. Also, I am concerned that the company thinks it will get some form of compensation by allowing me to have sex with a member of its staff."

I smiled.

"I am sure that's what Bernard Courtot thinks. And he doesn't know that we are having sex together, he's just hoping it will happen. Don't worry, my husband, who will be in charge of all operations in Australia, sees you as a close friend of his wife, who shares a common professional interest. He will probably ask you for advice or information, but he would never ask you to do anything non-ethical."

"Then why are we here together?" he sighed.

I laughed and pushed him back on the bed, hands working on his trouser belt.

"Because we enjoy having sex together, and it doesn't happen often enough."

An hour later, the phone rang and he picked up the receiver. It was the ambassador. While they talked, I continued to play, but very gently. The ambassador was being rudely inquisitive.

"Madame Duval?" Nigel said. "No, she's not here; I do believe she went out somewhere this evening. In fact, I'm rather pleased; I was hoping perhaps to organise a little entertainment for myself."

I could hear that the Ambassador was not amused. However, he was obviously totally unaware that while his Minister spoke, part of his anatomy was in close and loving contact with the elusive Madame Duval.

The ambassador rambled on for a few more minutes. The Minister nodded a couple of times, winked at me, but could not prevent a little sigh of pleasure, and the ambassador's voice stopped immediately.

"No, no, I'm sorry. You are not boring me; I'm just a little tired."

They exchanged a few courtesies and Nigel hung up. He roared with laughter and then proceeded to demonstrate that he was not tired at all. Never believe a politician!

I rang Pierre a couple of times, just to give him a little news. He was obviously terribly busy, there was a new investment project underway, and he only wanted to know if Nigel was happy and if I was not too tired. I confirmed that all was well.

It all ended too quickly, although I must admit that I was becoming eager to get back to my darling husband. Sex with Nigel is always good, but I was hungry for a little orthodox marital pleasure. The *Mystere 20* trip was very fast, and suddenly we were back in the world of officialdom. The Minister took the liberty of kissing his interpreter chastely on each cheek when parting company on the apron in Orly, and then it was all over.

I did receive a private phone call, the next day. Nigel knew we were going to Melbourne soon, and hoped that we would meet again in a few months. He asked if I had any professional plans, and offered to help if I was looking for a job. He was wonderfully kind and quite formal. It was just a nice conversation between good friends, and I knew that the line was probably not secure. I discovered, much later, that he'd had a drink with Pierre at the airport, before flying back to Sydney, and told him that I was the loveliest woman he had ever met. Pierre agreed.

ॐ ॐ

Before leaving Paris, I offered myself a last fantasy. I was about to turn 40, and although men still found me beautiful, I knew that the next few years would soon be leaving their mark. It was Pierre's crazy idea, but I accepted it tentatively.

At that time in France, people were using a National information system called 'Minitel', which was operated by a keyboard linked to the telephone. It was used to buy plane or train tickets, to check the weather or to book seats in theatres or restaurants. For others, it was a means of exchanging messages of love with complete strangers.

On the Minitel, I found Frederic. After a lot of cheeky banter and vain claims, he began to show definite interest. He pried, asked personal questions, boasted his own qualities, and insisted that we meet. Pierre sat beside me as I exchanged messages, and was surprised by some of the brazen, even outrageous, statements I made. Finally, Frederic begged to meet me. I told him that I lived in a nice apartment with my husband, and that Pierre was sitting there with me. Then I gave him my phone number. Generally, these Minitel conversations stopped well before this stage.

I loved his voice. He was obviously young, well-educated, and had a pleasant attitude. I told him I was 39, he confessed that he was only 23, and we both laughed. He said that he was eager to meet me, and I gave him our address. He lived close by and said he would be over in 20 minutes.

When Frederic arrived I was pleasantly surprised. He was beautiful: tall, slim, well-dressed and he had a seductive smile. He shook hands with us both and accepted a cup of coffee. As he sat down, I noted the small bag that he put on the floor beside his armchair. We exchanged harmless banter for about half an hour and he noticed that my eyes kept wandering to the little bag.

"It's a trimmer. I use it to shave my body."

"Why?" Pierre asked.

He smiled.

"Hygiene, I guess. Also, sex between two people with no pubic hair is an interesting experience."

"So why did you bring it here?" I asked, although I knew the answer.

"Because I was hoping you would like to try," he replied, simply, and with an engaging smile. "Would you like me to show you?"

Pierre smiled, and excused himself, ostensibly to make some more coffee in the kitchen. Frederic stood up and took off his clothes. When the groin is shaved, the penis is much more visible. I found that Frederic's sex, pointing straight at me, was terribly beautiful.

"You will notice that I lied," he said. "It's not 20 centimetres long, but, on the Minitel, people are inclined to exaggerate."

"I think it's beautiful," I assured him. "Would you shave me?"

"Sure. But you'll have to undress."

I took him up to the spare bedroom and left him there, slipping away to undress privately. Suddenly I was feeling shy. When I came back, Frederic and Pierre were sitting on the bed, drinking wine, instead of the promised coffee, and chatting. They both laughed when I walked into the room, and I was annoyed.

"You think I'm funny?"

Frederic shook his head.

"Oh, no, you are beautiful. But you forgot to remove one piece of clothing and if you keep that on, I won't be able to shave you."

I removed my panties and stretched out on the bed, parting my thighs to give him unrestricted access. The trimmer began to hum, and I felt the head, and his hands, moving softly across me. Occasionally, he lifted the tool, just to run his tongue gently across me. My vagina began to react to his attention, and he laughed.

"That's better," he exclaimed. "It certainly makes the job a little easier."

When he finished his job, I stood up and rushed to the bathroom to check his work. I came back to join the two men, still naked, face flushed.

"I feel more than naked," I complained. "If that's possible."

"But it is a wonderful opportunity to show your sex instead of hiding it," Frederic explained. "Would you like to try how it feels?"

He turned to Pierre.

"Is that okay?"

Pierre nodded.

"Go ahead. I'll fetch some more wine."

It was an extraordinary sensation. He was right, as our two bellies met, unencumbered by pubic hair. I found that the sensations of pleasure were accentuated. But, more extraordinary, I found that I was hopelessly enraptured by this handsome young man, and wanted him desperately.

There was no problem when Pierre came back into the room. Frederic continued to move inside me, and I continued to moan with pleasure. It was not often that Pierre could see me with another man, and I wrapped my legs around Frederic's waist to guide and encourage him, and this offered a more intimate view of my pleasure to my husband.

I reached a point where I began to beg him to finish me, digging my nails into his shoulders, pulling him in to me with my feet on his buttocks. He complied with my demands, still very gently, and I cried out with pleasure. As I came back to earth, I could see that Pierre was delighted.

"I'm not surprised that men love you," he exclaimed. "You are so beautiful, and you give yourself so generously. I think that this young man would be the perfect partner for our project."

Frederic was stretched out on his back, offering his nudity, I thought deliberately, to my husband. His attitude surprised me.

"What's the project?" he asked.

Pierre explained that he wanted to record my sexuality on video, and he thought it would be better to do this in Paris, before we went back to Australia. My husband thought that I was at the peak of my physical beauty and of my sexual enjoyment, so this was the right time. We were looking for a young partner, with good reserves. Frederic turned towards me and ran his fingers up my thigh.

"She is certainly quite beautiful, and she is a wonderful sexual partner. Is she very active, sexually, I mean?"

Pierre shook his head.

"Not really. We've been in Paris two, nearly three years. She's had sex two or three times with a couple of guys she knew in Australia, and she's looked after a couple of my business contacts. She likes sex, but she doesn't screw around, and we enjoy together a good sexual relationship."

Frederic nodded.

"For Paris, that's pretty reasonable. I guess that in Australia, that would be considered outrageous."

Pierre laughed.

"Very true. But then Australia is another world, even for Marie."

Frederic was thoughtful, but I could see that he was tempted. Pierre leaned forward, elbows on his knees.

"I need a total stranger who would be prepared to have two or three sessions, lending himself to her whims, while I use the camera. The film is for our private use, by the way, and we will be in Australia in about three months."

"And what do I get in return?" Frederic asked, playfully.

"Marie will cook a fine dinner before each shooting session," Pierre said, very simply.

The actual filming was completed over two Fridays, and took about three hours each time. Frederic would arrive for dinner, and he would be perfectly wined and dined. He would then stretch out on the bed and give his body to my hands, my mouth, and my sex. He was almost totally passive during the filming, and to Pierre's surprise, apparently able to restrain his ejaculations. Sometimes, I even became quite frustrated as he refused to deliver.

Sometimes, I would ride the handsome Frederic, sitting upright on his penis; at other times, I would be working his beautifully stiff cock with hands and mouth, moaning to him that his erection was magnificent. At all times, the inquisitive eye of the camera was on me, showing my eyes, my breasts, and even my sex as I rose and fell on his sword.

Now and again, he would take me in his arms and hug and kiss me, telling me that I was beautiful, stroking my face, caressing my breasts. Even these scenes of tender passion were recorded by my proud husband.

A few days later, we watched the film together. Frederic was proud, and we drank wine and laughed together. I never saw that young Parisian again, except on the odd occasion when I looked back at our film.

                                                      ഇ   ങ

It was in October 1992, just after my 40th birthday, that our stay in Paris came to an end. We packed and went to a few farewell parties and dinners. Madeleine kissed me. Bernard Courtot hugged me. Raymond cried.

12. Melbourne Becomes My New Home

I was pleasantly surprised by Melbourne. In some ways, it reminded me of Adelaide. It was another city whose inhabitants were attached to their European roots. In Melbourne, they did it better, because in winter you could almost imagine yourself in Europe. Like Adelaide, it did not have those magnificent Pacific beaches, which represent Australia in the eyes of the foreigner, and which are part of the everyday scenery around Sydney or Brisbane. We lived for ten years in Melbourne, and probably went to the beach four times.

Melbourne has probably more snobs per square kilometre than any other Australian city. There are streets where you *must* wander, shops where you *must* buy, markets where you *must* be seen, restaurants which you *must* frequent, and, above all, suburbs where you *must* live. I did not make a list of all the nice suburbs, but I do believe that Toorak, Prahran, Camberwell, Hawthorn, Box Hill, Malvern, Caulfield and Brighton are among the best. When you visit most of them you will wonder why they are so cherished: narrow streets, trams, noise, exhaust fumes, inadequate parking space. Of course, I have just explained why – it looks like Europe!

I must make a special mention of Brighton. This suburb, facing the bay, had houses worth well over $1 million. They looked out over a grey beach surrounded by scrub, washed by grey water while on the horizon a petrochemical plant offered an exotic backdrop. The palaces were separated from the waterfront by a two lane road with heavy traffic and enjoyed a light fragrance of diesel fumes from the semi-trailers going to Port Melbourne. On Sundays, the trucks were replaced by cyclists, some riding exclusive titanium frames and wearing the nicest gear. Just like Parisians.

After a few weeks, I discovered that there was another side to Melbourne. The low-income or no-income families seemed to settle to the west and north. Much of this pattern seemed to have been based on historical industrial activity, rather like the north of England or France, but now those industries are dead or dying.

The most populated part of Melbourne is the Eastern suburbs. Although the area is not as fashionable as the bayside suburbs, the surrounds are pleasant and the road network is excellent. Throughout this vast region, multi-lane main roads run north-south and east-west, and despite the density of population, the traffic flows well. This is a far cry from the despairing traffic jams of London.

Pierre and I found a nice house in a bayside suburb called Black Rock, which is a well-kept secret, but still quite exclusive. My husband then set about establishing the Melbourne head office and met, by extraordinary luck, a fine man, Paul Sterling, who would later be become his number two. Paul and Suzanne were to become our best friends, and I cherished their companionship.

As had been agreed with my darling husband, I would continue my research into prostitution, academically and physically, hoping that, one day, a publisher would be interested in my work. Melbourne was an excellent place to continue with my project, as it was one of the rare cities where the activities of sex workers were licensed, supervised, controlled and overseen. Admittedly, it also had the suburb of St Kilda where illegal street prostitution seemed to cause so many problems for some. But when Melbourne residents talk of the horrors of street life in this bayside suburb, I suspect that they have never delved into the dreadful ambience of Kings Cross, Sydney.

I realise now that there is a growing acceptance in many countries, but not in my homeland of France, that prostitution must be decriminalised and regulated. There is now a popular belief that illegal prostitution sponsors police corruption, supports other criminal activities and leaves sex workers without protection against human rights abuse. This is particularly true where prostitution is dependent on slavery, illegal immigration, or the exploitation of minors and children. It is obvious that the legalised environment in Victoria tries to address these issues.

I rang and visited half a dozen brothels in Melbourne, pretending to be a French author writing about legal prostitution in Australia. I did not mention that I was also looking for a new job. I was generally invited to come round early in the morning, when demand was slow. The brothels I visited were all in industrial estates, sometimes cleverly hidden from the ordinary passing traffic, but always offering a suggestive trade name. Many of the owners or managers were wary of what I would write about them, and were obviously not eager to see their professional activities discussed in a public forum. Others greeted me warmly and were happy to chat. Very few encouraged the workers to meet me, and most of the ladies seemed to deliberately avoid me, overcome by sudden shyness.

Some of the establishments I visited in the suburbs were converted houses, with basic facilities. But I visited two which, quite rightly, claimed to be most luxurious. In one instance, the house of pleasure was nestled in a pleasant park-like surrounding, but I was received on the doorstep, and not invited to cross the threshold. I visited another with a luxurious entertainment area, complete with grand piano. The rooms were spacious and beautifully, if erotically, furnished, and the owners even offered a small gymnasium where the ladies could work out when not undertaking more intimate exercises with their devoted clients.

The environment in Melbourne is quite special. One city-based bordello actually offers organised tours for local and overseas visitors; another is bidding for public investors. After these visits I began to feel more comfortable about working, at a later date, in this city. I would be offering professional sexual services within a legal and hygienic format.

During one visit, I was allowed to interview Cindy for my research. She was about 25, tall and very thin. She was wearing her working uniform, that is to say a mini-dress which had been designed to offer the punter an overall view of the goods on offer. As she talked to me, she shifted constantly on her chair, tugging at the hem of a dress which could hardly hide the fact that she was wearing white lace knickers. It was obvious that while she could probably show herself off well to a prospective client, she was embarrassed to be wearing such provocative clothing in front of another woman.

Her story was simple. A beaten child, she had left home at the age of 17 to live with a guy who also beat her. At 19, and with no formal education, she discovered that by working in the sex industry she could earn three times more than she was receiving as a cashier at K-Mart. Once she had become used to a better income, she spent and indulged herself accordingly, until she felt there was nowhere else to go. She admitted that she did not enjoy sex, that she did not give great satisfaction to her clients, and that there were 'real' professional prostitutes earning two or three times more than her in her establishment.

        ⁝ ⁒

Andy, a receptionist in another establishment, was the one who gave me the best analysis of what the situation should be between a brothel owner or manager and the people who sell sexual favours within the premises.

"It's a hotel," he explained. "The cheap and small brothels are just two star hotels with rooms. The big ones are the five star establishments with coffee bars, juke boxes, billiards tables, air-conditioning and spas. Nevertheless, the lucky punter might get a super service in a two star house, while a fistful of dollars will not always guarantee total pleasure in the up-market palace."

"If you ever get tempted, you'd be a knockout," he told me. "You have that look in your eyes."

I laughed and we went back to the interview. I made a mental note to come back to see him later.

Andy explained the commercial background to each operation. In the brothel-hotel, a visiting gentleman meets, individually, a few pleasant and well-disposed ladies. He discovers specific mutual interests with one of them, and together they decide that they would like to spend some time together, far from inquisitive eyes and ears. The brothel provides the room, the linen, the soft music and the hot water, but does not need to know what happens in the room. The sex workers are clients, not employees.

The system appears relatively simple, and closely related to the hotel-ex-brothel in Paris, but there were some discrepancies to Andy's theory. I noted that the room rental was always a fixed proportion of the gift offered to the lady by the visiting gentleman (often 50 per cent). In other instances, the rental might be higher if the visiting gentleman was interested in French or Greek culture, which contradicted his theory that the brothel owner would not need to know what was happening in the room. Nobody's perfect.

However, the theory does clearly demonstrate that the investor's returns are heavily based on two factors: the quality of the accommodation provided; and the beauty and talent of the house guests.

80   03

I was preparing a summary of my visits one glorious autumn evening, when Pierre announced that Claude was coming to dinner the following night. He was an old and close friend of my husband whom I had never met. I know that he had lived in Nouméa and that Pierre had subsequently caught up with him once or twice in Paris. Claude had arrived in Melbourne where he had been offered a job of marketing executive with a company exporting seafood to Japan.

I knew that Claude was divorced. He had been married to a girl whom Pierre had described as 'delightful' (which meant 'boring') and with whom he'd had two children. Unfortunately, at the age of 34, she had developed a great passion for spirituality, which had precluded, among other things, all sexual activity with her husband, but which had spiced family life with an intensified program of prayers and exaltations.

Claude had finally fled and filed for a divorce. He had buried himself in his work, marketing seafood, and had gone to Paris for two years to work in the import export business. He had apparently decided that he would exclude all women from his life, and I was not excited about preparing a good dinner for such an idiot. But Pierre was insistent, they were truly old friends, and Claude probably just needed to meet the right girl to get his hormones revving again.

"How about the little white dress from Paris?" I asked.

"Absolutely!" Pierre confirmed. "That would arouse a castrated monk."

I spent most of the afternoon concocting and preparing a menu to excite the tastebuds and, hopefully, stir the spermatozoids. Pierre had bought some nice Tasmanian wine and a bottle of All Saints matured port, so I knew that the evening would be relaxed.

Claude was expected at 6 pm but arrived at 7.30, blushing as he presented his lame apologies. I was preparing a sarcastic comment but was stopped in my tracks with dripping ladle in my hand; he was beautiful.

He was from the South West of France, and could not deny his Basque origins. He was dark-skinned with dark hair that was elegantly streaked with silver. He stood tall and slim, and his smile would have melted a nun's knees. He apologised about three times before I told him that I was simply delighted that he could come, even if it was a little late. After all, it was a Friday evening, so nobody had anything important to do the next day, and when Pierre served a second round of whiskies, with a wink to me, I knew that happiness was just around the corner.

Claude was an idealist. He admitted that he had not had a relationship with a woman since he had left his wife two years ago, and was in no hurry to build a new relationship. He wanted to wait for the right person to appear over the horizon, and explained that she should be beautiful, gentle, elegant, and have all the endearing qualities needed to make a man perfectly proud and happy. He was a little old-fashioned, but that can be nice, on occasions.

He added, with a wink, "And if she had a dress like that, I would be totally overcome."

Pierre laughed.

"It is a lovely dress, she bought it in Paris for some official functions."

Claude grinned, and showed that he was not as shy as I thought.

"A pretty frock is like an interesting job. It is totally dependent on what you put into it."

We all laughed. I decided that this friend was a person of quality, fine humour and good taste. He also enjoyed his food, and while the compliments and the wine flowed, I noticed that he was also enjoying my cleavage.

"This is delicious," he told me. "A bachelor rarely has the opportunity to enjoy fine food. You are a wonderful cook."

I had a sudden feeling that I might show him some of my other qualities before the night was over. I served raspberry mousse and Pierre opened the port. I could see that Claude's cheeks were flushed, and Pierre was looking worried.

"I don't think you should drive home," he suggested to his friend, after we'd finished dining.

"You're right. I'll get a cab back to the hotel."

I smiled, like a hungry cat gazing at an over-plump mouse.

"You can use our spare room. It's a bit crowded, but the bed's comfortable. Come and see."

We all wandered down to the 'spare room' which was, in fact, the largest room in the house. Pierre and I both used it as a study, and we had installed a desk, where my computer was set up, as well as two bookcases, a couch, an old TV and a double bed. Claude was impressed.

"If it's not putting you out, I'd love to sleep here. Have you got any computer games?"

Pierre laughed.

"Nothing exciting. But it's Marie's computer, nobody else is allowed to touch."

"That's not true!" I protested. "Would you like to see my project?"

Pierre went to fetch our glasses and I showed Claude the research I was undertaking. He was obviously fascinated.

"This is important to you, isn't it?" he asked.

"Very important. I hope to get it published one day."

He looked at me quizzically.

"Do you have somebody you know in the business?"

"Yes, a close friend. If and when you read the finished book, you'll understand. Do you know how to play Solitaire?"

Pierre sighed.

"I'll get you both a nightcap, and then I'm off to bed. Marie has a passion for this damned game."

I grabbed a second chair, sat Claude next to me, and opened the appropriate menu. He picked it up quite quickly, but was frustrated at not having a win. I moved a little closer, and had my hand on his thigh when Pierre came back with the glasses.

"For God's sake don't get too involved. She can spend hours trying to score."

"Don't worry, I won't," Claude assured him.

We played alternative games, and soon I had won three. He had still had no success when I decided to slip away.

"I think I'll go and have a shower before bed," I announced.

He looked disappointed and I knew he had been enjoying the view down the front of my dress when I leaned forward to play with the mouse.

"Come and see how I'm going before you tuck in," he suggested.

I promised that I would.

I had a hot and revitalising shower, in our small ensuite bathroom, while Pierre chattered about his friend. I dried myself vigorously, and pottered around a little, making some secret preparations. Finally, I walked into the bedroom. I had slipped into a short red silk kimono, but had left it open, leaving my breasts and my sex visible. Pierre gazed over his book and sighed.

"What are you up to? Are you coming to bed now, or am I going to have to come and fetch you?"

I smiled.

"Claude asked me to pop back to see how he was going with the game before I went to bed."

Pierre laughed loudly.

"Did he now? I think he might have been expecting to see something more demure."

I walked forward, took his hand, and slid it across my sex.

"I tried to shave a little, but I may have taken too much off. Is it prickly?"

He stroked me softly, slipping his finger into the place he loved.

"I don't think he'll mind, to be honest. I'll see you soon then."

"I won't be long," I promised.

"Take your time," he murmured, returning to his book.

Before entering the spare room, I ensured that the kimono was widely open. I wanted Claude to have a good impression. He gasped when I walked into the room.

"How are you going?" I asked, slipping into the chair next to his.

He seemed to have trouble breathing.

"I think I need a few more tips," he whispered.

I slipped my chair a little closer to his, our legs now touching.

"We'll play alternative games," I suggested. "You take the mouse first."

He began and as he progressed, I offered a few suggestions.

"Look, you can move the nine of diamonds under the ten of clubs, see?"

As he played, my hand rested on his thigh and began to move upwards, very slowly. By the time he had placed the four of clubs under the five of hearts, I had discovered magic.

"That's wonderful," I whispered. I wasn't talking about his game, and he knew it.

"It's your entire fault," he whispered back, proving the point.

Then it was my turn to play. I was disappointed that he was taking little interest in the game I was developing, but I loved the way his hands cupped my breasts.

"You should look at what I'm doing," I admonished.

My kimono was now on the floor. He continued to stroke my breasts with his right hand, and had placed his head on my shoulder.

"I'm watching all the time," he assured me.

Three games later, his clothes were on the floor and we were still pretending to play. He was holding the mouse without really looking at the screen, and I was softly stroking his magnificent erection.

"I don't think you'll score tonight," I warned him.

He grinned.

"I think I might."

Then, to my surprise, he picked me up and carried me over towards the bed.

"I hope Pierre is not going to pop in," he said.

"He's asleep," I answered. "But if you're worried, you can slip the latch."

He did. Then he was on top of me in a second, inside me, and he was enormous. I enjoy a little foreplay, but I realised that it had been a long, long time, between drinks.

"This is unbelievable," he murmured in my ear. "I'm going to try to take it slowly, or I'll explode straight away."

"Just enjoy yourself," I suggested. "You can always come back for seconds."

We moved slowly together for around half an hour, stopping regularly to avoid his ejaculation. We kissed softly, several times. Finally, I begged him.

"Please come Claude, I want to feel you come."

He stopped, and then withdrew himself slowly.

"I'm sorry. You are the wife of a good friend. I cannot come in you. That would not be right."

I pushed him back on the bed and sat up.

"I'll show you some of my other skills," I suggested. "I've done a lot of research. I know what I'm doing."

And then I went to work. I could hear him murmuring in amazement as his favourite member disappeared inside my mouth. It took little time to relieve Claude of several months of frustration. He hugged and kissed me for several minutes, before I asked an important question.

"Would you like to try again?"

He accepted immediately, and this time undertook his duties with more determination. The bed was actually squeaking in rhythm with his efforts, and I thought of poor Pierre who was trying to sleep just the other side of the thin wall. I would make it up to him afterwards, I promised myself, but for the moment I was having far too much pleasure with handsome Claude.

"Please, come for me," I begged him, and this time he could not refuse. Ten minutes later he was fast asleep, a smile of delight on his face. I kissed the corner of his mouth and slipped back into my bedroom, where Pierre was waiting.

"I thought the bed was going to give in at one stage," he commented dryly. "By the way, where's your kimono?"

I had forgotten it in the other room, but for the moment there were more urgent matters to attend to.

"You must take me now, please!" I begged my husband. "I need you."

Pierre never asked silly questions. He was ready for the fray and slipped inside me, commenting that I was terribly wet. I knew from my experience in Canberra and Paris that Pierre delighted in possessing his wife after she had been taken by another. I believe that it is a form of jealousy he will not recognise, but I enjoy every minute. Pierre began to moan, then he came and I cried out with pleasure.

"I hope he is sleeping soundly," my darling commented a few minutes later. "He might think that he did not make you happy."

I smiled in the darkness.

"I'm sure he is," I assured him.

Claude accepted a quick cup of coffee the next morning, but refused anything to eat. He looked very embarrassed. Then it was time to go, and the two men shook hands and I gave him a warm kiss on the cheek.

"I'll be leaving in about ten days," he explained. "The company wants me to work from its Sydney office."

"You must come and say goodbye," I suggested as I accompanied him to the door.

He never called.

                        80   08

I decided it was time to revert to what I wanted to call my 'physical' research. I decided that I would not work in a brothel too close to our own suburb, just in case the local butcher or newsagent popped in for a quickie. That would be embarrassing. But I wanted to stay in the South-East region of Melbourne because it was there I would find a wider spectrum of houses of pleasure, each with a different type of client. Also, I would continue to work daytime shifts.

I concentrated my research on the Cities of Kingston and Dandenong, which had the larger suburbs, and the largest concentration of industrial activity in Australia. My research had taught me that in Melbourne there were three categories of brothels: the upper class, for wealthy businessmen and overseas tourists; the middle class which generally served the needs of the white-collar community; and the lower class, which served the workers. The area where I wanted to work had a good selection of middle and lower class brothels, and I would aim for the middle of the road.

Because my experiences are recent, I will not mention the names of the places where I worked. I do not wish to denigrate, nor do I wish to offer free promotion.

The brothel I visited, one Friday morning, was in a beachside suburb. It was well furnished, attractive, and dreadfully, dreadfully busy. I decided that I did like a few breaks during the day, and this was not the place for me.

My next port of call was further south, in a large industrial estate, and not very far from the bay. It was beautifully fitted out, but seemed to be ignored by the punters. The girls there told me they would be lucky to have three clients each in a day. Maybe they were trying to scare me off.

80   03

In March of 1994, to encourage my passionate research, Pierre updated my computer and we connected to the internet where I found much more information about my industry. He read my work two or three times a week, and was most impressed. I discovered, for example, that it is difficult to determine the true volume of the industry in Victoria because of the number of illegal operations.

However, the illegal industry would probably not make much difference to overall turnover, as the illicit operations are generally short-term and cater for the same clientele. There may be official figures on the industry, but I have not found any. I can also confirm that I found no trace of industrial disputes, fraudulent or unfortunate commercial failures, takeover bids, State or Federal Government incentives or grants.

I tried to find out how the law defines 'prostitution'. Generally, it is described as vaginal, anal, oral or manual sex between persons of the same or different sexes for financial gain. I am sure that there were many task forces and strategic seminars held within the legal and public services to produce this short and bleak statement.

It led me to ask myself certain questions. When does a speculative investment in a box of chocolates, a bunch of flowers or a hamburger and fries become a 'fee for service' (if a successful outcome is obtained)? A girlfriend in Paris told me that when she dined out with another person, she always insisted on going 'Dutch' (although she was French), thus avoiding any suggested ultimate obligation on her behalf.

My research led me to the Department of Fair Trading, and although nobody believed my story about a literary project, somebody finally sent me the legislation concerning prostitution in the State of Victoria. I must confess that I had many problems trying to understand the archaic and stilted language, and so most of the research I did on the legal environment was with the help of my husband, Pierre, in the evenings.

I soon found out that not every sex worker or every house with pink curtains and a safety camera was licensed and approved. After all, every trade, profession or industry had its shady operators, why should the delivery of physical pleasures be any different, particularly with the advent of the GST? Yes, I discovered that the GST did apply to a blow job!

There was a fair amount of government initiative, intervention or persuasion in all of these wonderful developments during the 1980s and '90s, but we did not see the appointment of a Minister for Brothels, nor did we see the Premier laying the first stone of the House of Eternal Joy.

80   03

In September 1993 I decided to reduce my weekly service to three days, while staying faithful to the same premises, where I had built up a clientele of faithful lovers. I told Pierre that this would allow me more time for my research and writing, and that my 'visitors' would adapt. He laughed and noted that I was now becoming a cynical businesswoman. I worked in the same haven of love for nearly ten years. It was middle to lower class, it needed a good lick of paint, but the girls were friendly, the owner was a chatterbox, and many of the clients were absolute darlings. It was far from being top class, but it was also far from being the pits.

Within a few months, I became one of the most popular consultants on the job. I was good looking, friendly, sensual, comforting, and I gave satisfaction every time. I did try Sundays for a few months but gave up: sitting around for hours, often being the only girl on the job, waiting for a visitor, was too boring.

I noted every day I worked during those ten years. Each day I wrote down the number of guests I entertained, the length of each booking (from 15 to 60 minutes) and my gross and net income for the day. I also had a little code concerning some of my visitors and my special pleasures. But these will remain my secret. That part of my diary will not go into my story; it would be far too boring. I will simple tell you of the special events of my career, and above all about the special people I met.

The girls I work with all say that while the profession may be legal and licensed, it still carries a great stigma. Most of the sex workers I met were angry with society's attitude towards them. The profession has been active for thousands of years and has always met the needs of men and women from varied cultural backgrounds. One Filipino girl told me this stigma was just 'typical Anglo-Saxon hypocrisy'.

"I know guys who love what I do for them, who swear that they love me as they bang away, but who would spit on me if they met me in the street," she lamented. "I'm Asian."

I must add that there are two categories of visitors for each girl: the 'one-offs' whom you saw only once and who never come back, and the 'regulars', the ones I called secretly '*mes chéris*'.

There is often a little heart flutter of excitement when I meet a new client. Will this bring something different, something new? Or, more importantly, will he be a 'one-off' or become a new season's ticket holder? When you have worked several years, you find yourself with a large group of regular visitors, many of whom become boringly monotonous and painfully faithful. It's like multiple marriages. That's why a total stranger brings, occasionally, a breath of fresh air.

Some men may only pay one visit to a brothel in their lives, and you were simply in the right place at the right time. There are others who work on the principle of never visiting the same girl twice, either because they are motivated by the need for variety, or because they fear becoming sentimentally attached. Then there is the last category, those who were not satisfied: you were too fat, too thin, too chatty, too blonde, or you just refused to do what they wanted.

I told Pierre that my research led me to believe that in other times, and well before Thatcherism, we might have seen the establishment of State-owned brothels, which already existed in medieval Europe. We sat down with a bottle of wine one evening to develop, tongue in cheek, our own fantasy world of sex services being offered by the State public service.

Jobs would be scarce, we thought, on the interview panels whose duty would be to test the aptitudes of candidates for new positions (professional and physical). Would promotion be based on performance or be dependent on newly acquired skills? Of course, the training programs would be written by an expensive consultant. But who would judge if they were appropriate? How would the unions have handled inter-department transfers? Imagine a *Madame* being appointed Senior Trade Commissioner, or a clerk from the Department of Agriculture & Fisheries being moved to the National Brothels Services Commission. Flexibility, adaptability – such is the public service.

$$\text{\textcyrillic{80} \quad \textcyrillic{03}}$$

My research allowed me to better analyse my daytime job and my little darlings, some of whom came to visit me regularly for several years. Such customer fidelity is not unusual: I had a colleague who welcomed the same gentleman twice a week for many years. She reckoned that she had sex with him more often than with her own husband, and I can believe her.

A client named Ted made love with me practically every Wednesday morning at 11 o'clock for about six years. He was a widower who had loved his wife most dearly, but he discovered after about a year of solitude that he needed a woman. I became that woman, by sheer good fortune.

Another client, Tom, started after 11 years of marriage, and two children. He'd had a vasectomy to avoid his wife being obliged to undertake any form of birth control. For this reason, we enjoyed unrestrained and unfettered sex together, or, if you prefer, Tom was the only visitor with whom I had sex regularly without a condom.

$$\text{\textcyrillic{80} \quad \textcyrillic{03}}$$

Later in 1994 I met a new regular client who was to visit me every fortnight for five years. He was a Frenchman called Robert, who worked for a large French company and swore that I was the only woman with whom he was intimate during his stay in this country.

Like all my special visitors, I offered him oral sex without a condom, but the rubber was always ready for the final rush down the straight. While he was gentle, loving and generous during our meetings, he always insisted that to conclude he should be allowed to mount me vigorously. Like many of my clients, he liked to take me kneeling on the bed, while he stood, holding my hips firmly, to ensure his domination. He was so determined that he broke the condom on two occasions!

It was wonderful to be able to chat in French, my mother tongue, and like most Frenchmen, Robert was always careful to ensure that I had as much pleasure as him.

13. My Career Continues

In 1996, I told Pierre that I wanted to stay on in my work. He agreed, as he also planned to stay for at least another five years, and hoped that we would see the Sydney Olympics before Bernard Courtot called him back to France. I was also doing a workout in a local gym, twice a week, and was proud to receive flattering compliments from clients 20 years younger than me. Pierre declared that at the age of 46 I was a raving beauty. I agreed, totally.

∳   ∴

With many of my men, I had enjoyment, but I should qualify my use of that word. Tom, for example, was not a master of the art. We cuddled, we chatted, sometimes he talked about his wife for a while, then he would tell me how beautiful I was and I would know that he was about to climb aboard. He liked an early appointment with me, because he hated to take me after I had entertained other visitors. Early in the morning, I was in some ways his virginal mistress, and he preferred to ignore the services I might render to other men, once he had departed.

Another long-term visitor, although not as frequent as Tom, was Mark, the physiotherapist. To judge by the 5 series BMW he left in the car park, this little darling was not without means. If he had been a Parisian, he would have adopted a mistress. In Melbourne, he had me. Generally, our frolics always began with a wonderful massage, and he always succeeded in making me feel totally relaxed for the rest of his stay and for the rest of my day.

According to my diary records, he visited me more than 30 times. I knew that our gentle relationship was coming to an end the day he deliberately came inside my mouth without warning. He apologised afterwards, but I took him with pleasure because of the great affection which had grown between us.

                                                         80   CB

One evening, Pierre and I explored the *Yellow Pages*. We found ESCORT SERVICES, appropriately placed between ESCALATORS and ESSENCES AND FLAVOURING. Up you go, in you go, and out it comes.

For some reason, the classification BROTHELS did not exist but had been included in ADULT PRODUCTS OR SERVICES, itself appropriately placed between ADOPTION INFORMATION SERVICES and ADVENTURE TOURS. This could be why our receptionist received occasional calls from people looking for vibrators. She always provided an appropriate address and added that if the caller could not work out the operating instructions, he could come round and one of the ladies would be happy to help.

                                                         80   CB

Camilla, my favourite receptionist, told me about the boss she had when she was 19, in a high class house in the inner suburbs. During the job interview, the manageress told her that long-term business was based on a clean, neat, discreet household and ladies who were well dressed and kept their promises. She was told that she had to look elegant and distinguished, but, once in the room, was expected to 'fuck like a trooper'. Regular clients love that contrast, she was assured. The boss was right.

But not always. Camilla also remembers that same boss blowing her top when a girl called in to say she would not be at work that day. She was calling from the bedside of her child who'd had a serious accident.

"She could have chosen some other time to get her fucking kid killed!" the woman screamed from behind the desk.

80 03

The most wonderful lover I met in Melbourne was Johnny, another taxi driver. He walked in from the car park one day, looked at me and said that I was the woman he was hoping to meet. Each session began with his greatest joy, showing me how much pleasure he could offer me with his mouth and his tongue. He would book me every time for an hour, and would ensure that I had two or three massive orgasms each time. My pleasure was such that on his first visit Danni, my manageress, was close to breaking into the room, frightened that I was being beaten. I had to explain afterwards, blushing, that few men had ever had such an effect on me.

Once Johnny was sure that I was totally exhausted and satisfied, he would then decide that it was my turn to offer him oral pleasure. When he wanted to take me, I would slip a condom on to his lovely erection, without using my hands, sliding it down his stiff shaft, centimetre by centimetre, with my lips and teeth. He visited me eight times, and then he disappeared. For several weeks I spent many unoccupied hours standing at the back window, hoping to see his yellow taxi arrive.

ജ 🙰

I had a very long and gentle relationship with a wonderful man who was born on the island of Mauritius. Roger became a lover, a friend and a confidant. It was another case of the Catholic wife, and once again I became, in some ways, his mistress. He talked a lot about his family, his two sons and his daughter, his sister, and after a few years I found myself thinking of them as if they were members of my own family. Most people of his generation in Mauritius have continued to maintain their links with the French language, and we always chatted in French. After a few months, I realised that Roger was promoting my services within the Mauritius community, and at one time I had eight regular visitors of that origin.

ജ 🙰

Men who come to visit brothels may have sex with the girls, but do not know them as well as they may think. They see us with our working clothes and make-up, everything which is made to excite and entice them and make them believe that they will be having a good time with the lady of their final choice. Sex workers offering services to capture a punter are a little like politicians trying to win elections: they make promises they do not always deliver.

I, Marie, have always delivered what I promised. It was easy, because I never promised something I would later refuse to do.

But I am not unique. Often, I have been surprised by the quality of my co-workers over the years. Of course, there are others, those who think that vulgarity, foul language and crudeness is what the client wants. But there are a lot of gentlemen who like a little class, and luckily it is not too difficult to find.

There are also a lot of aggressive, rude, arrogant visitors who try to treat the prostitutes like animals. A good manager sends them packing if a girl complains of physical or verbal abuse. But not all brothels have good managers.

At one time, we had a lesbian who came to work with us. Personally, I could not understand how a truly homosexual woman could provide a good service to a male client. I do know that these girls never stayed for very long, and that there were a few heated telephone conversations and some loud screaming sessions in the car park now and again, when 'butch' came to pick up her girl. From what I saw, it seems that homosexuals were more likely to see the workplace put severe stress on their relationships than heterosexuals.

My colleagues jokingly called me the 'island girl', because I found myself adopted by another community; the immigrants from Sri Lanka. I had, at one time, 11 lovers from that country. Once again, Sam, this time a car salesman, was the first I met, and he was so happy with my services that he generously introduced me to a few friends. I confessed one evening to Pierre that the men from Sri Lanka, as a race, were the world's most accomplished lovers. Laughingly, he offered to take me to Colombo on holiday to test my theory, and I assured him that I would be delighted with the idea.

80 C3

I developed a good understanding with one of my co-workers, Julia. We both had our preferred visitors and neither poached on the other girl's territory. We both made our visitors happy, because we knew what they wanted and we did it well. I think it is fair to say, also, that we both enjoyed sex. I did not realise how much we had in common until we started doing 'twin' jobs for clients.

I quickly realised that Julia was quite happy to have sex with another woman, so I could probably safely say that she was bisexual. We played together, for the man's joy, and all was simply an exchange of stimulating caresses. Most of the time I was on the receiving end, and often I could not hide my pleasure from the excited male spectator. Then she would fit the condom into place and tell him to take me. As he rode me, she would excite him, tease him and encourage him.

Camilla, the receptionist, has some firm opinions on the way our business should be operated. We both agree that success depends very much on the state of the premises: firstly, the presentation, comfort and cleanliness of the establishment; secondly, heating in winter and air-conditioning in summer are vital.

We have been begging Danni to put in air-conditioning here, without success. Sliding up and down on a lazy gentleman's shaft of pleasure when the thermometer is tickling 38 degrees celsius can make a girl sweat, believe me. And, unfortunately, some guys love sweat. Jasmina, who does a five-day week, reckoned that she lost eight kilos last summer.

I told Camilla that I thought hygiene was an important issue. The sex workers and their patients need to feel comfortable and to know that the linen is clean and sanitised. We also talked about 'safe sex', which every brothel must announce as standard practice. But then how does Danni know that every girl always uses a condom with every client? Some, like me, will offer an oral or manual service without the little rubber charmer, but only if the partner is well known. But there are girls who will let the guy do whatever he wants without protection. When you are in urgent need of a 'fix', some rash whispered promises can be made. I agree with Camilla that a guy who asks for that is asking for trouble anyway.

℘   ℭ

When I arrived in the house of pleasure, there were two 'stars' working there; one of Spanish origin, the other English. I call them the stars because, between them, they entertained about seven visitors out of ten. They knew their job and they did it well. After a few months, I was beginning to give them a bit of competition, and the boss loved this. Then Stella, the English girl, ran away and married one of her clients, and I became a leading star.

There were many visitors who had simple needs. Some would simply like to hold me, lying face-to-face, and they would stroke my body while I stroked their manhood. They loved coming on my breasts or allowing me to watch their ejaculation. There were men who were totally amazed to see my own excitement as they climaxed, and to hear my groans of pleasure as the warm fountain of joy burst forth. I cannot explain why I find this moment so beautiful.

℘   ℭ

During my ten years of sex work in Melbourne, I learned many things: not about sex itself, but about those who provided it. Between clients, I would chat with my fellow workers or listen to conversations, and what I learned or heard made some interesting contributions to my research.

When we are not offering great joys and infinite pleasures to gentlemen, we sit around in the lounge. There is an old TV that grinds out rubbish that nobody watches; we drink tea or coffee and some of the girls smoke. Cissy paints her toenails, Diana picks her nose, Fanny scratches her buttocks, and we all talk. Julia, who has been in the business for many years, made me laugh one day by saying that she had seen 'more pricks than a dartboard in an Irish pub'. Their stories helped me greatly in understanding the hidden face of the industry.

14. Philosophy in a Brothel

My research, my job, and my husband's support and encouragement have allowed me to analyse my environment and to develop some personal beliefs and convictions about prostitution. Many of the professional and legalised sex workers I was employed alongside with go to the hairdresser, browse the same music shops as you, and visit the nicest coffee shops in Lygon Street or Southbank. Some have nice clothes, and I know one who has a swishy convertible. It is even possible that you have shared a secret and admiring smile with someone you took for a real estate agent, a financial consultant, a lovely mother, a lawyer or a TV actress, without realising that yesterday she was giving a blow job to a total stranger.

But the wealthy or successful sex workers are a minority; and most working girls are working class. You are more likely to meet them at Coles, MacDonald's or Big W, dressed in a t-shirt and jeans, looking tired and harassed, often with a couple of kids in tow. Outside of 'the job', they don't aim to please and often have a poor opinion of the average male.

Pierre has his own ideas about sex workers. He says that people who are good at figures become accountants, petrol-heads sell motor cars, lovely ladies aspire to being models or beauticians, and people who are sexually alert and gifted may decide for a few years to offer sexual pleasures. In fact, it's not always the case.

Some do it badly because they hate the job, and they are the ones who do not get many clients. It is the same in any other industry: commitment and professionalism pays. There are also tax consultants, public servants or hairdressers who hate their jobs but need to earn a living.

I told Pierre that sex workers are often like tennis champions: they need to earn a lot of money while they are young and active. Unfortunately, they do not enjoy the same late-life career opportunities, unlike the sports star who can open a retail shop selling appropriate accessories, or may become a coach for a group of snotty teenagers.

I must also tell you that some ladies I met have worked on the job for more than 30 years, and their experience and professionalism attracts most of the regular visitors. Sometimes I would hear the young chicks complain when another stranger chose me rather than their skinny teenage figures in miniskirts. The reason was in the provision of the service. All my clients left with a smile on their faces.

There were times when I would have liked to be able to talk to others, like Paul and Suzanne Sterling, about my job. After all, a sex consultant is not unlike a motor mechanic or any other trades person. They are both professional people attached to the service industries, licensed to operate a business. They work legally, pay taxes and make Medicare contributions like everyone else. Unfortunately, there is no Institute of TAFE offering Courses in Advanced Harlotry.

Sex consultants do it the hard way, learning on the job and doing what comes naturally. I have met those who HATE sex, those who simply know that it can be the fastest way to make a fast buck, and then there are those who ENJOY sex. I believe that it is the latter group which actually makes the most money.

I believe that as part of The Great Plan, the Creator decided to produce all Earthly species with sexual organs destined to extend and promote the race. That is good. But why did She have to add the Orgasm to the Organ? It is perhaps because without this, male humans, horses, goldfish and giraffes would not bother to ensure the continuation of their species.

What we do know is that most members of the human race, male or female, have always sought to enjoy the sensual pleasures of sexual stimulation, without necessarily wishing to have children every time. I know that the Pope does not agree, but he is not married, nor has he ever had to bring up screaming kids.

There are women who do not wish to reproduce and who do not wish to use a condom, often for religious reasons. Many have no desire to drop their knickers when the nearest male clicks his fingers. On the other hand, there are single women who do not wish to pick up a guy in a club or on the street, but who would be prepared to pay for safe sex. Few brothels cater for heterosexual women, but the escort services do now cater for their needs.

I know that there are many males who are either single, widowers or divorced. I can well imagine that often they do not want to waste time and money courting a woman in the hope of having sex with her a few weeks later, if all goes well. Dating is a long, sometimes expensive process, and often leads to deceptions or false expectations. They are BUSY, they have COMMITMENTS, they have CAREERS to nurture, a STATUS to massage. Some guys

HATE foreplay, DESPISE courting, or are AFRAID of the boredom of monogamy. The brothel provides a fast, friendly and hygienic solution to all these lonely men.

I remember a colleague telling me that one of her previous brothel managers occasionally kicked her in the ribs for fun. When she complained, she was told to 'shut her mouth, because she was only a fucking tart.' One day, her drunken husband punched her in the face and told her the same thing.

There are guys who come to a brothel, treat the girls roughly, throw in a few insults and tell them that all the other tarts do it better, and without condoms. These are the men who go to the pub or the club and, after a few beers, make crude jokes about sex workers or swear they have never paid for a service. In fact, they are perhaps regular customers, but only after a beer or two.

I was told that the best thing was to suffer the insults and the harshness in silence, happy to know in the end that you are taking the pig's money. Yes, you may suggest that there is recourse for sexual vilification. You must be joking. How can a whore complain about being called … a fucking whore? That's exactly what she is.

It takes guts, courage, patience and perseverance to persist in the profession. Add the crude jokes, the insults and the stigma, and you might begin to wonder why the career exists. The reply is simple: it has been servicing the basic needs of humanity for several thousand years. And making money.

My husband, Pierre, loves English literature, and once told me how Shakespeare understood all the hypocrisy behind the rejection of prostitutes from society. He gave me this from King Lear:

"Thou rascal beadle, hold thy bloody hand
Why dost thou lash that whore? Strip thine own back:

> *Thou hotly lust'st to use her in that kind*
> *For which thou whip'st her."*

I think this means "Don't whip the tart you wish you had enough guts to use." A literal translation from an ignorant French woman who cannot understand medieval English!

In my opinion the term 'sex industry' is not a good expression to apply to prostitution. It would be better used to describe businesses which manufacture artificial penises, eight-speed stereophonic vibrators or other stimulants. However, in this case, it concerns the provision of sexual relief or satisfaction to the needy, the depraved, the lonely, the rejected, the perverts or the sex-fiends, in legal and hygienic conditions, almost always along the officially prescribed guidelines. It is a service, a wonderful service, almost good enough to be covered by Medicare.

It is why I like to say that those who dispense pleasures are 'sex consultants', for their educational input, or 'sex practioners', for their contribution to the fight against stress and aggression.

There is a very old French joke which describes the scorn with which some people treat sex workers and how the latter may be tempted to retort. The joke is set in a large country town, where a 'nice' woman, full of moral convictions, jumps out of her car and angrily approaches a street walker to ask, "What kind of man would have anything to do with a bitch like you?"

And the sex worker replies, "Well your father, when he can afford it, your brother René who works at the Post Office, quite often, your husband twice a year and, would you believe it, last week I saw your son, the second one, Henri, for the first time."

Eva Rosta, the English sex worker, pointed out that all employment required that the worker use a part of his or her body: brain, hands, arms, legs, etc. To be different, or complimentary, she opted to add her vagina to the list.

80   03

Why is it that when a sex worker is raped, it is almost considered as an occupational health and safety issue? I doubt whether she or he would put in a claim to Work Cover. But if the victim were a school teacher, or any other 'honourable' member of the community, there would be a media outcry.

80   03

I talked about my research to some of my colleagues, when we sit around waiting for the next client to turn up. They often talked to me about the nice guys, the bad guys or the idiots who share our lives. Monday is the day some ladies are really happy to get back to work. It can be more enjoyable having sex or a cuddle with a total stranger rather than being bullied, kicked or insulted by the father of your kids.

Others talk of the past. Jan and Betty have been in the trade for several years. They were part of a team of 'lovely ladies' who went to Pentridge every year, just before Christmas, to put on a dance and strip show for the boys. I wonder whether today's experts in social welfare would consider adding this to their rehabilitation programs.

Brenda worked in a brothel in Brunswick, 20 years ago, where the rooms were upstairs. The Vice Squad would pay routine visits and when the constabulary arrived on the ground floor, buzzers would go off in the rooms. The girls and their customers would dress hastily and climb out of the windows to sit on the roof until the cops departed. The starting price in those days was $10 for three minutes. Each room had a mattress on the floor and a bowl of water with a sponge to check out and clean the visitor's tool kit. Most girls had managers called 'pimps' or 'hoons'. If charged with living off the earnings of a sex worker, they could face heavy fines and even imprisonment.

Danni once worked in a house where the owner believed that some of the ladies operating out of her premises were unreliable. She remembers, in particular, Wendy who called in one morning to say that her grandmother had died and she would be away for a few days. The manageress pointed out that the grandmother must be in very poor health, as she had already died three times that year.

"I know," said Wendy. "But this time I've got a death certificate to prove it."

The same owner discovered on opening one morning that the building was without water. A quick solution was needed to solve the problem, as water is an essential item for a clean house. The mystery was soon solved, thanks to a handwritten note which the culprit had slipped under the door. The previous night, the establishment had received this gentleman, a plumber who was extremely dissatisfied with the services offered. The angry client had come back during the night to switch the water off at the mains and remove the cock (as well as his own). Luckily, the honourable establishment counted more than one plumber among its regulars, and a new cock (among others) arrived that morning.

                                                                                ঙ   ও

I realise that when I talk about the workers and their visitors, I never mention money. Perhaps for the visitor, it is important to know where the money goes. If a gentleman books me for an hour of delight and pleasure, he pays $165. Of this, $75 goes into my pocket, $75 goes to the owner (provision of facilities, bed linen, condoms, laundry, etc.) and $15 is GST. So when a girl does a good job and makes the client happy, she is making, each time, a small contribution to the national budget.

15. Nelly, Venus and the Others

One of the important days of my professional life in Melbourne was when the door of my house of pleasure opened and Nelly walked in. She was terribly young, her skirt hem was close to her arm pits, and her hair was died white and fell to her knees. She wore more make-up than a coach-load of retired geishas.

She was applying for a job, so she was wearing her work outfit. As she stood there, in front of the desk, I swore that I would never become that tart's best friend. How wrong I was.

When all the artificial accessories to stimulate sexual hunger were removed, she looked like a little angel. I wanted to take her into my arms and smother her in maternal love. She was 19, and had decided to abandon her normal job, on the footpaths of St Kilda, to join us, the old women, in a warm and safe brothel, with solid mattresses.

Her life as a child within a family home ended when her mother arrived home too early, one afternoon, to find Nelly performing a professional oral service on a loving stepfather.

She was mystified by her mother's hysterical reaction, as she had been enjoying sex with Harry for several months, and thought that she was relieving Annette of at least one domestic chore she did not enjoy. A black eye and a broken arm proved that she had been guilty of a dangerous error of judgement.

There were a few attempts to bring the family together again. But the social worker was horrified to discover that Nelly was not interested in staying at home if her sexual freedom was to be taken away. If she was to leave home, she would need to earn a living, and there was only one trade she could practise. School was out of the question, she had no wish to pursue an intellectual career. Nelly was on her own, but not for long.

At the age of 15, Nelly was an illegal, underage street worker in St Kilda. She worked there for four years, mostly in the evenings, and her great success was to keep off drugs. She exercised her profession only as a living, and simply because it was what she did best.

She liked her stretch of footpath. She was known and respected by the faithful, but the danger was elsewhere. There were nights when a carload of teenage drunks would cruise down the street, offering cheap insults because they had neither the guts nor the money to use her services. Sometimes, there were even nocturnal sightseers and, like most of the girls, she did not like having her mug shots shown round a dinner table, accompanied by dirty jokes.

She gave a good service, because she liked men and enjoyed good sex herself, but on Greeves Street, good sex was rare. Her greatest success was the night she was picked up by a husband and wife in a new BMW and taken home for fun. She would never have believed that such 'nice' people could have an appetite for such pleasure, but she left their smart home the next morning in a taxi, relaxed and happy, her wallet full of banknotes.

Generally, the police she met were pretty indulgent. But there were the 'big boys', the upper levels of the constabulary who were still on the way up. To succeed, results were necessary. If a house was broken into, if a car radio was stolen, everyone knew that it was not the young office worker or shop assistant who would be the author of such a petty crime. Why look any further than the 'criminals' whose presence stands out in the street, the prostitutes and the transvestites?

She used rooms, hotels now and again, but sometimes offered her services standing up in a dark lane or spread wide on the back seat of a battered Commodore. She met young and old, black, yellow or white, and romance was never on the menu. She received almost as many punches as tips.

She lived through the great debate of whether certain streets should be reserved for prostitutes, while others would be devoted to neo-Georgian brick-veneer townhouses. She came to realise that the prostitutes, and their clients, were not the real problem. The threat to public safety came from the men who thought that bashing or insulting a tart was one way of having a good night out with the mates. She did not like footballers, whom she saw as guys with small brains, small balls and big fists.

She was forced out of her activity, not by the police, the pimps or the punters, but by the yuppies. This is the new generation of residents in the area, those who buy a derelict home in a hot street, renovate, move in, and then complain about the neighbourhood.

She lived happily in our midst, but sometimes dabbled in the rough night trade. She added another flavour, and, I must admit, we offered a few 'twin parties' together, and our visitors loved the wonderful contrast in education and culture of two girls who shared an overwhelming enthusiasm for pleasure.

She repeatedly told me how working in a brothel felt like 'cheating'. On the street, there are constant threats, and for some street girls this is part of the excitement. For her, a brothel was like an office, with a receptionist, staff amenities, cash box and diary.

I told her how lucky I was compared to all the girls around me. I was there because I was bored at home, because I loved making men happy, and also because I enjoyed sex. I confessed to an irresistible excitement each time I met a new client, eager to see a new penis, to listen to a different story, to experience another intimacy. And once the excitement and occasional pleasure was over, I slipped back to my happy marriage, my nice home, my wonderful husband. I could walk away whenever I wanted.

Other girls were so desperate to earn money, to feed the kids, to look after the family while the husband served time, or, worse, to satisfy a terrible addiction. I was sometimes ashamed to beat them at their own game, because it is not always easy to be attractive and sexy when you are worrying about serious family problems.

Nelly quickly realised another great difference, when comparing her new career to her past activities. She learned that she could be often booked just to lie next to a guy, to place her head on his shoulder, and to listen, while whispering advice and encouragement. These tender consultations usually reached their climax with a little friendly and agile handcraft.

Nelly and I discovered that we shared a terrible secret. We had both come to the conclusion that no two penises were the same, but they were all magnificent and beautiful. Luckily, men's thoughts are focused on bums and tits, and they do not realise the ravages which would be caused if they were allowed to walk around with those magnificent erections uncovered.

Venus was an attractive woman: she was pretty, she had class, she had a beautiful body, and a bubbling personality. She had been living for five years with a de-facto who was very much in love with her. He was a successful businessman, and showered her with gifts, fine clothing, expensive jewellery and even offered her a new car. He believed strongly that a wealthy man's wife should not have a job but should go shopping or sit at home and wait for her husband.

She began to work, once a week, on a daytime shift, in a luxurious bordello in the southern suburbs of Melbourne. Contrary to the majority of her colleagues, Venus did not come for the money. She was simply motivated by the excitement of having sex with total strangers.

She undertook her task with enthusiasm, and taught her clients how to give her pleasure rather than to just use her. This attracted a certain type of client, and she soon had a host of regular admirers. After a few months, Venus began to be less dependable, turning up at 11.30 am or midday instead of the normal opening time of 10 o'clock. The manager moaned but put up with it. Venus was always totally booked for her day, and the business was making good money. Some enthusiasts had to book a fortnight ahead.

But Venus was getting bored. There was no longer the excitement of meeting an enthusiastic stranger, every client was a regular. It was like being married to 30 husbands! She left and joined us. She turns up when she feels the need, refuses advance bookings, and meets lovely guys like forest workers or truck drivers, simple men with simple needs who, just once, find themselves with a beautiful, charming and enthusiastic partner.

She will leave us soon, I'm sure. Her lover is still ignorant of her extramarital activities, but she very nearly ran into one of his close friends visiting us a few weeks ago. Luckily, it was one of my regular clients, and he did not ask to see the others.

                                                                    ❧ ☙

Diana and Alex were the proud parents of young Frank who attended an exclusive grammar school. It was the mother's secret job which allowed the delighted parents to afford the fees. There was no doubt that if the charming little brunette had shown around one of her private business cards, the school board would have rocked on its puritan foundations.

Diana told me that the parents' association of a private school appears to be a preferred outlet for the frustrated energies of certain mothers. It is here that they overcome the restrictions of household management and sail forth to organise the lives of others. Mrs X was such a busybody. There was not one event concerning part of the school community where Mrs X was not bustling, cheering, handing round sandwiches, giving advice on the latest diets, booing, waving bunting, asking rude questions, interrupting private conversations or generally making herself noticed.

One evening, Diana and her husband, like many other doting parents, were attending the end of year sports trophy night. The usual woman (a strong, upstanding, respected member of the community in every way) was looking after the basketball section. That night, however, there was something new: she was introducing her shy little husband to all her friends. Diana saw the man, grabbed her husband's arm, and steered him forcefully away from the introductions.

"Poor guy," Alex whispered. "There's no joy being married to a woman like that."

Diana laughed.

"Don't worry, he gets his kicks elsewhere. I didn't realise that he was married to her."

Alex raised an inquisitive eyebrow.

"You're not telling me that he's one of your 'friends', are you?"

"For goodness sake keep your voice down. I see him for an hour every fortnight."

"I don't believe it. Let's get introduced, just for a laugh," Alex suggested.

Diana did not share his idea for fun. She shook her head vigorously.

"Certainly not. I would hate to embarrass him; he's such a nice guy."

                    ℘   ℘

One Saturday morning, Pierre and I ran into a co-worker, Tessa, at our favourite coffee place. She was excited to meet him and immediately invited us over for dinner, that same evening.

"Robert and I love to have a little foursome after dinner," she added, "but only with VERY nice people of course."

"Do you really?" Pierre asked. "With your daytime job, I would have thought you'd look for something different. Like ballroom dancing or growing mushrooms, for example."

I am afraid that Tessa decided she didn't like my husband, from that day on!

16. The Day the World Died

In the autumn of 1999, Pierre had been very busy setting up an important seminar in a large conference complex on St Kilda Road. He talked to me about it every evening, and I begged him to let me come and help, as I had done in France. He told me he would rather do it alone.

Late that morning, he was very busy and had lots of things to do; a lot of calls to make, a lot of suppliers to chase.

That's why he raced out of the hotel straight under the wheels of a semi-trailer.

He died an hour later, in the emergency ward of the hospital, while people were still trying to find his wife. Paul and Suzanne Sterling were horrified to see him pass away without being able to contact me. Nobody knew that I was working in a brothel, nor could they have imagined that at the very moment he died with my name on his lips I was being 'doggied' by a well-hung Italian.

Suzanne Sterling was sitting on my doorstep when I got home that evening. She must have been a little surprised by my heavy make-up and tacky jewellery, which contrasted with the shabby jeans. Luckily, I had not come home in my full work uniform, as I sometimes do, when I am running late. When I saw her I knew that the news would be terrible and I screamed, repeatedly. Two or three neighbours rushed out to restrain me while she told the terrible story, and then she called Paul on her mobile, begging him to come quickly.

I fought them. I wanted, desperately, to die, there, on my own doorstep. I was completely crazy, as I begged for a knife. I thought my life should have ended there so I could join him immediately. I could feel his hand trying to grab me, to drag me with him. Pierre was dead. The world had to end, immediately.

I was put into care for two days, as a protection against self-destruction. Paul rang both families and begged them not to come for the funeral, explaining that such were my wishes. They disobeyed. Finally, my mother came with her sister, and Pierre's father was on the same plane. Pierre's mother was in medical care.

My father in law walked with me behind the coffin. My mother and Aunt Madeleine walked behind us. Mr Duval was terribly dignified, stiff, upright and silent. I thought he was going to faint when the coffin slipped away towards the doors of the hungry furnace. Cremation is not popular in France. Michelle and Fabienne also came down from Canberra, and I wondered how they had received the news. And I saw Nigel, my favourite politician, who had come to be with me on my darkest hour.

Have you ever heard of people taking photographs at a funeral? Nelly did. She posted me a full set of her photos, several months later, and when I saw them it was the first time I laughed since Pierre's death.

There were many businessmen, colleagues and associates of Pierre's at the funeral, as well as the three members of our two families. They must have all been amazed by the group of ladies who came together and clustered, shyly. They were my colleagues from the brothel.

There were seven angels, all wearing black lace dresses and wide brimmed black lace hats. The hems were outrageously high, and the cleavages dreadfully deep; and their well-shaped calves were flattered by the black, patent leather stilettos. It was obvious from the shots that some of the businessmen, even in that hour of great sorrow, could not help casting an occasional, hungry glance in their direction. Funeral, perhaps, but business is business.

$$\infty \quad \infty$$

I never returned to the brothel. With the death of Pierre, I felt as if my own life had come to an end. I also realised the dreadful shame of being where I was and doing what I was doing while my dying husband was calling out my name in the emergency ward of a public hospital.

Pierre's father, my mother and my aunt flew home three days later. I could not leave Australia immediately, and they were too overwhelmed with grief to take any interest in visiting a foreign land. Paul and Suzanne Sterling were wonderful friends, and they helped me clear up my affairs as quickly as possible. I dearly loved Australia, but I could not stay there without my darling husband. Nelly wanted me to come back to work, but I did not believe that it was possible to live the life of a prostitute without the security of a home filled with love and affection.

Nigel invited me to Canberra for a few days, lending me a small townhouse he owned in the southern suburbs. I accepted, and Michelle rang me the next day. What she suggested was outrageous, and I screamed abuse at her over the phone. The next morning, I was on her doorstep.

I worked for eight full days, non-stop, on her premises. She and Fabienne watched over me closely, but after 48 hours, I was back in the old routine. Yes, my lover was dead, yes, my heart was broken, but I discovered that I could still enjoy a man's body, and even still achieve an orgasm. I fucked, vigorously, loudly, constantly, but the evenings were dreadful, as Pierre was not there to possess me, reclaim me as his own, or to fill my body and my dreams.

When I was cured, Michelle sent me home. And I spent my last night in Australia in Nigel's arms.

I flew back to France, back to see the winter cloak my hills and fields. Back to my nest. I lived with my mother, doing nothing.

ю cs

I saw the opening ceremony of the Olympic Games in Sydney on TV, and cried for my darling husband. He had been a passionate fan of Catherine Freeman, for who she was, for what she did and for what she represented.

I visited my in-laws a couple of times, but in the end I could not just sit opposite Pierre's mother and watch her waste away. It was not that they held me responsible for his death; it was simply that his disappearance had destroyed the links between us.

Bernard Courtot took the TGV (the very fast train) to come to visit me in my home. He offered me Madeleine's job, acting as public relations manager and organising his seminars. I thanked him most dearly, but told him that working there would only bring back memories of Pierre, which would destroy my soul. My sister, Brigitte, told me, after his visit, that he looked as if he was desperately hoping to climb into my pants. I told her that if I had taken the job offered this would have probably been part of my duties, an unwritten proviso I would have accepted. She looked at me strangely and shook her head.

"You have changed so much," she murmured.

"You would never understand," I assured her.

We went to Lyon for a weekend, just Brigitte and myself, and picked up two guys in a night club. We had a foursome that night, and my sister discovered that chaste little Marie was a hot operator. We decided that it would be better not to discuss our escapade with our mother, but slipped away for a few other dirty weekends until she decided to call it a day. My dear sister, who had almost raped half the boys in the village and who had openly declared that the only good thing about a man was whatever hung between his legs, my sweet little sister, fell in love. The object of her desire was unassuming, unattractive and totally boring, but her passion, thankfully, put an end to our assaults on the men of Lyon.

In the spring of 2001, I received a phone call from the Australian Embassy in Paris. They had an official visiting my region, and they asked if I would be free to act as interpreter. I accepted gladly, it was an opportunity to talk about Australia, the land which had given me so much pleasure and so much sadness. A driver would pick me up at my home address the following Wednesday morning, and the job would only last one day.

I should have guessed. The driver was Nigel, and there was no translating necessary.

In September he was leaving politics. Thanks to an English father he had obtained a European passport and had just bought a cottage in the hills above Cannes. He needed a caretaker while he cleared up loose ends in Australia, then a housekeeper once he had settled.

"Would you accept to make the housekeeper warm at night?" I asked, wistfully. "I feel so cold nowadays."

"Only if she sees an occasional siesta at my side as part of her duties," he confirmed.

I accepted and my parents were overjoyed. I announced that I would be living in sin with another man, for the rest of my life, because I had married and lost the only man I could truly cherish. They blessed me. My mother, who had overcome some of her old-fashioned ideas, thought that living in sin was a good idea. Bernard Courtot rang to congratulate me.

I have now spent nearly two years on the French Riviera, close to Nigel. Pierre is still in my heart, and Nigel knows and accepts this.

Tomorrow, I will be posting a large parcel to Paul and Suzanne Sterling, in Melbourne. It contains my past, my shame, my love, my pleasures and my confession.

I understand that the high-class brothel The Daily Planet has recently been floated on the Australian Stock Exchange, an event generously covered by the national press.

We are entering a new world.